Alexis Averbuck, Kate Armstrong, Andrea Schulte-Peevers,
Helen Iatrou, Vangelis Koronakis, Anastasia Miari, Sarah Souli,
Ryan Ver Berkmoes, Vesna Maric

Meet our writers

Alexis Averbuck
@alexisaverbuck

Alexis lives in Hydra, paints, writes and makes any excuse she can to explore her adopted land. Her favourite experience is walking coastal paths, like those in Hydra or the Small Cyclades, to swim in pristine waters, float and look back at the unspoilt coastline.

Kate Armstrong
@nomaditis and katearmstrongtravelwriter.com

Kate travels the world, frequently settling in one place, including Greece, to live locally. She writes about her experiences for global publications.

Andrea Schulte-Peevers
@aschultepeevers

Andrea has made her living as a travel writer and photographer for over a quarter century and has authored or contributed to well over 100 Lonely Planet titles.

Helen Iatrou
@heleniatrou

Born and raised in Australia, Helen relocated to her ancestral Greece in 1996. An island girl through and through, she can't bear straying far from the sea for too long and adores jungle-like landscapes. In Pelion she can have both.

Vangelis Koronakis

Vangelis was born and raised in Athens, where he works as a web editor. His favourite experience is re-discovering and introducing the city to his five-year-old son. He loves train journeys and spending summers in Crete.

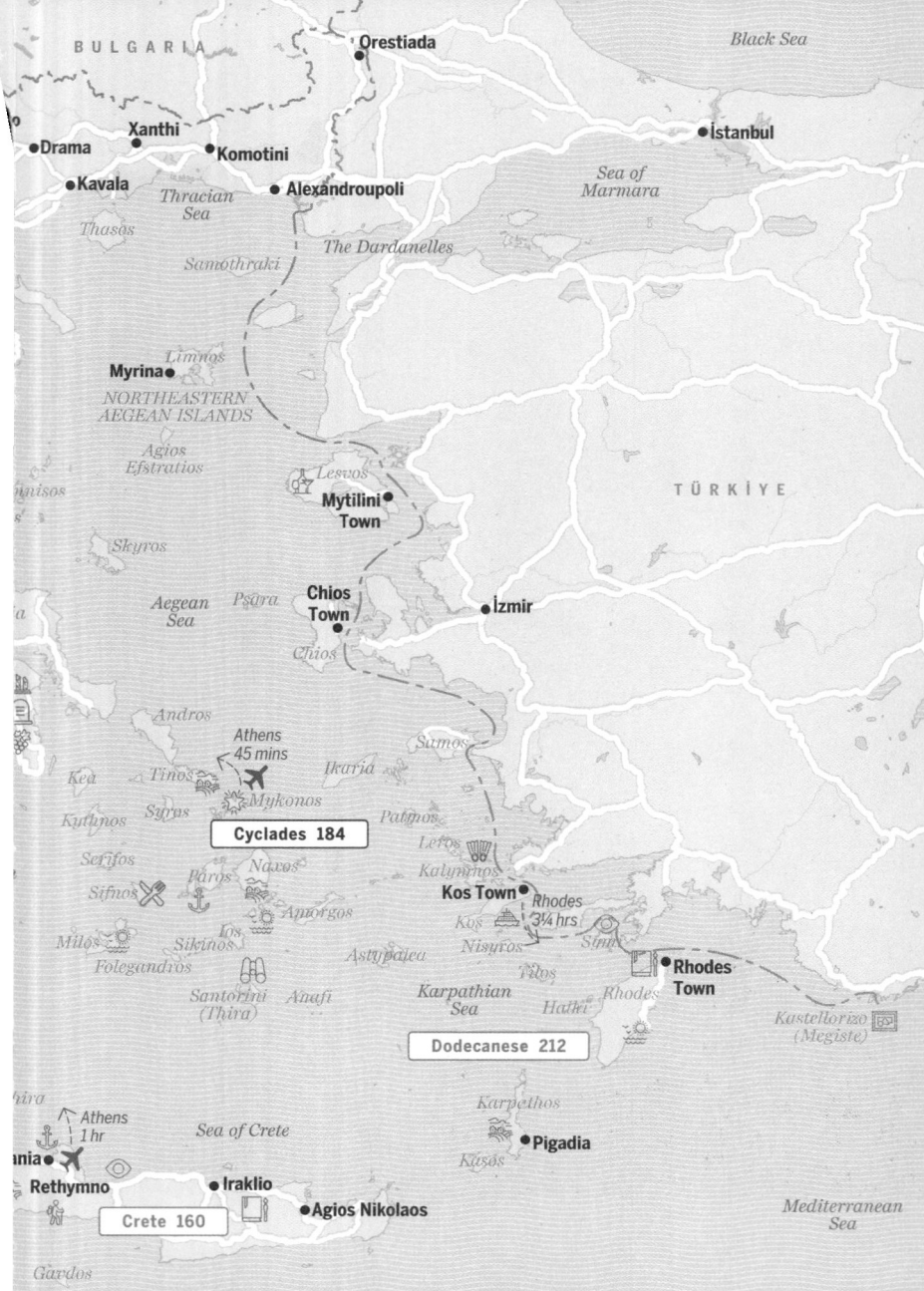

▬▬ Get seduced by sultry beaches where sands shimmer in shades of white, pink, cream, red, black. Surf and sail the azure seas, or strap on your boots to hike to remote shores and monasteries. Be amazed at the ease of hopping between islands, each with its own vibe. Dive into buzzy city life, then slow down to connect with rural culture over languid coffee breaks in village squares. Sample distinct regional flavours, from crusty cheese pies to hearty mountain stews. Rich, exciting, soul-restoring.

This is Greece.

TURN THE PAGE AND START PLANNING YOUR NEXT BEST TRIP →

Anastasia Miari
Based between Athens and Corfu, journalist Anastasia freelances for *Monocle Magazine*, *Konfekt Magazine*, the *Guardian*, the *Sunday Times* and is *Courier* magazine's Greece correspondent.

Sarah Souli
@sgsouli

Sarah is a US journalist based in Greece. Though she mostly lives between Athens and Tinos, she's a firm believer that the north is actually the country's best secret. She has a penchant for slow travel and wild swimming. (Photo credit: Marco Arguello)

Ryan Ver Berkmoes
@ryanverberkmoes

Ryan first visited Greece in 1985 and has lived on the idyllic island of Hydra part-time since 2012 – shortly after he met the love of his life, his wife Alexis Averbuck. He has written more than 130 books for Lonely Planet.

Vesna Maric
@vesnamarx

Vesna writes travel guides, and critically acclaimed literary fiction and non fiction, as well as essays.

Contents

Best Experiences	6
Calendar	20
Trip Builders	28
7 Things to Know about Greece	40
Read, Listen, Watch & Follow	42

Athens — 44

Among the Monuments	50
Unlikely Gallery	54
Athenian Landmarks	56
Around Central Market	58
Picnic under an Olive Tree	60
Wine Tasting in Attica	62
Breathtaking City View	64
Party Like a Greek	66
Art During Economic Crisis	68
Riviera to Sounion Temple	70
Listings	72

Thessaloniki & Northern Greece — 74

Taking a Bite	80
Urban Pedigree	82
Up in the Clouds	84
Ottoman-Era Road Trip	86
Zigzagging Zagoria	88
The Cuisine of Northern Greece	90
No Place Like Halkidiki	92
Ioannina's Magic	94
Listings	96

Delphi & Central Greece — 98

Delphi Done Differently	102
Tsipouradhiko Ritual	104
Action-Packed Peninsula	106
Cavorting in Karpenisi	108
Small but Mighty Messolongi	110
Escape to the Country	112
Listings	114

Peloponnese — 116

Kalavryta Rail Journey	120
Following Literary Footsteps	122
Admiring Arkadia	124
Olive Oil, Lunch & More	128
Meander Through the Mani	130
Fortresses & Ancient Sites of the Peloponnese	132
Listings	134

Saronic Gulf Escape — 136

Ionian Islands — 140

An Ionian Sailing Adventure	144
Country Life on Corfu	146
A Window onto Italy	148
Corfu Town Secrets	150
Eating All Over Corfu	154
A Smashing Easter	156
Listings	158

Crete — 160

Unmissable Hania	166
Ancient Knossos	168
Exploring Gorges	170
Alluring Beaches	172
Enchanting Rethymno	174
Mountain Villages	176
Foods of Crete	178
Mysterious Minoans	180
Listings	182

Cyclades — 184

Volcanic Santorini	190
Beach-Hopping Milos	192
Taste of Sifnos	194
Treasures of Tinos	196
Uninhibited on Mykonos	198
Adventures on Land & Sea	200
Magic Mountains & Beaches	202
Get Away from It All	204
Ancient Art from the Cyclades	206
Wines of the Islands	208
Listings	210

Dodecanese — 212

Stroll Medieval Alleys	218
Breathtaking Harbour	220
The Greenest Island	222
Nisyros' Volcanic Beauty	224

Knossos (p168)

Ancient Remains & Beaches	226
Astypalea's Beauty	228
Cliffs & Quiet Beaches	230
Listings	232

Accommodation	248
Essentials	250
Language	252

Index   **253**

Drinking Ouzo on Lesvos   **234**

Practicalities   **238**

Arriving	240
Getting Around	242
Safe Travel	244
Money	245
Responsible Travel	246

ESSAYS

Art During Economic Crisis	68
Urban Pedigree	82
Escape to the Country	112
A Window onto Italy	148
Mysterious Minoans	180
Wires of the Islands	208

VISUAL GUIDES

Athenian Landmarks	56
The Cuisine of Northern Greece	90
Fortresses & Ancient Sites of the Peloponnese	132
Foods of Crete	178
Ancient Art from the Cyclades	206

WIDE OPEN
SPACES

Greece is a land of grand spaces, where towering mountains dominate the horizons and drama fills the windswept coasts – it's the stuff of Homerian tales. No matter your landscape preference, you can find a dose here. From the forested villages of Zagorohoria alongside Vikos Gorge, to the lush springs of Naxos and Santorini's insane crescent of sunken caldera, dazzle your mind and awe your soul.

→ NYMPH-SPOTTING
Greek nature is imbued with mythical creatures. Keep an eye out for *dryads* (tree nymphs), *oreads* (mountain nymphs), *Naiads* (freshwater nymphs) and *Nereids* (sea nymphs), among others.

Left and right Vikos Gorge (p89)
Below Wild boar

MAGICAL PELION
Donkey trails zigzag over rolling, forested hills to quiet, sandy coves and quaint villages on the Pelion Peninsula, the reputed home of the centaurs.

Best Outdoor Experiences

▶ Be virtuous as well as exalted on green-energy Tilos, where birdwatching, beachcombing and hiking all take centre stage. (p190)

▶ Follow ancient trails up the thickly forested slopes of Mt Olympus, once the lair of the Ancient Greek pantheon. (p84)

▶ Hike Crete's gorges from spectacular Samaria Gorge to equally breathtaking Imbros and Aradena gorges. (p170)

↑ HUNTING SEASON
Late August to late February is hunting season in Greece. When hitting the trails, look for signs saying Κυνηγετικός χώρος (hunting area) – many are handmade.

AZURE SEAS & SANDY SHORES

Greece is virtually synonymous with beaches – broad sweeps of white sand, grey or even red-pebble coves, and black volcanic shores. Summer season is a tradition here, when families return to home islands and holidays are a call for R&R. A siren song for travellers, too, summer means crowds but also the best swimming of your life.

→ **TAKE A DIVE**
Greeks at work don't forego the sea. They head out for a *voutiá*, a quick dive. Early mornings and twilight are perfect for solo swims.

Left Antipaxi (p145)
Right Paros (p200)
Below Crete (p160)

ACCESSIBLE BEACHES

Increasingly, Greece is installing ramps and providing assistive devices and wheels at popular beaches for getting into the sea. Not ubiquitous but on the rise (check *extramilers.eu*).

Best Beach Experiences

▶ Surrender to sun and clear, blue water on Antipaxi, for some of Greece's best swimming. (p145)

▶ Sample beaches on Naxos, where one glossy strand merges right into the next. (p202)

▶ Discover Milos' surreal rock-formation-backed volcanic beaches. (p192)

▶ Stroll on foot from beach to glorious beach in the Small Cyclades. (p204)

↑ **PINK SANDS**
It's minute bits of coral that create the long pink-hued sand dunes on Crete's west coast from Falasarna to Elafonisi.

Part of Greece's allure is its well-preserved buildings. Casting your eyes around its cities you'll find architectural styles ranging from ancient to sleek 21st century.

In the city, people are polished and the younger crowd is trendy, so pack a few of your more stylish clothes, especially for bars or high-end restaurants.

BUZZING
CITIES

Greece's cities are magnets for people from all over the country, who come to work, shop and play. Always dynamic, they sizzle with modern innovation, creativity, street life, and dining and partying scenes. Jump from cool Athens with its epic ancient sites to elegant Thessaloniki and its Ottoman-style architecture, to Iraklio, Crete's vibrant capital.

Best Active Experiences

▶ Explore Athens' world-class ruins and trendy shops before sipping cocktails and partying til dawn. (p44)

▶ Shop for vintage treasures and stroll grand plazas in Thessaloniki, northern Greece's laid-back seaside city. (p74)

▶ Discover your favourite among the lively bars and tavernas lining Hania's sparkling Venetian harbour. (p167)

▶ Hopscotch from Byzantine fortresses and neoclassical palaces to Parisian-style arcades in Corfu's Old Town. (p150)

The word *xenos* means both 'stranger' and 'guest'; Greeks see *filoxenia* (hospitality) almost as a matter of personal pride and honour.

You can still see older men in the villages playing with the *komboloï* – they may look like prayer beads, but are only used for relaxation.

VILLAGE LIFE

Greek life has always taken place in the public sphere, whether it's talking politics at the local *kafeneio* (coffee house) or families gathering in neighbourhood squares while the kids play into the evening. And Greek villages, from seashore to mountain valley, are a quintessential place to experience daily life.

Left The Temple of Olympian Zeus, Athens (p44)
Right Zagorohoria (p89)

Best Village Experiences

▶ Tramp ancient paths between Zagorohoria's stone villages near Vikos Gorge. (p89)

▶ Wander among the neoclassical mansions cascading down a steep hill on picture-perfect Symi. (p125)

▶ Delight in the sheer variety and beauty of Crete's mountain villages. (p176)

▶ Stroll the cobbled paths of Apiranthos, one of Naxos' many multifaceted villages. (p203)

▶ Snap selfies in Cycladic white-cube harbour villages on Paros and Antiparos. (p200)

Paxi & Antipaxi
Shimmering Ionian jewels

Explore beyond grand Corfu to diminutive Paxi and its even smaller friend, Antipaxi. Hidden in plain sight, they offer azure waters with some of the best swimming in Greece, peaceful harbours with bobbing yachts and pensions tucked into olive groves.

🚢 *30mins from Corfu*
▶ p145

Kefallonia
Sea to Mountain Paradise

Chill on pristine beaches, enjoy dazzling views from the Ionians' highest peak and taste exquisite wines made from the indigenous *Robola* grape in magical Kefallonia.

✈ *75mins from Athens*
▶ p148

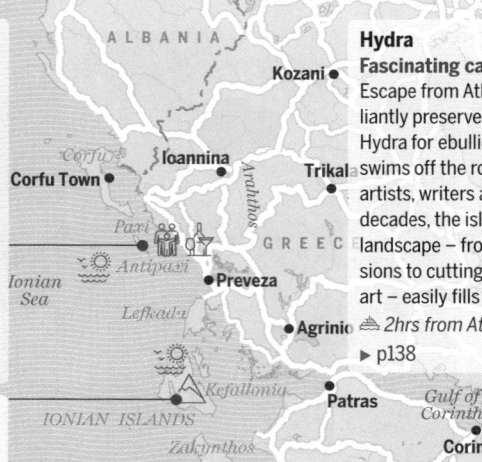

Hydra
Fascinating car-free getaway

Escape from Athens to the brilliantly preserved, car-free island of Hydra for ebullient harbour life and swims off the rocks. A beacon for artists, writers and musicians for decades, the island's rich cultural landscape – from historic mansions to cutting-edge international art – easily fills days.

🚢 *2hrs from Athens*
▶ p138

Milos
Parade of sensations

Circle the array of beaches on volcanic Milos, a gentler option than busy Santorini. Sarakiniko is a star, with creamy rock formations and blue, blue water, as is the hamlet of Klima with its colourful seafront fishing dwellings.

🚢 *4hrs from Santorini*
▶ p192

ISLANDS GALORE

▬▬ Stereotypes don't work on Greek islands, and marquee names may not always be the best fit for you. Each island has its own character, its own culture. And many have vastly different terrains, weather patterns and, certainly, histories. So a trip in the islands is an incredible smorgasbord – sample widely.

CLOCKWISE FROM TOP LEFT: IMAGIN.GR PHOTOGRAPHY/SHUTTERSTOCK ©, SVETLANA RYAJENTSEVA/SHUTTERSTOCK ©, HECTOR CHRISTIAEN/SHUTTERSTOCK ©

Paros & Antiparos
Traditional Cyclades and easy fun
Entertain the whole family in Paros and Antiparos, where you can mix village strolls with beach play and even nightclub crawls. Parikia and Naoussa harbours are resplendent with blooming bougainvillea draping over cubist, white lanes packed with cafes and boutiques.

✈ *1hr from Athens*
▶ p200

Crete
Something for everyone
Dive deep into all aspects of Greek life on its largest and most diverse island, Crete, almost a country unto itself. Discover its pink-sand western beaches, its vast gorges begging to be hiked and its vibrant cities and mountain villages with top cuisine.

✈ *1hr from Athens*
▶ p160

CULINARY RICHES & WINE

■ Greek food has been exported across the world, but there is simply no way to recreate the delight of sampling it in the spot where it is produced. Cheeses are made fresh in the mountains and herbs and greens picked from their slopes. Goats and lambs graze free, while small fish and calamari are harvested from the seas. And, of course, there are the subtly brilliant creative variations on how each region and each chef prepares them.

→ HONEY, HONEY

Rich honey is a product of native flowers and trees. Many are only available in homemade batches sold locally – look for these in smaller markets.

Left Greek salad
Right Cretan honey
Below Local wines

SEAFOOD LUNCH & SIESTA

A summertime cultural mainstay is a seafront taverna lunch, with its parade of dips and dishes, followed by a decadent siesta. Embrace it.

↑ KNOW YOUR WINES

You'll find Greek wines at supermarkets, but know your regions to learn how to tell the solid sips from truly delightful treats.

Best Food & Drink Experiences

▶ Village-hop on Tinos to discover some of Greece's best regional food. (p196)

▶ Tour volcanic vineyards, then taste top *asyrtiko* white wines on Santorini. (p190)

▶ Savour the Italian-inflected cuisine of the Ionian Islands in charming Corfu Town. (p154)

▶ Sip delicate ouzos in Plomari on Lesvos, the island of Sappho. (p234)

▶ Relish glorious Cretan meals in Hania's excellent restaurants. (p166)

Delphi
Centre of the Ancient Greek world
Listen for the oracle's whisper at majestic Delphi. Zeus released two eagles at opposite ends of the world and they met here, on the slopes of Mt Parnassos with the Gulf of Corinth shimmering below, thus making Delphi the centre of the world.
🚗 3hrs from Athens
▶ p102

Ancient Olympia
Birthplace of the Olympic Games
Sprint around the stadium at Ancient Olympia, a 3000-year-old World Heritage–listed sanctuary to sporting glory, which hosted the original Olympic Games.
🚗 4hrs from Athens
▶ p132

Ancient Mycenae
Mighty kingdom rich in gold
Climb to the citadel of Ancient Mycenae with its immense royal beehive tomb of the Treasury of Atreus. It was home to magnificent gold masks and jewellery now in Athens' National Archaeological Museum.
🚗 30mins from Nafplio
▶ p131

EPIC ANCIENT WONDERS

World-renowned ancient sites – some featuring in the greatest tales of all time, the Greek myths – carpet the country. With every layer excavated, another civilisation is revealed. And the architecture and artefacts created to honour the gods – Athena, Poseidon, Apollo, Zeus, to name just a few – remain ready for us to marvel at and explore.

ABOVE: CONSTANTINOSA/SHUTTERSTOCK ©
TOP RIGHT: JON DAVISON/LONELY PLANET ©
RIGHT: TIMOFEEV VLADIMIR/SHUTTERSTOCK ©

Athens' Acropolis
Wonder of the Western world
Make the pilgrimage to Athens' beautifully preserved Acropolis with its temples to Athena, columns shining above the city. Looking down, you'll see the Ancient Agora – the civic, political and commercial centre – plus Roman ruins and Byzantine churches, legacies of rulers past.

🚆 *6hrs from Thessaloniki*
▶ p52

Delos
Centre of the Cyclades
Sail from party-hard Mykonos to the epic sanctuary at Delos, the centre of the Cyclades and birthplace of Apollo and Artemis. This uninhabited island is chockablock with ruined temples, treasuries and residences bedecked in mosaics; it also boasts a museum of priceless statuary.

⛴ *30mins from Mykonos*
▶ p199

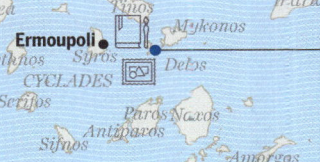

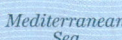

Knossos
Palatial Minoan capital
Imagine the mysterious Minoan culture at Crete's marquee site, Knossos, as you ascend to monumental terraces with vibrant fresco restorations. It's ideally paired with the Heraklion Archaeological Museum, packed with elaborate finds from the site.

⛴ *30mins from Iraklio*
▶ p168

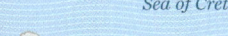

HIKING COASTS & MOUNTAINS

Whether you're just getting started or your boots are covered with the dust of a thousand hikes, Greece has a trail for everyone. Rove through the national parks to uncover roiling cascades or feel the salt on your skin as you ramble coastal trails. Islands are primo for exploring on foot, beckoning with well-marked pathways.

EXPLORE WIDELY & GO DEEP

The social cooperative Paths of Greece (*pathsofgreece.gr*) creates new hiking routes across the country, many with cultural links.

Best Hiking Experiences

▶ Hike through Kefallonia's olive groves and vineyards. (p159)

▶ Walk the hilltops, hamlets and chapel-studded beaches of Sifnos. (p194)

▶ Drop out of time on Iraklia and follow well-marked trails over its small mountains. (p204)

▶ Stroll pine-covered dirt tracks to azure coves on Angistri. (p137)

← HIT THE E4 TRAIL

The long-distance route from Portugal to Cyprus encompasses ancient paths in Greece, like those from Livadi plateau (near Arahova) down to Delphi, or others near Mystras.

Above Mt Olympus (p84)
Left Sifnos (p194)

PALACES OF CULTURE

If there's one thing Greece has in spades, it's art and culture and the museums dedicated to their veneration. Any list of places to go is by definition incomplete. Grand city museums hold world-class treasures, and so do many humble village collections. Entry prices tend to be low, so explore widely.

Best Art & Culture Experiences

▶ Admire ancient sculptures in the Acropolis Museum's spacious, superbly designed galleries. (p56)

▶ Browse the last several centuries of Greek painting at Athens' new National Gallery. (p56)

▶ Imagine the life of a great artist on Hydra at the Studio of Panayiotis Tetsis. (p138)

JACKPOT
When visiting ancient sites – from Olympia and Delphi to Naxos' Temple of Demeter – leave time for their museums where countless prizes found on-site are protected.

← **MUST SEE**
Quietly filling a full block in Exarhia, the National Archaeological Museum is a treasure chest of ancient art from across Greece. Don't miss it.

Above National Archaeological Museum (p56)
Left Acropolis Museum (p56)

The *meltemi* (north wind) is a summer wind whipping across the Aegean from the north, mainly between June and September.

→ **Miaoulia Festival**
In June, Hydra ignites in celebration of its contribution to the War of Independence with a spectacular boat burning, fireworks and folk dancing.
📍 Hydra

← **Athens Epidaurus Festival**
The most prominent summer festival (June to August) features music, dance and drama at the ancient theatre on Athens' Acropolis and at Epidavros in the Peloponnese.
📍 Athens and Epidavros
▶ aefestival.gr

Feast of St John the Baptist
On June 24, bonfires blaze across Greece, with people leaping over them as part of a ritual of purification.

JUNE

Average daytime max: 29°C
Days of rainfall: 1

JULY

Greece in SUMMER

↓ Cool Pindos

Seek fewer crowds and cooler temperatures in Greece's northern mountains like the Pindos range.

Naxos Festivals

May to September concerts fill the Venetian *kastro* (castle), the Bazeos Tower hosts art exhibitions, and celebrations abound with food and music.

📍 Naxos

Delphi Festival

In June and August, trip the light fantastic with musical and theatrical events in and around Delphi and Dorida.

📍 Delphi

▶ delphifestival.gr

Demand for accommodation peaks during summer. View tours and overnight adventures in advance at *lonelyplanet.com*.

AUGUST

Average daytime max: 32°C
Days of rainfall: 0

Average daytime max: 32°C
Days of rainfall: 0

🧳 Packing Notes

It's fiercely hot: Bring a big hat, sunglasses, sunscreen and a refillable water bottle.

Autumn is tops for peaceful, late-season swims and excellent walking. Services begin closing on some islands, but those in popular locales remain open.

↘ Great Days of Nemea Wine Festival

Sample widely at this wine festival in September that celebrates Nemea's *agiorgitiko* grape with tastings, concerts and more.
📍 Nemea
▶ nemeawineland.com

↖ Ohi Day

A simple 'no' (*ohi* in Greek) was the famous response when Mussolini demanded passage for his troops on 28, October 1940. Now, it's a national holiday with remembrance services and parades.

SEPTEMBER   Average daytime max: 28°C   **OCTOBER**
                  Days of rainfall: 1

Greece in AUTUMN

↘ Thessaloniki International Film Festival

In November, around 150 films are crammed into 11 days of screenings, alongside concerts, exhibitions, talks and theatrical performances.

📍 Thessaloniki
▸ *filmfestival.gr*

↖ Olive-picking

Autumn sees temperatures drop. Olive-picking is in full swing in places such as Crete and feta production picks up, giving you the opportunity to taste some seriously fresh cheese.

NOVEMBER

Average daytime max: 23°C
Days of rainfall: 3

Average daytime max: 18°C
Days of rainfall: 4

 Packing Notes
Both bathing suit and light sweater or scarf, plus hiking boots for prime walking season.

The holiday season in Greece is understated and joyful, with Christmas bringing light-festooned harbours, honey cookies and good cheer on into the new year.

↗ Feast of Agios Vasilios (St Basil)

New Year's Day sees a church ceremony followed by gifts, singing, dancing and feasting. The *vasilopita* (golden glazed cake) is cut; if you get the slice with a coin, you'll have a lucky year.

↘ Epiphany (Blessing of the Waters)

Christ's baptism is celebrated throughout Greece on 6 January, when seas, lakes and rivers are blessed, with the largest ceremony at Piraeus.

📍 Piraeus

↓ Snow in Athens

Greece sees snow in the north and on its mountaintops. Freak storms even occasionally powder Athens or the islands.

DECEMBER

Average daytime max: 15°C
Days of rainfall: 6

JANUARY

Greece in
WINTER

FROM LEFT: FOXYS FOREST MANUFACTURE/SHUTTERSTOCK ©, VASILIS VERVERIDIS/ALAMY STOCK PHOTO ©, SVEN HANSCHE/ SHUTTERSTOCK ©, PIT STOCK/SHUTTERSTOCK ©, AERIAL-MOTION/SHUTTERSTOCK ©
BOTTOM: MANOS FIKARIS/SHUTTERSTOCK ©

↘ Thessaloniki Nightlife

The islands may be quiet but Thessaloniki (along with Athens) is in full swing. Nightlife there peaks during winter.

↓ Carnival

Carnival season culminates in a wild weekend (February/March) of costume parades, feasting and dancing. Patra's is the largest and Skyros' the most unusual.
📍 Patra and Skyros

↖ Quiet Acropolis

With fewer tourists, you won't have to push through crowds at the major sights like the Acropolis or Roman Agora (pictured).

FEBRUARY

Average daytime max: 13°C
Days of rainfall: 5

Average daytime max: 14°C
Days of rainfall: 5

🧳 Packing Notes

Bring jumpers, a rain slicker and sturdy shoes for potential chilled rains and slippery marble cobbles.

Spring is grand for hitting Greece's trails, when temperatures are mild and wildflowers splash colour across the land.

↘ Independence Day

The anniversary of the hoisting of the Greek flag is celebrated nationwide with parades and dancing on 25 March.

Prioritise islands that get overcrowded in summer since the droves haven't yet arrived: Santorini, Mykonos, Corfu, Rhodes and Hydra.

MARCH   Average daytime max: 16°C   **APRIL**
Days of rainfall: 4

Greece in
SPRING

↓ Easter

The Greek Orthodox calendar is chock-full of festivals and saints' namedays, but the biggest by far is Easter (April or May). Experience it on Patmos with fireworks, dancing in the streets, goats roasting and plenty of ouzo.
📍 Patmos

← Farmers Markets
Seek out farmers markets, known as *laïki agora* in Greek, which overflow with seasonal produce.

→ May Day
On 1 May, picnic in the country and gather wildflowers to make wreaths *(stefania)* to decorate houses.

MAY

Average daytime max: 20°C
Days of rainfall: 3

Average daytime max: 25°C
Days of rainfall: 2

🧳 Packing Notes
Layers, layers, layers – plus a swimsuit for variable weather.

ISLAND CRUSING
Trip Builder

TAKE YOUR PICK OF MUST-SEES AND HIDDEN GEMS

First trip to Greece and looking for island highlights? The Cyclades and Crete supply some of the country's top islands, most beautiful beaches, cultural highs and special villages. Mixing and matching is easy when island hopping, so a diversion anywhere along the way just adds to the fun.

📍 Trip Notes

Hub islands Mykonos, Naxos, Santorini

How long Allow 10 days

Getting around Frequent ferries run between islands in summer, but decrease dramatically in winter. Some Cyclades islands as well as Crete have an airport.

Tips For larger islands where you need wheels, it's easier and cheaper to hire on each island than take a vehicle on ferries. Summer traffic is chaotic on popular islands like Santorini, Paros and Mykonos.

Paros
Stroll traditional Cycladic whitewashed lanes, then surf the waves between Paros and Antiparos or boat around their golden beaches.
⛴ 1hr from Santorini

Sifnos
Walk, swim, eat...what's not to love? On this chic island with rainbow-prism waters, alternate between see-and-be-seen Apollonia with its excellent eateries and deep R&R.
⛴ 2½hrs from Piraeus

CLOCKWISE FROM TOP LEFT: SVETLANA RYAJENTSEVA/SHUTTERSTOCK ©, SYLVAIN SONNET/GETTY IMAGES ©, DZIEWUL/SHUTTERSTOCK ©

Delos
Examine and imagine ancient sanctuaries at the sacred island of Delos, the treasury of the Delian League and reputed birthplace of twins Apollo and Artemis.

🚢 30mins from Mykonos

Mykonos
Slather on the sunscreen for see-and-be-seen lounging at fashionable bars and crowd-pleasing beaches on this world-famous island ideal for social butterflies and lovers of action.

✈ 45mins from Athens

Naxos
Hike to stone-topped peaks, mountain villages and ancient ruins, then recline on soft-white-sand beaches after a bountiful seafood taverna lunch.

✈ 45mins from Athens

Small Cyclades
Roam the teeny, tiny and out-of-the-way in this series of delectable islands hugging Naxos, each with its own vibe.

🚢 1hr from Naxos

Crete
Struggle with abundant choices: the Minoan palace of Knossos and Iraklio wine country; charming Hania, a harbour city that's happily alive year-round; or gorgeous beaches and gorges beckoning to be hiked.

✈ 1hr from Athens

Santorini
Thrill in the awe of floating in the middle of a volcanic caldera, water sparkling and whitewashed villages perched above.

✈ 45mins from Athens

MAINLAND HISTORY
Trip Builder

TAKE YOUR PICK OF MUST-SEES AND HIDDEN GEMS

Greece's iconic ancient sites and thrilling multifaceted history are layered across the land. Trace the trail from Ancient Greece to more modern marauders while touring some of the country's most beautiful terrain.

🗺 Trip Notes

Hub towns Athens, Ioannina, Thessaloniki

How long Allow one week

Getting around It's best to tour with your own wheels and add extra days to hike or simply sip a drink on a shade-dappled terrace.

Tips Cultural sites are open year-round, so visiting outside summer will ensure quieter experiences. Always check ahead for winter hours, which can be significantly shorter than summer. See the Peloponnesian trip (p116) for more epic ancient ruins.

Zagorohoria
While away time in these immaculately preserved slate-stone villages spread along the ridges of Europe's deepest canyon, the Vikos Gorge. Here, the air is clear and cool, the views astounding.
🚗 *1hr from Ioannina*

Ioannina
Embrace raw Epiros, home of the Pindos Mountains and lovely lakeside Ioannina. Peruse Ali Pasha's castle, the Ottoman-era architecture and the car-free island in the lake with its historic monastery.
🚗 *5hrs from Athens*

Meteora

Clamber up stairs carved into soaring pillars of rock to reach magnificent 14th-century monasteries perched on their summits.

🚗 4½hrs from Athens

Thessaloniki

Enjoy a seaside sojourn in cultured Thessaloniki with its Ottoman-era architecture and vibrant arts scene, sipping coffee, dining in high style and sampling local sweets while you're there.

🚆 6hrs from Athens

Vergina

Have your mind blown at the Vergina Royal Tombs, where you descend to unspoiled royal Macedonian burials crammed with gobsmacking riches.

🚗 1hr from Thessaloniki

Athens

Pay homage at the grandest ancient sites like the Acropolis, Ancient Agora and Roman Agora. Dip into world-class museums, then emerge into modern life at markets and award-winning restaurants.

🚆 6hrs from Thessaloniki

Delphi

Seek advice at Ancient Delphi, the former home of the mysterious Delphic oracle. Gaze out over the Gulf of Corinth and understand why the ancient Greeks chose this as the centre of their world.

🚗 3hrs from Athens

GREECE BUILD YOUR TRIP

IONIANS & PELOPONNESE
Trip Builder

TAKE YOUR PICK OF MUST-SEES AND HIDDEN GEMS

If you have a hankering for island life along with beautiful towns, historic sights and dramatic scenery, tour the Ionian Islands – with their cooler climate and luxuriant olive and cypress trees – and the wonderful Peloponnese, with lofty, snowcapped mountains, vast gorges, sandy beaches and azure waters.

Trip Notes

Hub towns Corfu, Nafplio

How long Allow eight days

Getting around Ferries run between Ionian Islands (but plan ahead as schedules change) and Lefkada is connected to the mainland by a small bridge. Corfu has an airport with flights from European cities. In the Peloponnese, hire a car and cruise beautiful country lanes.

Tips The Peloponnese's west-coast highway has high crash rates. Stick to smaller roads when possible.

TOP LEFT: BALATE DORIN/SHUTTERSTOCK ©
BOTTOM LEFT: MEVZUP/SHUTTERSTOCK ©
TOP RIGHT: MARK READ/LONELY PLANET ©
BOTTOM RIGHT: SERGIO CONSOLI/SHUTTERSTOCK ©

Corfu
Wander through the amazing blend of Italian, French and British architecture in Corfu's Old Town, indulging in gourmet cuisine, exploring picturesque coastal villages and lounging on sandy beaches.
✈ *1hr from Athens*

Ithaki
Hike through dramatic island scenery and past archaeological sites in Odysseus' homeland (aka Ithaca).
⛴ *30mins from Kefallonia*

Lefkada

Investigate the little-known, thrillingly pure-white-pebble beaches backed by cliffs along Lefkada's west coast. Spend the night in charming Lefkada Town and zip into the mountainous interior for excellent taverna fare.

🚢 1hr from Kefallonia

Vouraïkos Gorge

Chug through the mountainous Achaïa region and the dramatic Vouraïkos Gorge aboard a vintage rack-and-cog railway.

🚗 90mins from Nafplio

Nafplio

Embrace the charm of graceful Nafplio, with its Venetian-era mansions, intriguing museums, and vibrant port and café scene. A natural spot for romantics and families alike.

🚗 2hrs from Athens

Ancient Olympia

Stand in the 3000-year-old ruins of the stadium that hosted the first Olympic Games imagining the crowd roaring, then browse the site's excellent museums crammed with masterpieces.

🚗 4hrs from Athens

EASTERN ISLANDS
Trip Builder

TAKE YOUR PICK OF MUST-SEES AND HIDDEN GEMS

Strung along the Turkish coast, the Dodecanese and Northeastern Aegean Islands have endured a turbulent history that endowed them with a fascinating diversity. These far-flung islands harbour unspoilt scenery, and some remain relatively calm even when others are bulging with tourists at the height of summer.

Trip Notes

Hub towns Rhodes Town, Mytilini Town

How long Allow at least a week

Getting around The islands are interconnected by ferries and there are airports at several islands both in the Dodecanese and in the Northeastern Aegean with flights to Athens and some European cities.

Tips You can also ferry over from the Cyclades. Visiting Turkey's Aegean coastal resorts and historical sites from Samos, Chios and Lesvos is easy.

Lesvos
Bathe in thermal springs on Lesvos, birthplace of the poet Sappho and producer of some of Greece's finest olive oil and ouzo. Mytilini Town offers fantastic cultural life.
✈ 1hr from Athens

Patmos
Experience Patmos' artistic and religious vibe: visit the cave where St John wrote the Book of Revelations and explore beautiful villages like Skala, barely disturbed bays and pine- and heather-coated hillsides.
⛴ 5½hrs from Rhodes

Kos
Dine on the day's catch at waterside seafood restaurants, then follow in the footsteps of Asclepius and Hippocrates, or stretch out on volcanic-sand beaches.
⛴ 3¼hrs from Rhodes

CLOCKWISE FROM BOTTOM: PISAPHOTOGRAPHY/SHUTTERSTOCK ©, PHOTOBAC/SHUTTERSTOCK ©, FRANZ MARC FREI/GETTY IMAGES ©

Kalymnos

Test your mettle learning how to dive for sponges or down to wrecks and climbing the island's limestone cliffs.

⛴ 40mins from Kos

Symi

Explore ravishing Symi whose pastel-coloured harbour houses cling to a hillside and burst into shades of pink, violet and gold as the setting sun casts it glow.

⛴ 1½hrs from Rhodes

Rhodes

While away a couple of days exploring the walled medieval Old Town and checking out its nightlife, plus diving in crystal-clear waters and touring its stunning Acropolis of Lindos.

✈ 1hr from Athens

Nisyros

Explore the striking caldera, wander through traditional villages with charming narrow streets, and enjoy serene, unspoiled beaches on this slow-paced volcanic island.

⛴ 1hr from Kos

Tilos

Slow down in this serene, eco-friendly gem with stunning meadows, mountains, and secluded beaches, perfect for peaceful travel, good food, hiking, and sustainable living.

⛴ 2hrs from Rhodes

ATHENS & CRETE
Trip Builder

TAKE YOUR PICK OF MUST-SEES AND HIDDEN GEMS

Combine the bustle of Athens with Cretan landscape, which unfolds from sun-drenched beaches in the north to the rugged canyons and the cove-carved, cliff-lined southern coast. Trek through Europe's longest gorge, then dine in history-imbued Hania and Rethymno, whose lanes are lorded over by fortresses, Renaissance mansions and mosques.

Trip Notes

Hub towns Iraklio, Hania

How long Allow five to eight days

Getting around Buses crisscross Crete but having your own wheels definitely makes things more spontaneous.

Tips Get used to unusual driving – motorists may slow to a crawl, intending you to pass or, conversely, may zoom by you. If you want to hike a gorge, tour companies can drop you at one end and pick you up from the other.

Athens
Take in Athens' greatest hits, from the Acropolis to the National Gallery, stroll its chameleonic streets, then trip the light fantastic in its bars, restaurants and nightclubs.

6hrs from Thessaloniki

Mediterranean Sea

Western Beaches
Surrender to the shimmering turquoise waters lining the craggy Gramvousa Peninsula, the broad sweep of pink-cream Falasarna beach and Elafonisi's rose-hued sand and undulating dunes.

1hr from Hania

Rethymno

Bask along commanding bastions of a 15th-century fortress and the azure waters of the Mediterranean. The Venetian-Ottoman quarter is punctuated with graceful wood-balconied houses and the occasional minaret.

🚗 1¼hrs from Hania

Hania

Stroll the charming Venetian-style harbour and labyrinth of bougainvillea-draped pedestrian lanes, perfect for adjusting to a Greek rhythm, then enrich your Cretan culinary tour at the town's excellent restaurants.

🚗 2½hrs from Iraklio

Iraklio

Bounce between seafront tavernas and cultural sights like the superb archaeological museum in town before sampling fine vintages in Iraklio Wine Country, a mosaic of shapely hills, sun-baked slopes and lush valleys.

✈ 1hr from Athens

Knossos

Imagine the palaces filled with life at the captivating Minoan ruins of Knossos, with its vibrant frescoes and elaborate apartments and terraces.

🚗 25mins from Iraklio

Southwest Gorges

Connect with Crete's wild side on a trek through the famous Samaria Gorge or one of its lesser-trodden cousins, some of which spill out onto remote, attractive villages and beaches lapped by the crystal-clear Libyan Sea.

🚗 1½hrs from Hania

Amari

In the heart of pastoral Amari Valley, this village has an enchanting medley of Venetian buildings and a square filled with cafes and overflowing flowerpots.

🚗 1½hrs from Rethymno

SLEEPER HITS
Trip Builder

TAKE YOUR PICK OF MUST-SEES AND HIDDEN GEMS

Slide a tad off the beaten track to find a combination of low-key islands featuring strong *filoxenia* (hospitality), some of Greece's best food, wild walking mountains and exceptional swimming waters. Throw in the ruins of multiple great civilisations and there's something for everyone.

Trip Notes

Hub towns Athens, Nafplio

How long Allow 10 days

Getting around This far-flung trip combines islands served by frequent ferries from Piraeus and a couple of Peloponnesian sights reachable from Hydra or by car from Athens. Kefallonia has an airport.

Tips You can hire wheels on each island (except Hydra, where all transit is on foot or by boat). Each spot beckons for a longer stay.

Paxi & Antipaxi
Splash around crystalline neon-blue waters at tiny, glorious Paxi and Antipaxi, where olive groves provide shade on secluded white-pebbled beaches and yachts bob in taverna- and bar-lined harbours.

⛴ *30mins from Corfu*

Kefallonia
Savour the flavours at waterfront restaurants in Fiskardo, daydream on soulful beaches from majestic Myrtos to terracotta-hued Xi, trek through lush forests to the Ionians' highest peak and embrace the cosmopolitan flair of Argostoli.

✈ *1hr from Athens*

Epidavros
Catch a starlit performance from the well-worn stone seats at this ancient theatre amid pine-clad hills, or come during the day to also explore the adjacent Sanctuary of Asclepius, god of healing.
🚗 35mins from Nafplio

Tinos
Explore marble-ornamented villages dotted across the terraced hillsides and misty mountaintops before paying your respects at the sacred Church of the Annunciation.
⛴ 35mins from Mykonos

Hydra
Grand stone mansions embrace a marble-cobbled quay lined with cafes and bobbing boats on this car-less, history-rich island, inviting a side step out of time with rejuvenating swimming, too.
⛴ 2hrs from Athens

Mystras
Find your way through citrus groves to the captivating World Heritage–listed ruins of Mystras, a massive ancient fortress town that was the last stronghold of the Byzantine Empire.
🚗 10mins from Sparta

7 Things to Know about GREECE

INSIDER TIPS TO HIT THE GROUND RUNNING

1 Shopping Hours

Large stores are open from 9am to 9pm (Saturdays until 8pm), but many smaller businesses adhere to traditional shopping hours and close early (2.30pm or 3pm) for the time-honoured siesta, before reopening at 5pm on Tuesdays, Thursdays and Fridays (they remain closed on Monday, Wednesday and Saturday afternoons). On Sundays, all but the most essential stores and those in tourist areas are closed.

3 Late Nights Out

Greeks go out late. They rarely have dinner before 9pm, and drinks usually begin after midnight. Many bars stay open till the wee hours of the morning.

4 Essential Summer Gear

Summers can be extremely hot, so never go out in the daytime without a bottle of water (available everywhere for €0.50), a hat and sunscreen. Sunglasses are also recommended during the day's bright hours.

2 Coffee Culture

Greeks love spending hours outside, sipping coffee, conversing and watching the world go by. This leisurely pastime is one reason for the relatively high prices in popular cafes. Iced coffee is the preferred beverage, even in winter, although the famous frappé (shaken instant coffee served with ice) is no longer so popular. Instead, practically everyone drinks *freddo* (cold) espresso or cappuccino in myriad varieties.

5 Local Lingo

The Greek alphabet may look daunting, but once you know how to pronounce every letter and a few combinations of letters, you can actually read Greek

Most Greeks speak at least some English, but they are always impressed by a visitor who makes the effort to say a few Greek words to them.

▶ See the Language chapter on p252.

6 Etiquette

Greeks like lively conversations and when they speak, it frequently sounds like they're arguing, but you'll know it when you witness a public squabble.

Drivers are not always considerate, and pedestrians must remain vigilant at all times.

If you go out to dinner with locals, it's very common to order an assortment of dishes, place them in the middle of the table and share everything. And, of course, when it's time to pay, your local hosts are highly unlikely to let you pay your share of the bill.

When you visit religious sites, avoid shorts and generally overly exposed attire.

Greeks enjoy discussing their rich history and the impact of Greek civilisation on the world. Politics is also a popular topic, but discussions can become heated – avoid discussing the Civil War, and don't forget the full name when you mention neighbouring North Macedonia. Plain 'Macedonia' is a Greek region and a sensitive issue for many Greeks.

Greek–Turkish relations are tense and unless your views are generally Greek-friendly, it's better to talk about the weather.

7 Stray Dogs

Many stray dogs and cats roam the streets, although the majority are not abandoned pets. They are actually born and raised on the streets, where they are cared for and fed by concerned citizens. Authorities run vaccination and sterilisation programmes for them, and the majority are safe and friendly.

Read, Listen, Watch & Follow

 READ

Mani/Roumeli (Patrick Leigh Fermor; 1958/1966) Classics by one of the best travel writers of all time.

Austerity Measures (Ed Karen Van Dyck; 2016) Contemporary Greek poetry inspired by the economic crisis.

Zorba the Greek (Nikos Kazantzakis; 1946) Superb classic explores the contrast between intellectualism and a zest for life.

Greeks Bearing Gifts (Philip Kerr; 2018) Hard-boiled mystery in Athens 60 years ago.

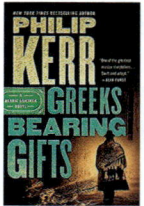

 LISTEN

Gioconda's Smile (Manos Hadjidakis; 1965) A timeless instrumental masterpiece by one of the greatest Greek composers of all time.

Greece Goes Modern (Mimis Plessas; 1967) Traditional songs from around Greece conducted in a wonderful jazzy and bossa-nova style. Recently reissued.

2XXX (Lex; 2019) Stadium-filling Greek hip-hop with strong social and political concerns.

Anime (Fivos Delivorias; 2022) One of the hottest names on today's Greek music scene.

Athens Unpacked (*sofkazinovieff.com/podcast*) Writer Sofka Zinovieff tries to make sense of Athens' complexities.

WATCH

Never on Sunday (1960, pictured right) Rom-com about an American's efforts to pull a kind-hearted sex worker out of her lifestyle.

Summer Lovers (1982) A ménage à trois on glorious '80s Santorini, before the hordes.

The Big Blue (1988) Sublime cinematography of Amorgos and the Aegean Sea.

The Two Faces of January (2014, pictured bottom right) Film adaptation of Patricia Highsmith's atmospheric thriller novel.

The Durrells (2016–19) A family resettles from England in 1935 to a simple but fulfilling life on Corfu.

UNITED ARCHIVES GMBH/ ALAMY STOCK PHOTO ©

PICTORIAL PRESS LTD/ ALAMY STOCK PHOTO ©

FOLLOW

Visitgreece
(*visitgreece.gr*) The official Greek National Tourism Organisation website.

eKathimerini
(*ekathimerini.com*) News and analysis by the leading Greek broadsheet.

Greece Is
(*greece-is.com*) All about Greece in English.

Discover Greece
(*discovergreece.com*) A complete guide by the Greek tourism industry.

More
(*more.com.gr*) Listings and tickets for all events.

ATHENS

CITY LIFE | CULTURE | HISTORY

- **Trip Builder** (p46)
- **Practicalities** (p48)
- **Among the Monuments** (p50)
- **Unlikely Gallery** (p54)
- **Athenian Landmarks** (p56)
- **Around Central Market** (p58)
- **Picnic under an Olive Tree** (p60)
- **Wine Tasting in Attica** (p62)
- **Breathtaking City View** (p64)
- **Party Like a Greek** (p66)
- **Art During Economic Crisis** (p68)
- **Riviera to Sounio's Temple** (p70)
- **Listings** (p72)

ATHENS
Trip Builder

A city with millennia-long history, the capital of Greece is a modern metropolis that attracts throngs of visitors with the abundance of cultural sights, the blessed climate and the laid-back, fun-loving lifestyle. There's plenty to experience for the lovers of the outdoors, food and nightlife alike.

Spend a day by the sea in the bustling port of **Athens Riviera** (p70)
🚃 *45mins from central Athens*

⚓ *Piraeus (6km)*

Delve into Athens' glorious past at the **Acropolis** and the surrounding sites (p50)
🚶 *15mins from Plateia Syntagmatos*

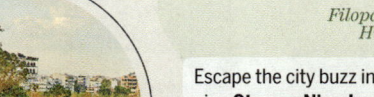

Escape the city buzz in the stunning **Stavros Niarchos Park** (p60)
🚃 *30mins from Plateia Syntagmatos*

⛺ *Stavros Niarchos Park (3.5km)*

Enjoy the sunset with a panoramic view of the city from **Lykavittos Hill** (p64)
🚶 *20mins from Plateia Syntagmatos*

Browse vintage bric-a-brac and antique furnishing around Plateia Avyssinias in the **Monastiraki Flea Market** (p73)
🚶 *10mins from Plateia Syntagmatos*

Tour Attica's ancient wine-producing region of **Mesogeia** (p62)
🚗 *1hr from central Athens*

See world-class modern art in **Basil & Elise Goulandris Foundation** (p69)
🚶 *10mins from the Panathenaic Stadium*

Visit a solemn open-air sculpture museum in **Athens' First Cemetery** (p54)
🚶 *20mins from Plateia Syntagmatos*

FROM LEFT: PIT STOCK/SHUTTERSTOCK ©, NATALIIA SOKOLOVSKA/SHUTTERSTOCK ©, THEASTOCK/SHUTTERSTOCK ©, PREVIOUS SPREAD: TOMAS MAREK/SHUTTERSTOCK ©

Practicalities

ARRIVING

Eleftherios Venizelos International Airport is located 27km east of the city. The metro runs half-hourly until 11.30pm, and it takes approximately 40 minutes to get to Plateia Syntagmatos (€9 single, €16 return). Bus X95 (€5.50) takes about an hour and runs 24 hours. A taxi takes 30 to 40 minutes (flat rate €40/55 day/night). There are also car rental companies in the airport, and ride hailing apps Uber and Free Now.

HOW MUCH FOR A

Souvlaki
€3

Water bottle
€0.50

5-day sites pass
€30

WHEN TO GO

JUN–AUG
High and hot season; the city is packed with visitors.

SEP–NOV
Still pleasantly warm, mainly sunny and less crowded.

DEC–FEB
Mild winter, perfect to see the city's true colours.

MAR–MAY
Glorious spring, when Athens is at its best.

GETTING AROUND

Public transport The quickest and easiest way to move around the city is by metro and tram, operating between 5am and midnight with an extra hour on Fridays and Saturdays. There's also an extensive bus and trolleybus network – a decent mode of transport, traffic permitting.

Tickets (*oasa.gr*) A single 90-minute trip costs €1.20 but you can buy a five-day pass for €8.20 or a three-day pass including a return ride to the airport for €20.

Taxi You can hail a taxi in the street or use one of several apps: Free Now, Ikaros, Taxiplon, Uber (only professional drivers). The cost is €0.90 per kilometre (€1.25 midnight to 5am); minimum charge is €4.

EATING & DRINKING

Greek food is generally healthy and nutritious and Athens is full of street-food joints – souvlaki, of course being the king among them. Every neighbourhood has its own *souvlatzidiko* and the vast majority are above par. The restaurants run the full range for all budgets and tastes, from ethnic and traditional Greek eateries to Michelin-starred establishments. Booking is usually required in most upmarket restaurants. For a true Athenian experience try a traditional taverna, retsina barrels and all.

Best old-school food joint Diporto, Agoras (p59)

Must-try Greek wines Attica region (p62)

WHERE TO STAY

Every neighbourhood in Athens has a distinct character. The city centre is relatively compact, so wherever you stay you'll be within walking distance from the main attractions.

CONNECT & FIND YOUR WAY

Wi-fi There are hundreds of free Wi-Fi hotspots around Athens, but the connection can be lousy during peak times. There's almost universal 5G coverage in the city and all three mobile operators (Cosmote, Vodafone and WIND) offer internet-only packages.

Navigation Any navigation app is good in the city centre – you can download an offline Google map when you're on Wi-Fi.

Place	Pro/Con
Koukaki	The hottest neighbourhood these days is buzzing with tourists and options for going out.
Kolonaki	Posh, elegant, central and relatively quiet but pricey.
Plaka	Picturesque but touristy, with many dining options and close to the ancient sites.
Historic centre	The beating heart of the city, between Ermou, Stadiou and Athinas streets. Commercial flurry in the daytime, vibrant at night.
Exarhia	Youthful and alternative; probably the most affordable option.
Pangrati	Hip neighbourhood slightly away from the centre but with many dining and drinking options.

FREE-ADMISSION DAYS

All museums and archaeological sites are open to the public for free on the first Sunday of the month from November to March, the last weekend of September, 28 October, 18 April, 18 May and 6 March.

MONEY

Credit and debit cards are accepted everywhere; some taxi drivers may frown but the ones working with apps should be fine. Shops catering to tourists can be pricey – you can always ask for a better price but avoid hard haggling.

01 Among the MONUMENTS

HISTORY | ART | FOOD

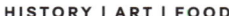 A day spent hopping around Athens' ancient sites is an experience of a lifetime. It starts with the absolute highlight, the sacred rock of the Acropolis, followed by its glorious museum, including dinner on its terrace facing the floodlit Parthenon, and ideally culminates in a concert at the Odeon of Herodes Atticus.

How to

Getting here The main entrance to the Acropolis is the Propylaia at the southwest side of the hill, but there's a less busy southeast entrance gate.

When to go Early in the morning is the best time to beat the tour groups, or go in the last two hours when crowds thin out. The Acropolis Museum restaurant stays open until midnight every Friday and Saturday year-round (book by phone or email).

Combo tickets The best option is a €30 five-day ticket valid for many archaeological sites.

Awe & Inspiration

Getting an early start will allow you to avoid both the crowds and the heat (if you're visiting in summer) at the **Acropolis**. Climb the rock and wander around the magnificent site to fully immerse yourself in the ambience and marvel at the classical beauty and harmony of the enduring monuments.

Try to imagine the place through the centuries and be captivated by the magic of classical Greece. Democracy, science, art, drama and philosophy flourished centuries ago in these very surroundings. The likes of Socrates, Plato, Aristotle, Pericles, Thucydides and Solon once trod these same grounds. It's impossible not to feel the Acropolis' magnetic pull as you roam among the living manifestations of ancient Athens' loftiest ideals.

The World's First Theatre

Built on the southern slope of the Acropolis rock and originally part of the sanctuary of Dionysus Eleuthereus, the **Theatre of Dionysos** is considered the world's oldest theatre, the place where ancient tragedy, comedy and satire were first formally performed to celebrate the cult of Dionysos.

Top left Propylaia
Top right Theatre of Dionysos
Bottom left Odeon of Herodes Atticus

Marble Wonders in the Home They Deserve

After a break for a light snack or a refreshment in the winding alleys of Plaka, the old town, head to the **Acropolis Museum**, one of the finest and most important in the world.

The museum building, an architectural masterpiece in itself, is a short walk away from the Acropolis and houses original marble sculptures taken to safety from the ancient site.

Take a guided tour or simply wander around the four flours to admire the stunning sculptures, friezes and other exquisite artefacts, and conclude in the glorious **Parthenon Gallery** reflecting on timelessness, beauty and human achievement.

The Most Uplifting Dinner of Your Life

The Acropolis Museum boasts a fine restaurant, with tables on its terrace facing

The Acropolis Monuments

The crowning glory of the Acropolis and the city, **The Parthenon** is the apex of classical Athenian monuments and the city's eternal trademark. Dedicated to goddess Athena, the temple was constructed during the Golden Age of Athens (5th century BCE).

The **Erechtheion** features replicas of the glorious Caryatids, the larger-than-life maiden columns that held up the temple. The originals were moved to the Acropolis Museum – but one of the positions remains empty, awaiting the lone Caryatid kept in the British Museum.

On the rock you can also admire the imposing **Propylaia** entrance and the small but beautiful **Temple of Athena Nike**.

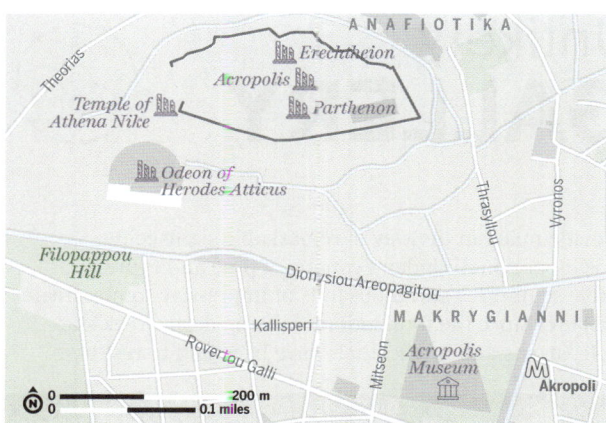

Left Propylaia
Below Aerial view of the Acropolis

the Acropolis – an al fresco dinner here will perfectly complement a fulfilling day.

The fare is traditional Greek, carefully prepared with high-quality local seasonal ingredients, and the prices are surprisingly affordable for a location every restauranteur in the world would kill for.

Both the restaurant and the museum cafe also serve a rich traditional Greek breakfast until noon, in case you prefer to reverse the schedule and start your day at the museum.

A Worthy Close to a Unique Day

The **Odeon of Herodes Atticus**, built in 161 CE at the foot of the Acropolis, hosts almost daily performances of music, theatre, dance and opera during the summer's **Athens and Epidaurus Festival** (*aefestival.gr*). Many international and local stars have performed in this spectacular setting since the 1950s, when it was fully restored.

If you can get tickets for any performance, don't miss this opportunity for a grand finale of a day that will stay in your memory forever.

02 Unlikely GALLERY

WALK | ART | HISTORY

Cemeteries rarely provide much in the way of remarkable sightseeing, but Athens' First Cemetery is exceptional. Under a canopy of pine and cypress, hundreds of wonderful marble sculptures and thousands of impressive tombs create an eerie but tranquil atmosphere. Since the foundation of the modern Greek state, the most famous statespeople, artists and intellectuals have been laid to rest here.

How to

Getting here The cemetery is within walking distance of the Panathenaic Stadium in the district of Mets.

When to go It is open every day from 8am to 8pm; entrance is free of charge.

Be mindful This is a functioning cemetery where funerals take place daily, so try to be discreet and respectful. On a hot day, bring a bottle of water.

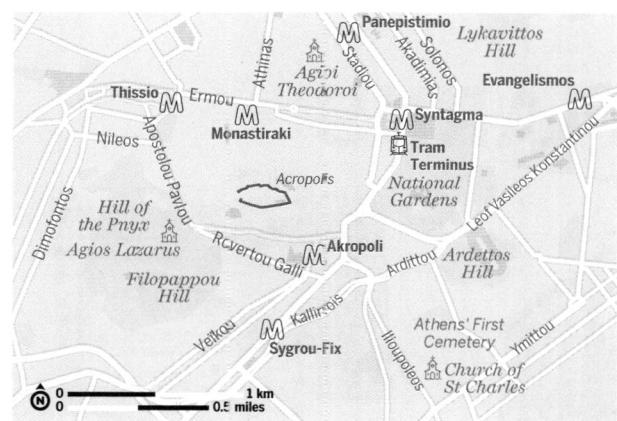

Left and below left Athens' First Cemetery

A peaceful stroll in an art garden The tombs, mausoleums and the grassy alleyways between them are lavishly decorated with marble tombstones, statues and every imaginable adornment. More than 800 magnificent works of art may be found here, while some of the tombs are so large that they resemble ancient temples. Don't miss the mausoleum of archaeologist Heinrich Schliemann (1822–90), decorated with scenes from the Trojan War. A visitor can even admire a reproduction of the **Choragic Monument of Lysicrates**, whose original is located near the Acropolis. The cemetery is also home to three churches: the Greek Orthodox **Agioi Theodoroi** and **Agios Lazarus**, and the Catholic **Church of St Charles**.

A lesson in modern Greek history Take notes or look up some random names you see in the inscriptions on the tombstones, and you could instantly be transported to different periods of modern Greek history through the stories of the deceased. Actor and politician Melina Merkouri, songwriter and musician Demis Roussos, poets Elytis and Seferis, film director Theo Angelopoulos, as well as former prime ministers, mayors, painters, actors, writers, state benefactors, church figures and fighters from the Greek Revolution, are buried here among ordinary Athenians. The caretakers are friendly and used to answering questions, and when they have the time, some lucky visitors even get short impromptu tours.

📖 Sleeping Beauty

The *Sleeping Maiden* is the highlight of the cemetery's art and probably the most famous and recognised modern Greek sculpture.

It was created by the famous Greek sculptor Yannoulis Chalepas in 1877 on the commission of a wealthy, prominent Greek to adorn the tomb of his 18-year-old niece, Sofia Afentaki, who had died from tuberculosis in 1873.

The white-marble statue is a life-size depiction of the young girl, lying on her bed with her eyes closed and holding a cross to her chest. It's widely considered a neoclassical masterpiece and one of the greatest works ever created by the artist from Tinos island.

Athenian
LANDMARKS

01 Parthenon
The eternal Athenian symbol and main sight at the sacred Acropolis, built in the 5th century BCE during the city's 'Golden Age'.

02 National Archaeological Museum
Housed in a magnificent neoclassical building, one of the most important Greek museums has a huge and splendid collection.

03 Panathenaic Stadium
Constructed as the exact replica of an ancient stadium that existed on the site to host the first modern Olympic Games in 1896.

04 National Gallery
A brand-new impressive building for the capital's largest collection of paintings by Greek masters.

05 Acropolis Museum
The state-of-the-art home to all artefacts discovered in and around the Acropolis rock.

06 Parliament
Originally the royal palace of the first king of modern Greece, Otto,

it now houses the Greek parliament.

07 Ancient Agora
The heart of public life in ancient Athens, where democracy was born and flourished.

08 Hadrian's Arch
The monument to the Roman Emperor Hadrian, built in 131 CE, combines Roman and Greek architectural elements.

09 Odeon of Herodes Atticus
A magnificent open-air Roman theatre that still hosts almost daily performances every summer.

10 Athenian Trilogy
The three-building architectural spectacle consists of the old National Library, the University of Athens ceremonial hall, and the Academy of Athens.

11 Roman Agora
Together with Hadrian's Library, this is the most important Roman-era site in Athens.

03 Around Central MARKET

SENSATIONS | FOOD | SHOPS

▬▬ Wander the stalls inside Athens' huge late-19th-century wrought-iron central market hall, as hawkers sell fresh-caught fish and shellfish, as well as freshly butchered meat. Next head to the vegetable market across the way, then browse nearby shops overflowing with spices and the local delis to work up an appetite for lunch.

How to

When to go If you set an alarm and arrive around 7am, deliveries are happening and it's all at its most bustling. But any time from 7am to 6pm Monday through Saturday will do.

Getting there It's an easy walk from Monastiraki, or the Omonia metro (green and red lines) is closest to the market area.

Hangover helper Tavernas within the market, many open 24/7, are an Athenian institution for hangover-busting *patsas* (tripe soup).

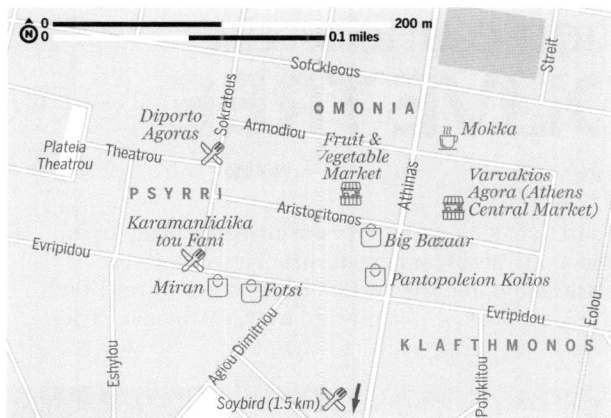

Left Central Market
Below left Olives, Central Market

Getting going For peak energy, before you visit the **Central Market** (Varvakios Agora), fuel up with a Greek coffee at **Mokka** (mokka.coffee) – they use the traditional technique of brewing coffee on hot sand and serving it in copper pots.

The markets Start with the market hall itself, which is dedicated to fish and meat, especially row upon row of lamb carcasses. Wander west across Athinas street to the little **fruit and vegetable market**, piled high with colourful displays of fresh produce.

Fascinating stores After the market, pick through fantastically crammed bric-a-brac at the aptly named **Big Bazaar** junk shop. Plenty of stores sell traditional Greek foods, but **Pantopoleion Kolios** stands out for its scope, stocking Santorini capers, boutique olive oils, Cretan rusks, preserves and countless other edible souvenirs, p us Greek wines and spirits. Evripidou is the street for spices, a couple of highly aromatic blocks of Mediterranean herbs and imported seeds, barks and other wonders. Check out **Fotsi** with its bags overflowing with fragrant herbs and spices.

Make it vegan Lamb carcasses not your thing, but you love Greek food and want to learn how to make it vegan? Take a cooking class at **Soybird** (soybird.com; class from €60) where they'll pair what you prepare – from mousakas to dolmadhes – with beer and wine. They also offer packages that include market shopping – so can join you on this market adventure.

Lunchtime!

Near the market, **Miran** (miran.gr) specialises in cured meats, such as pastourma (pastrami, but spicier). **Karamanlidika tou Fani** (karamanlidika.gr), a modern-day pastomageireio (combo tavern-deli), offers Greek cheeses and cured meats, as well as good seafood and rarer wines and craft beers. Each have tables to enjoy treats on the spot. Or, experience one of Athens' most unique eateries, **Diporto Agoras**, tucked away in a cellar with no signage. There's no set menu, but tuck into the speciality, revythia (chickpea stew), followed by grilled fish and wash it down with metal jugs of cheap wine from giant barrels.

04 Picnic under an OLIVE TREE

OUTDOORS | ARCHITECTURE | CULTURE

In the labyrinthine paths snaking under cypress, olive and plane trees, and through the array of blooming herbs and green shrubbery of the vast seaside Stavros Niarchos Park, you'll find the perfect cool shade to escape the city bustle. Bring a picnic, enjoy a book or just unwind in true Athenian style.

How to

Getting here
There's an hourly free shuttle bus from Plateia Syntagmatos; most bus lines to Piraeus also pass by. A taxi takes 10 to 15 minutes from the centre.

When to go The park is open year-round from 6am until midnight (2am during summer weekends). Of course, its full glory can be best enjoyed on a warm, sunny day.

Tours Entrance to the park is free; there are also daily free guided tours in English for groups of up to 20 people (booked online at *snfcc.org*).

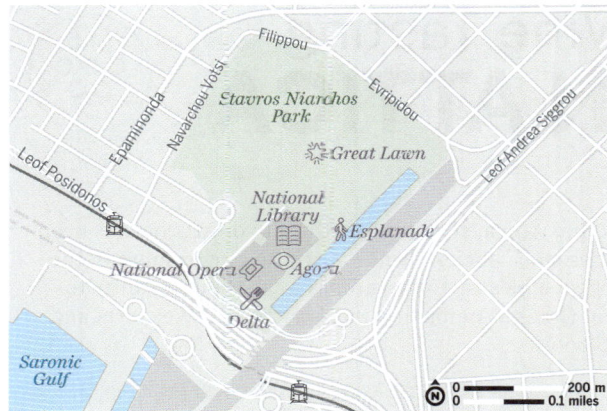

Top Stavros Niarchos Park
Bottom Stavros Niarchos Foundation Cultural Center

Fragrant blossoms and lush greenery Large trees native to Greece such as olives, pines, carobs and laurels abound, and a variety of typical Mediterranean herbal plants like lavender, oregano and thyme have been carefully arranged around the park's 21 hectares to provide a seasonal feast for the senses all year round. Even during the park's busiest days (summer weekends), there's always a quiet shady corner under the greenery where you can indulge in a spontaneous picnic or a carefree rest, complete with the archetypal cicada song.

World-class architecture The Stavros Niarchos Foundation Cultural Center is a magnificent Athenian landmark, designed by the renowned Italian architect Renzo Piano, and hosts the **National Opera** and the **National Library**. The lighthouse on top of the building offers splendid 360-degree views, while the **Agora**, an open space inspired by the ancient concept, is the focal point of the building complex. Along the 400m canal, the **Esplanade** allows for an idyllic stroll to and from the rest of the park.

Dancing fountains, free concerts and open-air movies
The choreographed fountains are one of the most spectacular aspects of the park. They are daily water shows in the canal, put on by water jets and rotating fountains to the sounds of jazz, classical and pop music. The **Great Lawn** is the park's main open space, where visitors can enjoy free concerts and screenings of classic movies during the summer.

※ A Greek Feast

If you don't want to bring your own snacks and drinks, there are kiosks, canteens and a bistro scattered around the park and inside the buildings.

And if you are looking for an exceptional culinary experience, **Delta** – the only Greek restaurant with two Michelin stars – offers contemporary Greek cuisine accompanied by stunning views of the city. With an emphasis on high-quality ingredients and sustainability, the restaurant boasts an exceptional wine list featuring the best wineries from Greece as well as the rest of the world.

05 Wine Tasting IN ATTICA

WINE | NATURE | FOOD

The sun-drenched soil of Attica, surrounding the city of Athens, has been producing fine grape varieties since ancient times. A trip to one or more of the many wineries in the Mesogeia area's vast vineyards is a great opportunity to learn all about the emerging Greek winemaking industry from the experts and try some delicious wines to boot.

How to

Getting here Most wineries are a short drive outside Athens, and the best way to reach them is by car or taxi.

When to go The wineries are usually open to the public during working hours, but most of the larger ones accept visitors at weekends too.

Booking ahead You must call a few days in advance to schedule a visit.

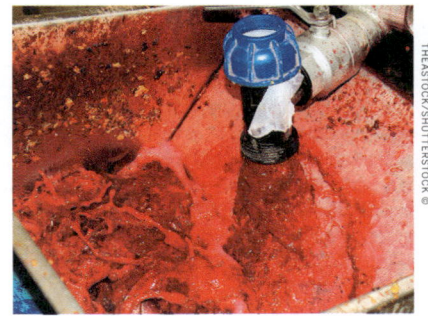

Top Attica vineyard
Bottom Wine making in Attica

🍷 Let's Drink to That

Domaine Papagiannakos This bioclimatic winery was built on the site of an old monastery.

Kokotos Estate A family winery that's been producing organic wines for more than 40 years.

Nikolou Winery For a century and a half, it's been producing wines in Koropi from selected vineyards in Attica and the rest of Greece.

Oenotria Land Established in Kapandriti in 2000, it's a branch of the famous Drama estate.

Strofilia Estate Located in Anavyssos as well as Nemea, the famous *agiorgitiko* region of the Peloponnese.

Zeginis Winery Located near the archaeological site of Ramnous in Marathon.

Heritage and tradition Wine has been produced in Greece for millennia, and there are vineyards with uninterrupted production since antiquity. However, during the last few decades, a new generation of winemakers has invested in all stages of production, and as a result, Greek wines are finally taking the place and credit they deserve on the world stage. There are about 200 distinct regional varieties, many with a 'Protected designation of origin' indication. Attica boasts the world-famous retsina, considered inferior in the past but making a quality comeback these days. The most frequent grapes in this region are *savatiano*, *roditis* and *malagouzia*, but in recent decades Attica has seen the cultivation of a plethora of other varieties – both indigenous and international – that harmoniously marry the grapes' core qualities with the Greek climate and terroir.

An experience to thrill your senses Visiting a winery on the outskirts of Athens is the perfect opportunity to learn about the history of Greek winemaking, walk around magnificent vineyards, have a peek into their cellars and, of course, savour their wines, usually accompanied by matching delicacies. Most places offer guided tours, tastings and the chance to buy your favourite bottles straight from the producers at very affordable prices. The larger estates even have their own wine museums and they often host events on the grounds, such as music concerts, masterclasses and family-friendly activities.

06 Breathtaking CITY VIEW

VIEWS | WALK | SUNSET

Lykavittos Hill looms above central Athens, dominating the city's glorious skyline along with the Acropolis. It's a cherished natural park, with meandering footpaths among shrubs, pines and other greenery, topped by the whitewashed Chapel of Agios Georgios. The 360-degree panorama of the city is stunning – this is arguably the best place in Athens to watch the sun setting.

How To

Getting here You can either walk, catch a taxi or take the funicular to the 277m summit of Lykavittos.

When to go Late afternoon, when the heat subsides and the sun goes down, is the perfect time to go.

Funicular The 10-minute service operates half-hourly between 9am and 2.30am. Return/one-way tickets cost €10/7 (children €6).

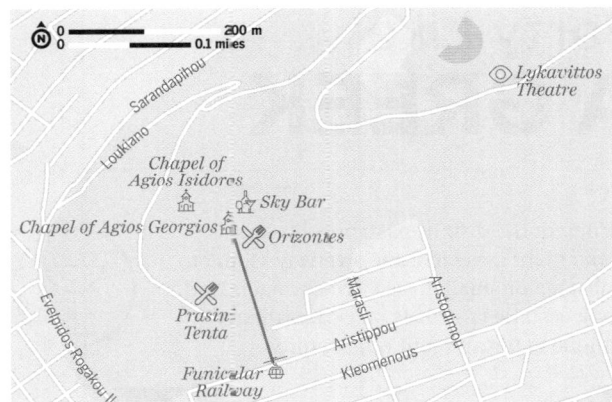

Top Lykavittos Hill seen from the Acropolis
Bottom Chapel of Agios Georgios

Take a break from the city's buzz with an invigorating urban hike up **Lykavittos Hill**, the so-called 'Hill of Wolves', an Athenian landmark you can't miss no matter where you stand in the city centre.

If you're up for some serious hiking, start your ascent from Plateia Dexamenis in Kolonaki and follow the footpaths or go along the road that will take you to the hilltop car park. On the way you'll meet locals from the nearby neighbourhoods of Kolonaki and Exarhia jogging, walking their dogs or just enjoying a stroll on the leafy paths. The hilltop is also one of the favourite romantic spots for Athenian couples.

Located on the site of a former stone quarry, the open-air **Lykavittos Theatre** next to the car park is a time-honoured cultural facility that has seen outstanding performances throughout the years.

From the car park, another footpath ascends to the **Chapel of Agios Georgios**, where weddings and baptisms often take place. The tiny **Chapel of Agios Isidoros** in a nearby cave is one of the oldest in Athens, built after the city became the capital of Greece.

From the open viewing area around the church, as the afternoon progresses, the spectacle is reminiscent of a low flight over the metropolis.

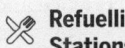 Refuelling Stations

If you want to complement your visual experience with a gastronomic one, there are several options for grabbing a cup of coffee, a quick bite to eat or a full-course meal on Lykavittos Hill.

The historic **Prasini Tenta**, located on the southern slope of the hill, was closed for many years but has recently been restored and is the perfect place to rest before continuing up the hill.

The **Sky Bar** serves appetizers and cocktails alongside the breathtaking views, while **Orizontes** is the more upscale alternative for fine dining with an extensive wine selection.

Finally, outside the theatre there's a canteen where you can get a quick snack or a drink to go.

07 Party Like **A GREEK**

FUN | NIGHTLIFE | MUSIC

Plate-smashing is a thing of the distant past, but the Greeks have never ceased partying the night away in their own way. Going to one of Athens' many live clubs, big or small, to see Greek singers and musicians perform live among ecstatic crowds is an extraordinary cultural experience and a unique entertainment opportunity.

How to

Where to go Check out listings when in Athens, as shows are usually on for a limited time. The action moves from the city to the coast in summer.

When to go Clubs usually open after 10pm, but the fun doesn't start before midnight.

How much If you want to be seated at a table, you must share a bottle of spirits between four or wine between two (roughly €40 to €50 per person). If you just stand, a drink costs €10 to €20.

What about food Although food is sometimes offered, these are not places to dine.

Top left and right Bouzouki players
Bottom left Athens nightclub

Huge clubs, big names, heaps of fun The largest clubs (*bouzoukia* or *pistes*) are impressively glamorous venues that regularly feature the hottest names on the Greek contemporary *laïka* and pop scene, both genres based on the sounds of timeless Greek bouzouki. The clubbers tend to overdress and show up well after midnight. The show kicks off with the supporting acts, and the atmosphere and fun build up until it's time for the real stars to appear. At this point the night lights up and there's singing and dancing all over the place until the morning hours. The audience quickly floods the stage, dancing around the performers and the band while whole trays of carnations are tossed at the stage.

Low-key, high emotion The Greek *entekhno* music scene is more subtle, with elements of Greek folk. It's known for being gloomier and more artistic, and its devotees consider it classier and more upscale than its 'rival' mainstream and mass-market *bouzoukia* world. The respective artists are equally popular and have a large fan base, yet they are very different and prefer playing in more intimate settings without the extravaganza of their pop counterparts. Despite the lack of dancing, the atmosphere and the intensity of the singing are on par with the *bouzoukia* experience, but the average cost is slightly lower.

🎵 Name-Dropping

Nikos Vertis, Konstantinos Argyros, Anna Vissi, Giorgos Mazonakis, Antonis Remos – these are only a few of the most popular performers currently active on the Greek pop scene. During the winter, you may catch them at clubs on **Iera Odos** and **Pireos** streets, while in the summer they play at open-air venues along the coast.

On the other hand, Socratis Malamas, Giannis Charoulis, Foivos Delivorias, Natassa Bofiliou and Miltos Paschalidis are all luminaries in the field of *entekhno*. They perform largely in outdoor summer concerts and only a handful of winter events in more modest venues like **Stavros tou Notou**, **Kyttaro** and **Sfiga**.

Art During Economic Crisis

IN ATHENS, ART ENDURED AND FLOURISHED

Art in Athens not only endured but also flourished during the decade of economic crisis – and it continues to be one of the city's most dynamic cultural offerings. To understand why this is the case, we'll take a look at the big picture.

Tough Roots

During Greece's financial crisis that peaked in 2012 – a time when the status quo was being openly questioned – a feeling of social solidarity and creativity coalesced. The Athens Biennale, the city's largest international exhibition of contemporary art, first raised the question 'And now, what?' in 2013. The next one, in 2015, brought into focus activist cultural groups and self-organised art ventures.

Then Athens co-hosted Documenta – the largest European exhibition of contemporary art – in 2017. It was unprecedented for such a large event to focus on Athens, and it changed the dynamics of the city's art scene. The spotlight of the world's art community turned on the Greek capital.

Suddenly, Athens became a laboratory where one of humanity's greatest experiments was being carried out: the search for a better and more just society. The Greek capital appeared to be an (artistic) land of opportunity, and people from all over came to be part of the ongoing artistic crescendo.

The Onassis Foundation's cultural hub, **Onassis Stegi**, embraced the alternative scene, and dozens of small independent galleries sprang up – many underground and formed by artist cooperatives. Older galleries tended to address the Athenian middle and upper classes and big collectors, while the new ones targeted 'the people'. International street artists joined their Athenian counterparts, creating murals and graffiti that are still a huge attraction in central Athens.

The Scene Today

Now, crisis banished, as stylish hotels mushroom and tourism booms, artistic expression continues to flourish. The revamped **National Museum of Contemporary Art** (EMST),

Left National Opera at the Stavros Niarchos Foundation Cultural Center
Centre Odeon of Herodes Atticus
Right National Theatre

under the direction of internationally renowned curator and art historian Katerina Gregou, hosts exhibitions of great Greek and foreign artists, with a social footprint. It advocates for the rights of communities such as LGBTIQ+ people and showcases their work.

The impressive **National Gallery** complex is complete, and the **Basil & Elise Goulandris Foundation** – a dream museum for every metropolis – houses one of the richest collections of modern, mainly European art. Small galleries still show some of the city's edgiest work.

> Athens became a laboratory where one of humanity's greatest experiments was carried out

Journalist and expert on the Greek art scene Yannis Konstantinidis' take on the future: 'It is very important that the people who live, work and create here are happy because they produce important work. But the next day largely depends on whether they stay in the city, and that in turn has to do with several things: whether life in the city continues to become more expensive and whether the city itself will continue to be interesting.'

Performing Arts

Athenians also love going to the theatre. From neoclassical buildings to tiny basements, hundreds of venues stage an array of performances each season (at the height of the economic crisis, more than 1500 plays premiered). The most important venues include the **National Theatre**, the **National Opera** (in the Stavros Niarchos Foundation Cultural Center, p51) and the **Athens Concert Hall** (aka Megaron). In summer, the action moves outdoors, like to the magnificent **Odeon of Herodes Atticus** (p53).

Best Private Galleries

There are more than 50 private art galleries in the city. Here's a selection of the most representative venues:

Backspace An experimental space for visual arts in Exarhia.

Callirrhoë An independent exhibition space for contemporary art in Koukaki.

Carwan Gallery An international contemporary design gallery in Piraeus.

ERGO Collective A creative platform founded on the premise of collaboration.

Hot Wheels Athens Individual and group exhibitions and collaboration with other art spaces internationally.

Rodeo An international gallery in Piraeus – a 'production house' with a London branch.

08 Riviera to Sounion TEMPLE

BEACHES | SEASIDE | LANDMARK

Attica's western coastline, dubbed the Athens Riviera (or Apollo Coast), stretches for around 50km from Palaio Faliro to the grand Temple of Poseidon at Sounion. It's lined with beaches, resorts and summer nightlife to suit all tastes and pockets.

Trip Notes

Getting here/around Athens' tram runs to Voula, via Glyfada. For Vouliagmeni and beyond, transfer to a bus. It's all easier with your own wheels.

When to go Avoid heavy traffic on summer weekends and set out by 9am; without traffic the drive from Glyfada to Sounion takes about an hour.

Local flavour For excellent seafood, stop off at Sardelaki me Thea with sea views and beach access to Vouliagmeni Bay.

Kicking Back at Sounio

You can get refreshments at the site's **Naos** cafe with its brilliant views, or follow the steep path down to small **Sounio Beach** with its couple of seafood tavernas (try **Aegeon Beach Hotel** or **Akrogiali**). Then rent sunbeds or stake out a bit of free sand for a dip with temple views.

Listings

BEST OF THE REST

Museums & Art

National Archaeological Museum
Superb permanent collections, including the best Greek sculpture, span the Neolithic and Bronze Age, Cycladic and Mycenaean civilisations, as well as the Roman era. Unmissable!

Kerameikos
Browse the museum then the sculpture-filled ancient burial grounds which dates to 1200 BCE.

Benaki Museum
A complex of five top museums featuring works of art. The concise and beautiful Museum of Islamic Art, near Keramikos, is a real gem.

Byzantine & Christian Museum
Based in the 1848 Villa Ilissia, a
nd crammed with religious art, an expansive maze of glimmering gold leaf, mosaics and illuminated manuscripts.

Technopolis
Old gas factory transformed into a cultural hub hosting exhibitions and concerts.

Maria Callas Museum
Museum dedicated to Greek soprano, Maria Callas (1923–77) with close to a three-octave range, a career that dazzled and a life that titillated.

Public Tobacco Factory
Ground-floor spaces, including a glass-roofed courtyard, house epic-scale art installations.

Local flavours

Nikitas €
Tried-and-true taverna serving reasonably priced, refreshingly simple and tasty traditional food since before Psyrri became a hot spot.

Klimataria €
A family-run restaurant in the heart of Athens that dates back a century and is known for its beautiful garden and regular performances of live Greek music. Open all day.

Kriti €€
Tucked away in an arcade on Plateia Kanigos, this is the place to enjoy Cretan cuisine with fresh ingredients sourced from the island.

Kostas €
Arrive early at this pretty Plateia Agia Irini hole in the wall for its excellent pork souvlaki or *bifteki* (seasoned hamburger).

Café Avissinia €€
Classic bistro vibes in the heart of the antique market for live music and varied mezedhes. Acropolis views from upstairs.

A Little Taste of Home €€
It's summed up in the name, with a range of global dishes – all delicious and fresh.

Kanella €€
Housemade bread, retro crockery and brown

National Archaeological Museum

paper on tabletops set the tone for this modern taverna in Gazi.

🍴 Gourmet Gems & Fine Dining

Nolan €€

Fusion cuisine with Greek and Asian touches, under the watchful eye of Sotiris Kontizas, a judge from the Greek MasterChef TV show.

Seychelles €€

Gourmet tavern in trendy Metaxourgio. Greek food with unexpected twists and a peasant setting on Plateia Avdi, ideal for a leisurely alfresco meal on a warm day.

CTC Urban Gastronomy €€€

Treat yourself to an extravagant multicourse tasting menu by Michelin-starred chef Alexandros Tsiotinis in a romantically lit courtyard.

Spondi €€€

The dining benchmark in the Greek capital for more than a quarter of a century – world-class cuisine and service.

Varoulko €€€

Michelin-star chef Lefteris Lazarou offers Athens' finest seafood experience coupled with a terrific location on the promenade of Mikrolimano in Piraeus.

🍷 Vintage Drinking

Galaxy Bar €

This narrow bar with a '70s vibe has been serving regulars and celebrities for 50 years. Come to drink and chat in a quaint ambience.

Au Revoir €

The oldest bar in Athens, unchanged since 1957. The 'time capsule' has served most living Athenian night owls.

Jazz in Jazz €

With a heritage going back to southern Crete in the '70s, this is an old-school jazz den.

Batman €

A small bar in Neos Kosmos that plays Greek retro music and gets packed every night, after midnight until the morning. A cult institution on the Athenian nightlife scene.

Gazarte €€

Respected arts complex with a rich schedule – ground-level theatre hosts live music and rooftop restaurant-bar is glorious on warm nights.

🛍 Shop Till You Drop

Monastiraki Flea Market

In the flea market at Plateia Avyssinias, sift through the piles of junk for strange findings, antiques and retro objects.

Apivita

A Kolonaki-based 'experience store' that features a spa, a fresh juice bar and a 'green' hairstyling service, in addition to retailing a line of natural cosmetics.

Mastihashop

Spirits, cosmetics, remedies and food products, all with the touch and flavour of the unique mastiha (mastic tree resin) grown exclusively on the island of Chios.

Chrisanthos

Shop for beaded bridles and shepherd bells – or, if you don't have a donkey, a set of worry beads. Around the corner, Mompso is the upscale version, catering to Athens' horsey set.

Olgianna Melissinos

Get fitted for custom leather sandals or browse handmade smart belts and bags.

Ermou

The main commercial street in the centre of Athens. Large department stores, international and local boutiques create a brand-name shopper's paradise.

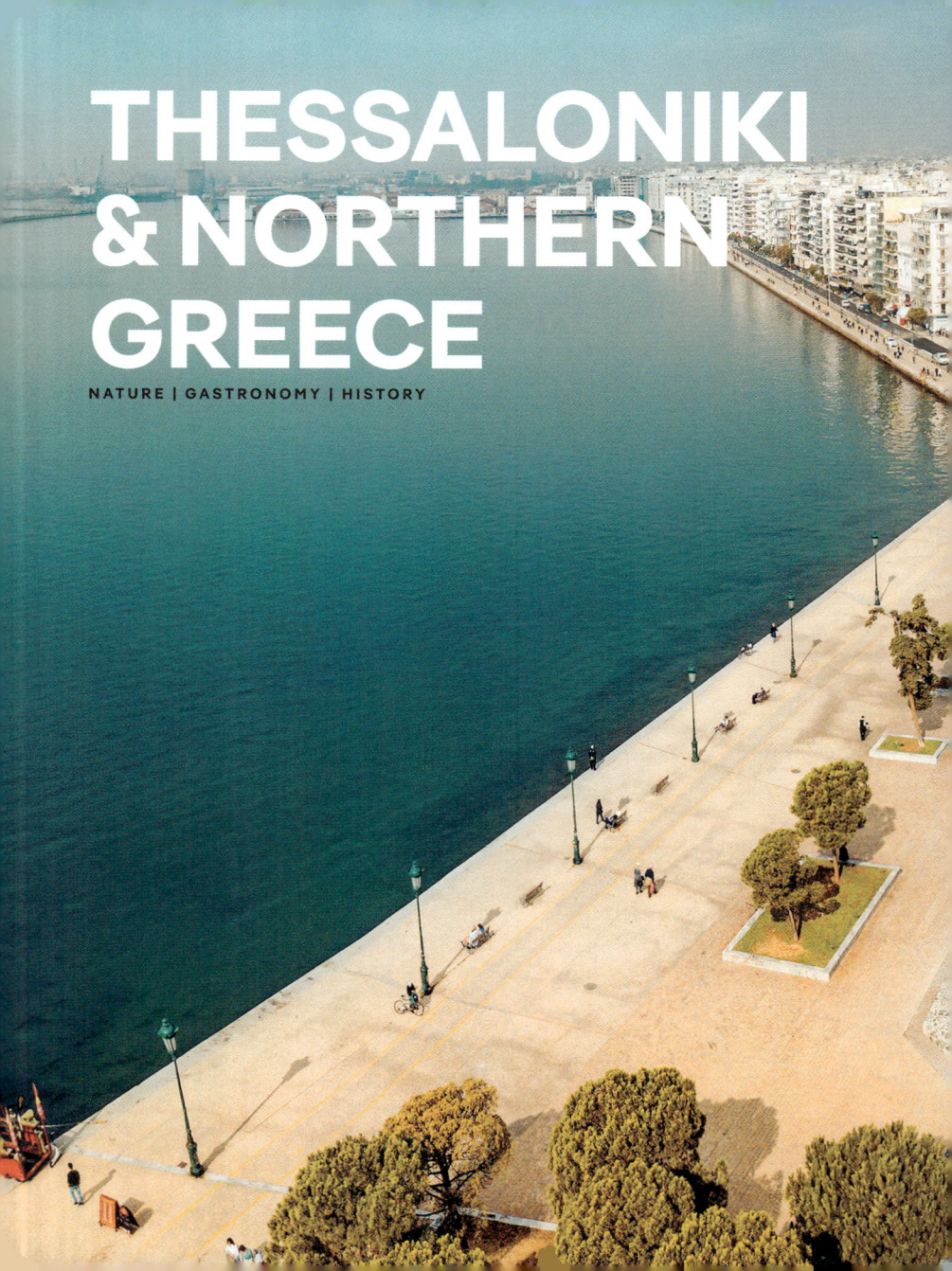

- **Trip Builder** (p76)
- **Practicalities** (p78)
- **Taking a Bite** (p80)
- **Urban Pedigree** (p82)
- **Up in the Clouds** (p84)
- **Ottoman-Era Road Trip** (p86)
- **Zigzagging Zagoria** (p88)
- **The Cuisine of Northern Greece** (p90)
- **No Place Like Halkidiki** (p92)
- **Ioannina's Magic** (p94)
- **Listings** (p96)

NORTHERN GREECE
Trip Builder

Rugged mountains, magical waterfalls, crystalline beaches, perfectly preserved ruins that demonstrate a deep history, limestone villages seemingly lost in time, excellent cuisine – northern Greece is one of the least-visited regions in the country, which is all the more to the benefit of the adventurous traveller.

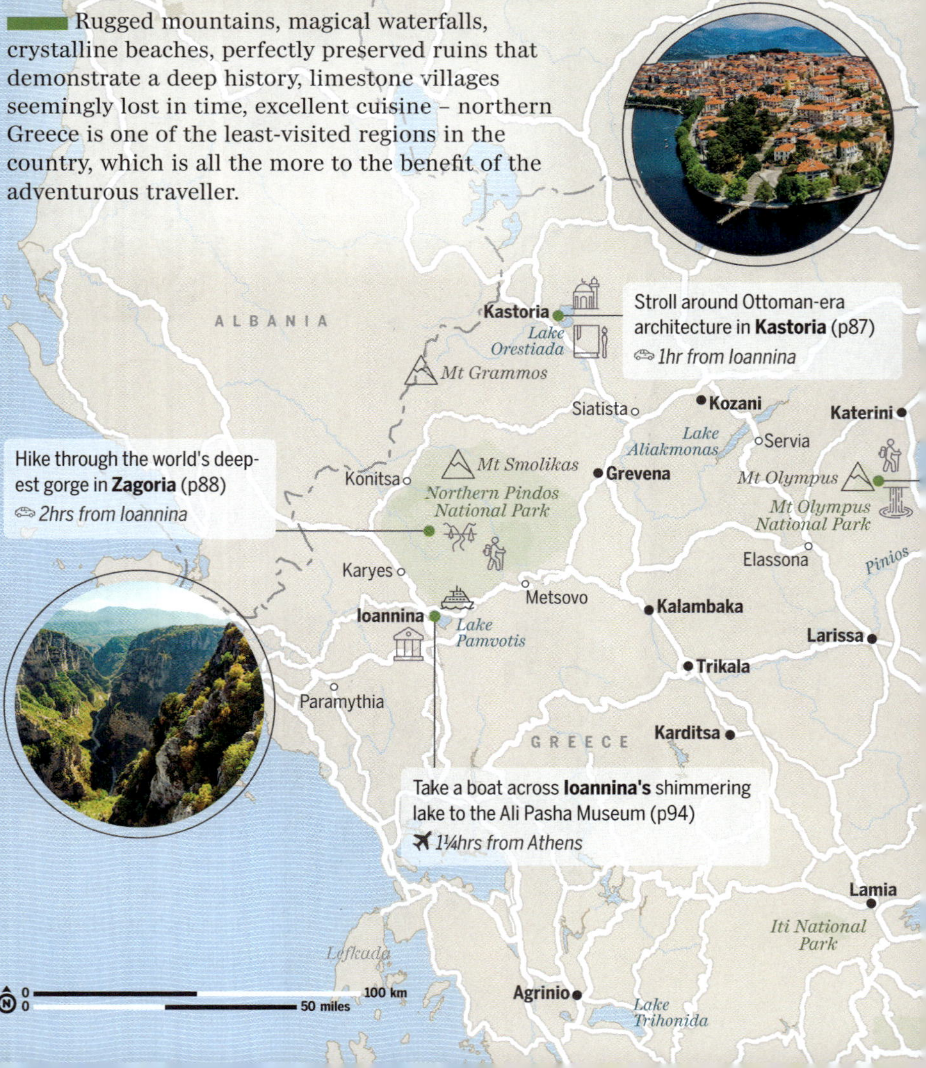

Stroll around Ottoman-era architecture in **Kastoria** (p87)
✈ 1hr from Ioannina

Hike through the world's deepest gorge in **Zagoria** (p88)
🚗 2hrs from Ioannina

Take a boat across **Ioannina's** shimmering lake to the Ali Pasha Museum (p94)
✈ 1¼hrs from Athens

Practicalities

ARRIVING

Makedonia International Airport The region's main transport hub for international and domestic flights; there are smaller regional airports servicing domestic flights in Ioannina, Kavala and Alexandroupoli. Taxis to the centre of Thessaloniki cost between €20 and €30 depending on the time of day or night, and take about 30 minutes. Bus X01 comes every 40 minutes, and takes between 50 and 70 minutes to reach the centre, depending on traffic; tickets cost €2.

WHEN TO GO

JUN–AUG
Hot and humid days, perfect for the beach.

SEP–NOV
The tail end of summer, when you can beat the crowds.

DEC–FEB
Wet, cold, occasionally snowy weather.

MAR–MAY
Warmer days, perfect for city jaunts and hikes.

HOW MUCH FOR A

Gyros
€2.70

Tsipouro
€7

Freddo **espresso**
€1.90

GETTING AROUND

Walking Thessaloniki's centre is compact, and most of the sites are within close distance, so exploring by foot is your best bet. For cities like Ioannina, Xanthi and Kavala, you can also rely on your feet to get around.

Bus The metro is still under construction so for public transport, hop onto the city's bus system. You'll need exact change (€1) to purchase a ticket from the *periptera* (kiosks) or the onboard blue machines.

Car You'll definitely want to rent a car to travel across the region. Driving in Thessaloniki is not for the faint of heart, though – double parking, running red lights and kamikaze pedestrians are seemingly the norm.

EATING & DRINKING

Northern Greece has some of the best food in the country, and Thessaloniki is the gastronomic capital (don't tell the Athenians). In the city, you'll find world-class restaurants and plenty of casual places dishing out souvlaki and *gyros* (rotisserie meat eaten with pitta bread). Along the coast, expect fresh fish and seafood, while in the mountains, grilled meat, boiled greens and fragrant cheeses are the norm. Northern Greece also makes the country's best pies and baked goods. There's a distinct Ottoman influence on the cuisine thanks to the many Anatolian refugees who settled here in the 20th century.

Best restaurant Mourga, Thessaloniki (p81)

Must-try *bougatsa* Select, Ioannina (p95)

CONNECT & FIND YOUR WAY

Wi-fi Buy a SIM card from Vodafone or WIND in stores and at the airport; special tourist packages cost €10 and provide ample data. Most cafes and restaurants have wi-fi, but service can be spotty in the more rugged areas.

Navigation Google Maps works well in most of the region. In some areas, like eastern Zagoria, you won't have good mobile service; pre-load maps to avoid getting lost.

WHERE TO STAY

From atmospheric guesthouses to design hostels, you'll be spoiled for choice. In Thessaloniki, note that hotels in the centre can be a bit noisy even at night.

Place	Pro/Con
Thessaloniki	A cosmopolitan hub with a diverse range of places to stay. Ano Poli is quiet, but an uphill hike. The waterfront has the best views, but can be noisy with nightlife.
Zagoria	Atmospheric stone guesthouses nestled in the mountains.
Halkidiki	Beachfront hotels and apartment rentals to suit any budget.
Ioannina	Ottoman-era boutique hotels with views of the lake.

ARCHAEOLOGICAL SITES

A handy app to download is Topos Text, which geolocates ruins and provides a historical overview.

MONEY

Most places in northern Greece now accept contactless payment through card or phone, but it's always a good idea to have small notes on you to pay for taxis and more off-the-beaten-path restaurants.

09 Taking a BITE

FOOD | DRINKS | HISTORY

▬ As the gastronomic capital of Greece, Thessaloniki is a place where you can literally taste your way through the city's history. With countless bakeries, *tsipouradhika,* souvlaki spots, tavernas and wine bars, each bite and sip will delight your senses and bring new understanding of its layered past.

How to

Getting here/around Fly direct from across Europe, or take a five-hour train from Athens. Most of the listed restaurants and bakeries are within walking distance; for locations slightly further away, a taxi is your best bet.

When to go Summer in Thessaloniki can be brutally hot and humid. The best time for a culinary tour is in May or September, when it's warm enough to dine outside.

Dress code Thessalonikians are known for their style and grooming – you'll look out of place if you're dressed shabbily!

Tyropita After the 1923 Greek-Turkish population exchange, Thessaloniki experienced a culinary boom, as Christians brought over Turkish cooking techniques and traditions – including the best way to make filo pastry. In the district of Neapoli, try the city's best cheese pie at **Milano Bakery**. Started by Anatolian refugees, it hasn't changed the recipe in nearly a century.

Gyros A hallmark of Thessaloniki cuisine, gyros is slow-roasted pork or chicken shaved off with a blade and stuffed into pitta bread with a smear of tzatziki, onions, tomatoes and plenty of French fries. The perfect hangover lunch, the best gyros is found in Toumba district, known for its football stadium and a drink called tuba libre (mix of Coca-Cola and retsina). The best of several rival gyros spots is **Giotis**.

Neo-taverna As a port city, Thessaloniki is better known for fish than meat, with countless tavernas to feast on octopus, sardines and fish fillets. The most interesting seafood dishes can be found at neo-taverna **Mourga**. The menu changes daily – expect dishes like amberjack ceviche, giant grilled prawns and white taramasalata (fish-roe purée). The produce is regional and fresh; the wine list features Greek natural wines.

Sephardic cuisine During WWII, the city lost most of its once-prominent Jewish population, and only whispers of Sephardic culture remain. One such place is **Akadimia** in the historically Jewish neighbourhood behind Tsimiski. Sample (by pre-arrangement) a menu of typical Sephardic dishes, like meatballs with walnuts and parsley and huevos haminados (braised hard-boiled eggs).

Left Greek food
Bottom left A Greek restaurant

A Day at the Market

You could easily lose track of time at the **Kapani Market**, an atmospheric jumble of stalls selling everything from hunks of lamb to mastic from the island of Chios to mountain tea from nearby Mt Olympus.

It is the oldest continuously operating market in the city – since the time of the Ottomans – and the perfect place to stock up on picnic supplies or gifts to take back home.

■ **By Amber Charmei**
Amber's favourite aspect of life in Greece is the graceful way locals embrace the beauty of the moment.

Urban Pedigree

CONTEMPORARY CULTURE WITH PLENTY OF CONTEXT

With its sun-kissed Mediterranean glamour, Roman gravitas, lots of Byzantine glory and sounds and flavours of Asia Minor, Thessaloniki offers a compelling urban experience. This shimmering port city has reinvented itself many times since its founding in 315 BCE. Its latest manifestation is an engaging destination for contemporary art and culture.

Left Thessaloniki International Film Festival banner outside the Olympion cinema **Centre** Museum of Byzantine Culture **Right** Stream in Pozar

In a world where secrets are ever scarcer, Thessaloniki offers that rare quality of being a discovery. With over two millennia of continuous urban life, it has an easy confidence – a city with nothing to prove. Yet it can't help but make a dazzling first impression, with a row of elegant facades so close to the sea you'll taste the salt on a stormy day. Poised between east and west, Thessaloniki has been a magnet for empires – Roman, Byzantine, Ottoman – and a nexus of cultures and faiths. With the arrival of Sephardic Jews expelled from the Iberian Peninsula in the 15th century, it became the main Jewish city of Europe. The lilting cadence of Ladino (Judeo-Spanish), along with Ottoman Turkish, Greek and French, filled the streets of sophisticated Salonica, as it then was called. This petite multicultural metropolis finally joined modern Greece only on the eve of WWI. A decade later, the great influx of Greek refugees from Asia Minor reinforced the city's Greek identity, while underscoring its eastern cultural orientation.

Thessaloniki has absorbed a lot and abandoned little, forging a deeply cosmopolitan culture and complex urban landscape. Worldly yet disarmingly quaint, this is a city of juxtapositions. Roman ruins and Ottoman mosques and bathhouses punctuate ungentrified stretches of grand prewar apartment buildings, belle époque beauty and juicy bites of '60s pop. More than a picturesque backdrop, history is integrated into the city's contemporary life. Bells peal at Byzantine churches, some over a millennium old (13 of them UNESCO-recognised monuments), and locals still shop at the Ottoman-era Kapani Market; join them as they break for a *tsipouro* and mezedhes amid swirling crowds and fresh fish.

With such wealth to draw on, Thessaloniki's **Archaeological Museum** and **Museum of Byzantine Culture** are superb. Engagement with modern and contemporary culture is equally inspiring. At the **MOMus Museum of Contemporary Art**, A-list collections and special exhibitions explore currents in 20th- and 21st-century art. The Costakis Collection, one of the most complete collections of Russian avant-garde art outside Russia, is at the MOMus Museum of Modern Art. Museums at the pier feature experimental art, photography and cinema. The city adores film – cinephiles and luminaries converge for the Thessaloniki International Film Festival, as well as the Short Film Festival and notable Documentary Festival. The highlight of the visual arts calendar is the Thessaloniki Biennale of Contemporary Art, encompassing a performance art festival when the city shines as a surreal stage.

Nightlife here is an art itself, with many expressions both Greek and international. As a city with a large student population, Thessaloniki has always had a famously active music scene. Thanks to its excellent crowds and a couple of choice venues, it's also a favourite stop for touring bands of all genres. Over a dozen music festivals supplement a full concert programme. And with an after-hours food scene to match, no one goes home hungry; there's *patsas* (tripe and trotter soup) for the bold, and many other choices for the rest of us.

> With a row of elegant facades so close to the sea you'll taste the salt on a stormy day.

Bathhouse Culture

Bathing in one of the city's grand public baths was part of Thessaloniki's culture for centuries; the last closed only in the 1960s. But you can still enjoy the experience at **Loutra Lagada**, half an hour from town.

Natural warm waters fill the Byzantine pools (dating from 900 CE and 1400 CE), separated by gender in the daytime and reserved for private use in the evenings.

At the gorgeous **Loutra Pozar**, about two hours from Thessaloniki, you can bathe in warm natural pools and waterfalls as steam rises into the trees above. It also has private indoor baths, and stays open until late.

10 Up in the CLOUDS

HIKING | WATERFALLS | RUINS

As the loftiest peak in Greece, Mt Olympus has a history as impressive as its height (2918m): here, after all, is the mythical home of the ancient Greek gods, and the palpable energy of the 12 Olympians remains. Today it's better known as a hiker's paradise, with wild nature full of endless waterfalls and natural pools, and the unmissable ruins of Ancient Dion.

How to

Getting here/around Mt Olympus is an hour's drive from Thessaloniki. You'll need a car to get around the area (aside from hiking in the mountains).

When to go Hiking is best in spring, summer (when the water is most refreshing) and autumn. The temperature can drop quickly at night, so bring layers. Avoid hiking in winter, as the top of the mountain becomes very unsafe.

Where to sleep Litohoro makes a practical base, though you can also stay in the refuges that dot the landscape. Wild camping is not permitted.

Pay your respects In the shadow of Mt Olympus lies **Ancient Dion**, one of the most important sites in classical Greece – this is where Alexander the Great made sacrifices to Zeus before going to war. Take your time walking through the grounds, sitting by the river and eating figs that generously grow off the trees. Don't miss the **Sanctuary of Isis**, goddess of fertility; in the heat of summer, watch out for the snakes that slither through the tall grass (in ancient times, they were believed to protect the temples). Entry includes access to the park and the **Archaeological Museum of Dion**.

Wild swimming There's a number of hiking trails around **Mt Olympus**, among them the E4 European path that begins in the village of **Litohoro** and ends in Prionia at an altitude of 1100m (the hike takes about five hours). The springs of Prionia feed the mountain with gushing waterfalls and deep natural swimming pools, beckoning you to jump in. Most are accessible just off the main hiking trail, and the further up the mountain you go, the icier the water gets.

A bacchanalian evening What would the gods want you to do after a day in nature? Get drunk, of course. In the village of Litohoro, make a beeline for **Disco Romeiko,** an all-day cafe-bar that sits by the Enipeas River. Run by a former DJ and her husband, it always has excellent music, generously poured drinks and delectable mezedhes. Most evenings, the party goes on until late and the bar turns into an impromptu dance floor.

Left and bottom left Mt Olympus

✖ A Small Feast

Fasoladha (bean soup) is, surprisingly, the national dish of Greece – and one of the best places to eat it is at the entrance of **Prionia**.

There, a tavern by the same name welcomes weary hikers with fiery shots of raki and steaming bowls of bean soup, flecked with red pepper and served with warm, homemade bread.

11 Ottoman-Era ROAD TRIP

HISTORY | RELIGION | ARCHITECTURE

The legacy of the Ottomans is still tangible in the north, and the best way to soak up the history is on a road trip. From the lakeside city of Kastoria to Xanthi, where a distinct Islamic presence is still felt, you'll feel like you've stepped back in time.

How to

Getting here/around Thanks to the Egnatia Odos highway, completed in 2017, it's never been easier (or safer) to drive through the mountainous terrain connecting these once distant cities.

When to go Spring or autumn is the best time to visit. Avoid winter, when the roads can become icy and dangerous.

Road-trip snacks The most portable snack is *koulouria* – a yeasted bread ring coated in sesame seeds. It's crunchier and thinner than its Turkish counterpart, *simit*, but the culinary parallels are obvious.

Ottoman-Era Thessaloniki

Don't miss the **Bey Hammam** (the old public baths, pictured), **Alaca İmaret Mosque** and **Eptapyrgion** (or Yedi Kule, a defensive fort turned into a prison).

History buffs should also stop at the birthplace and residential home (now museum) of **Mustafa Kemal Atatürk**, the founder of modern Turkey.

02 It's a two-hour drive to **Thessaloniki**, one of the Ottoman Empire's most important cities. A walking tour around the centre will reveal many architectural gems, though most buildings are today used as markets, cafes and churches.

03 A former Islamic seminary built by Pasha Mohamed Ali in **Kavala**, Imaret features vaulted stone ceilings and a jaw-dropping hammam. The impressive grounds and delightful restaurant are open to the public, or splurge and spend the night.

04 Some 600 Ottoman-style mansions built in **Xanthi** include the impressive Kouyioumtzoglou Mansion. Xanthi has Greece's largest Muslim population, with working mosques and shops selling Islamic books and prayer rugs.

01 The atmospheric lakeside city of **Kastoria** has some of the most interesting Ottoman-era buildings around. The single-domed Koursoum Mosque in the historic centre is the only one surviving in the area.

12 Zigzagging ZAGORIA

HIKING | VILLAGES | GASTRONOMY

Nestled between the Pindos Mountains and the Ionian Sea, Zagoria, located in the region of Epiros, is one of the last relatively unknown parts of Greece – largely thanks to its isolation. With nearly 50 villages dotting the landscape, stone forests, gorges, waterfalls and musical festivals, it's a truly entrancing part of the country.

How to

Getting there/around Ioannina serves as the gateway to Zagoria, but you'll need a car to get around the mountain.

When to go Winter: ice climbing and snowshoeing. Summer: foraging for blackberries and cooling off in mountain springs.

Pop on some tunes A special kind of Greek blues comes from Epiros; Grigoris Kapsalis is the most prolific *klarino* (clarinet) player – load up a playlist for melodic beats.

Pack a map The eastern side of Zagoria has no mobile service; make sure you pack a paper map.

Top Vikos Gorge
Bottom Monodendri

Bridges There are more than 100 soaring stone bridges across Zagoria, built in the 18th and 19th centuries by craftspeople trying to connect isolated villages to each other. These impressive feats of engineering are artworks, seamlessly built into the environment. Some can be easily spotted from a car, like the **Noutsos Bridge** on the road from Dilofo to Koukouli. To reach others, such as the **Plakida Bridge**, with its triple arch on the edge of the village of Kipoi, you'll need to hike.

Hike the gorge The 12km-long, 900m-deep **Vikos Gorge** is the world's deepest gorge relative to its width. Those who have no fear of heights can head to the **Beloï Viewpoint** for jaw-dropping views of the canyon (the acoustics up here are pretty great, too). You can also trek through the gorge along the **Voïdomatis River**; it's best to do this in summer. The classic route starts in **Monodendri** and ends in Vikos or vice versa; in either case, follow the O3 signs and budget up to seven hours for the hike.

Villages Collectively, the 44 villages of Zagoria are known as **Zagorohoria**, and each one is seemingly more beautiful than the next. All are built out of limestone, with quiet squares shaded by plane trees and framed by bougainvillea – you'll feel like you've stepped into a fairy tale. For a truly magical experience, don't miss the three-day mid-August *panigyri* (religious festival) in the village of **Vikos**, where you'll experience traditional Epirot music and dance

Metsovo Magic

You'll smell **Metsovo** before you see it – a heady mix of chimney smoke, pine trees and, most importantly, grilled meat.

The most delectable can be found at **5 Fs**, an outdoor taverna that has been doling out perfect portions of grilled meat, unceremoniously served on butcher paper, for decades.

This is the best place to try *provatina* (female sheep), and more adventurous eaters should go for *kokoretsi* (lamb sweetbreads and liver wrapped in intestines).

Round out the meal with smoked cheese and fried potatoes.

The Cuisine of
NORTHERN GREECE

01 Florina pepper
A sweet red pepper that is pickled, grilled or preserved in olive oil. Around Greece, it is revered for its delicate taste and structure.

02 Tsoureki
Greece's answer to challah, this yeasted, braided bread has a complex flavour thanks to the addition of mastic and *mahlepi* (wild cherry bark).

03 Bean soup *(fasoladha)*
Some of the country's best beans come from the north, around the Prespes region. Boiled until creamy and tender, it's the perfect post-hike or winter meal.

04 Kokoretsi
No part of the animal goes to waste in Greece. *Kokoretsi,* or offal wrapped in intestines and grilled to perfection, are a favourite in the north.

05 Tsipouro
Triple-distilled grape alcohol reminiscent of grappa, served in tiny glasses – you can easily have 20 before realising what's happened.

06 Bougatsa
This breakfast pastry is made with filo dough

and stuffed with either sweet custard cream or salty cheese.

07 Soutzoukakia

These oblong kebabs spiced with cumin are usually grilled over an open fire and served with a little pile of crushed *boukovo* (red-pepper flakes).

08 Galotyri

A combination of sheep's cheese and yogurt, this delicious spread originated in Epiros. It's often eaten with meat to aid digestion.

09 Metsovone

This semi-hard, smoked cheese is a mountain speciality from the village of Metsovo. It's eaten plain or served grilled and sprinkled with paprika.

10 Spoon sweets

Ultra-sugary preserved fruits suspended in unctuous syrup. It can be made with any fruit and is usually served with Greek coffee or yoghurt.

11 Mushrooms

There are more than 2000 varieties of mushrooms in central northern Greece, and during the autumn you can go mushroom-hunting yourself.

13 No Place Like HALKIDIKI

BEACHES | BOAT TRIPS | DIVING

▬▬ Forget the islands – some of Greece's best beaches are actually on the three-fingered, potbellied peninsula just an hour's drive from Thessaloniki. 'There's no place like Halkidiki', the local saying goes, and it's true. From crystalline beaches to the most important site for the Greek Orthodox Church, Halkidiki has something for everyone.

 How to

Getting around
For travelling around the peninsula, opt for a car rental.

When to go Try and avoid August, when crowds are at their peak.

Choose a peninsula Kassandra Peninsula is the most developed for package tourism. Sithonia has the best beaches and a more relaxed vibe. Athos is the holy prefecture and only part is accessible.

Religious permits Men wishing to visit Mt Athos will need to apply for a special permit (called a *diamonitirion*) from the Pilgrims' Bureau in Thessaloniki or Ouranoupoli.

Boating Ever dreamed of being a captain? You don't need a special licence to rent a small boat and navigate the turquoise waters between the Sithonian Peninsula and Mt Athos. In **Vourvourou**, you'll find dozens of retailers renting out boats for the day; bring your own food or snacks and set sail for **Diaporos Island**. You'll be able to drop anchor wherever your heart pleases.

Holy mountain One place you can't visit unaccompanied is **Mt Athos**, the most holy place for the Greek Orthodox Church and a World Heritage Site with a 1700-year-old history. Women aren't permitted to visit the area, so for a more inclusive experience, book a three-hour cruise from Ouranoupoli with **Athos Sea Cruises**, which will give you a glimpse of the 20 monasteries from a distance.

Diving As impressive as Halkidiki's shores are, what's going on underneath is even more jaw-dropping. At the village of **Nikiti** in Sithonia, **Atlantis Diving Center** offers one-day diving excursions. There's no need to be a professional – they have options for first-time divers and children, and you're guaranteed to spot silvery schools of fish.

Beaches There's no shortage of beaches in Halkidiki. Organised beaches (with lounge chairs, bars and pulsing music) can be found in Kassandra (the most beautiful is **Glarokavos**), while undeveloped beaches are the norm in Sithonia (check out **Armenistis** or **Karidi**). Alternatively, head to the hidden naturist beach of **Kalamitsi**. Here, people pitch tents and drop their clothes for weeks at a time. Nudism and free camping is a big part of the Greek summer experience, and this is the perfect place for it.

Top Mt Athos
Bottom Beach in Sithonia

 For the Free Thinker

Philosophy buffs should make a pilgrimage to the seaside village of **Stagira**, the birthplace of Aristotle, one of the greatest names in European philosophy and Plato's most famous student.

Nearby, a 'theme park' has been erected in his honour, and while you won't find rollercoasters or Ferris wheels, you will see replicas of many scientific inventions mentioned in Aristotle's textbooks, including optical discs and a playable pentaphone (sounding bars).

14 Ioannina's **MAGIC**

HISTORY | CRAFTS | GASTRONOMY

Set on Lake Pamvotis, Ioannina has an atmospheric city centre, perfectly preserved ruins and a strong arts and crafts scene. The air smells like figs or firewood, depending on the season, the morning fog rolls in over the silvery lake, while the chants of the Orthodox priests float above the abandoned Ottoman-era minarets.

How to

Getting around
Unless you're planning on travelling outside the city, Ioannina is compact enough that you don't need a car or public transport.

When to go Ioannina is stunning year-round but particularly magical around Christmas, when the city is awash in twinkling lights and snow caps the mountains.

Where to stay Book a room in the Its Kale district, which is pleasantly quiet but still close enough to the centre that you'll be in on the action.

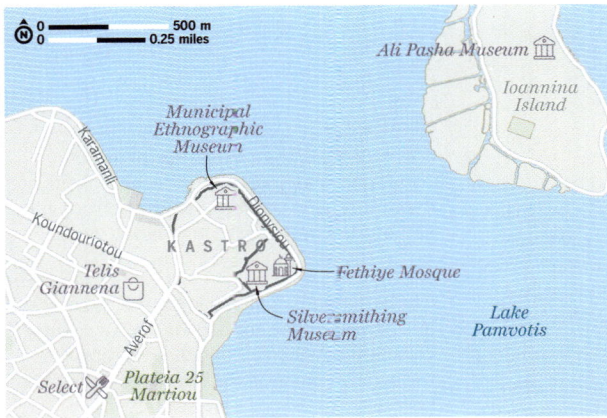

Catch a ferry to the tiny island on Ioannina's **Lake Pamvotis**, famous for being the summer residence of Ali Pasha, one of the most important figures in Epirian history – and the place where his life came to a gruesome end. The enchanting island has been inhabited for centuries and today, aside from some local residents, it hosts the small **Ali Pasha Museum**, located in his former home. The islet is also famous for fried frog legs, which you can munch on at **Prasini Akti**.

Spend some time wandering around the **Kastro**, where you can soak up centuries of Ioannina's history in a few hours. Start at the **Municipal Ethnographic Museum**, housed in the former Aslan Pasha Mosque (keep an eye out for the ketubahs, or Jewish wedding contracts), before heading onto the ruins of the fortress, the 1430 **Fethiye Mosque** and the ornamented tomb of Ali Pasha. Here you can also check out the **Kahila Kedosha Yashan Synagogue**, which is the oldest Romaniote synagogue in the Balkans (visit by appointment only). The whole fortified area is now wheelchair-accessible; you can purchase one ticket that will give you access to all the sites.

As the former silversmithing capital of Greece, Ioannina is known for all things shiny (and for being the hometown of Bulgari). Head to the **Silversmithing Museum** to learn about the city's historic contributions to this ancient craft. While you'll find plenty of jewellery stores along the town's main drag, a much more unique gift is a hand-forged knife – and the best ones can be found at **Telis Giannena**.

Top Autumn in Ioannina
Bottom Fethiye Mosque

 Bougatsa Breakfast

Make a beeline to **Select**, a family-owned *bougatsa* (a type of pastry) spot in downtown Ioannina serving two things: custard-filled *bougatsa* and cheese-filled *bougatsa*.

Served piping hot and haphazardly cut with a double-handled knife, this is the most traditional – and delicious – way to start the day.

Select is one of the oldest bakeries in town, and it's been doling out *bougatsa* for decades.

Listings

BEST OF THE REST

 Local Flavours

Souvlaki Kostas €
Little cubes of pork, chicken or lamb are grilled to perfection on a wooden stick, basted with olive oil and garnished with lemon juice. You can eat them plain or in a sandwich, and the best ones in Thessaloniki can be found here.

Bantis €
Since 1969 this little corner shop in Thessaloniki has been doling out *bougatsa,* crispy filo pastries filled with cheese or vanilla cream. Served piping-hot out of the oven and sold by the weight on an old-fashioned scale, they make the perfect breakfast.

Ktima Bellou €€€
On the eastern side of Mt Olympus, where few tourists venture, lies this hotel-restaurant where all the (organic) ingredients are grown on their own land.

Thomas €€
Opened in 1970, this family business in Sklithro is one of the best in Greece. Come here to try wild-mushroom orzo, local *saganaki* cheese with red-pepper jam, and any of their meat dishes. All regional ingredients and only Greek wines.

Ta Psaradika €
A very cute cafe next to the Prespa Lakes that's the perfect place to try the famous Prespes beans and smoked trout.

Kanella & Garyfallo €€
Northern Greece is abundant in mushrooms, and this mountain restaurant in the Zagori village of Vitsa is the best place to try them in a million different ways – stuffed, fried, sautéed, or pureed into soup are just a few examples.

Genteki €€
This little restaurant in Florina takes slow cooking very seriously – all the ingredients are hyper-local and cooked over an open fire. It's some of the best food in northern Greece.

Akanthos €
One of the oldest *kafeneia* in Greece, Akanthos in Tzoumerka has been serving honest country cooking for decades. Sit under the grapevines in the summer or inside the cafe in the winter. The speciality is *provatina* (female sheep).

Coffee & Wine

Kofi Microroastery €
A cute third-wave coffee shop for takeaway; perfect for strolling Ioannina's town centre.

Its Kale Cafe €
In the castle ruins of Ioannina, with a breathtaking view of the lake and mountains, this is the most atmospheric place to have a cuppa.

Domaine Ligas €€
The winery that put natural Greek wine on the map, now in its second generation in

Papingo Rock Pools

Giannitsa. Come here to sample some of the most interesting wines in Greece. Visits by appointment.

SHED €
One of the best in Thessaloniki: a third-wave coffee shop with outdoor seating located next to a sunken Byzantine church.

Domaine Karanika €
The only winery in Greece producing sparkling wine is run by a gregarious Greek-Dutch winemaker near Florina. By appointment.

Chatzivaritis Estate €€
One of Greece's only female winemakers runs this family business in Goumenissa, making low-intervention natural wines from local grapes. Visits by appointment.

Outdoor Thrills

Arcturos Bear Sanctuary
The brown bear, Europe's largest land mammal, exists only in small numbers – and several of them have been placed in the Arcturos Bear Sanctuary near Kastoria. It's a delightful outing.

Tzoumerka National Park
The Arachatos River in Tzoumerka, south of Ioannina, has some of the country's best whitewater rafting – you'll float through gorges and under stone bridges. Whether you're an experienced rafter or a newbie, there are cascades for any skill level.

Prespa Lakes
Near the border with Albania and North Macedonia lie the twin Prespa Lakes, Greece's most impressive. Swimming, strolling and birdwatching are all fun activities around the lakes.

Papingo Rock Pools
In Zagorohoria, millennia of erosion have created a karst terrain with natural rock pools and

Archaeological Museum, Pella

waterfalls. Come in spring or early summer, when the water is still high enough to bathe.

Historical Vibes

Art of Silk Museum, Soufli
Just across the border from Turkey, Soufli is the former epicentre of silk production in the Ottoman Empire. This informative museum is a great place to learn about the trade and purchase a few silk items.

Vergina Royal Tombs Museum
The ancient royal tombs of the Macedon Kingdom make for an arresting experience – the *tumulus* (burial mound) has been turned into an underground museum. The undisputed star is the marble tomb of Philip II, Alexander the Great's father.

Archaeological Site of Pella
Pella rose to fame in late 5th century BCE when King Archelaos made it Macedon's capital. Also visit the adjoining Archaeological Museum, where burial treasures including remarkable gold jewellery are on display.

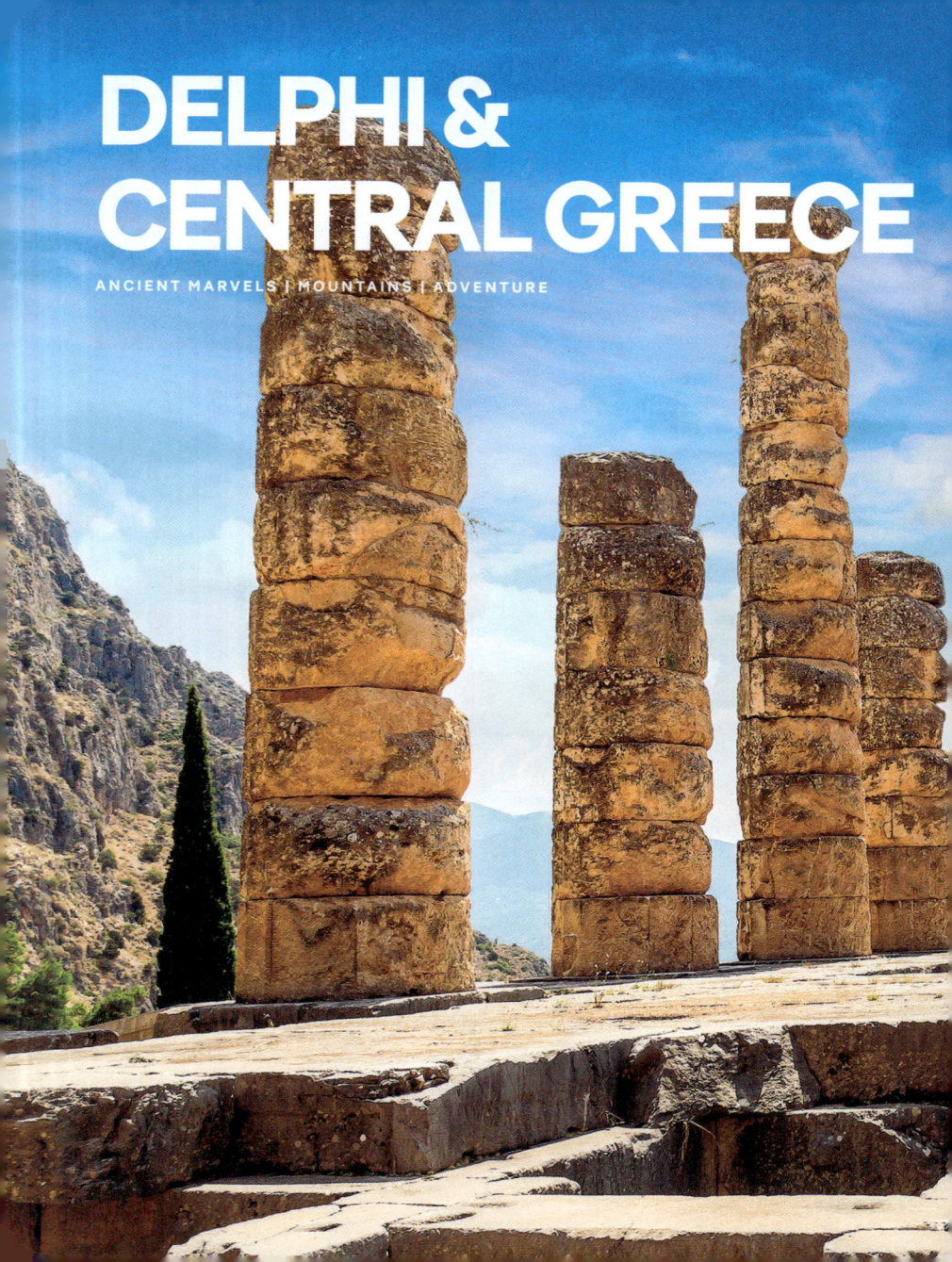

DELPHI & CENTRAL GREECE

ANCIENT MARVELS | MOUNTAINS | ADVENTURE

- ▶ **Trip Builder** (p100)
- ▶ **Practicalities** (p101)
- ▶ **Delphi Done Differently** (p102)
- ▶ **Tsipouradhiko Ritual** (p104)
- ▶ **Action-Packed Peninsula** (p106)
- ▶ **Cavorting in Karpenisi** (p108)
- ▶ **Small but Mighty Messolongi** (p110)
- ▶ **Escape to the Country** (p112)
- ▶ **Listings** (p114)

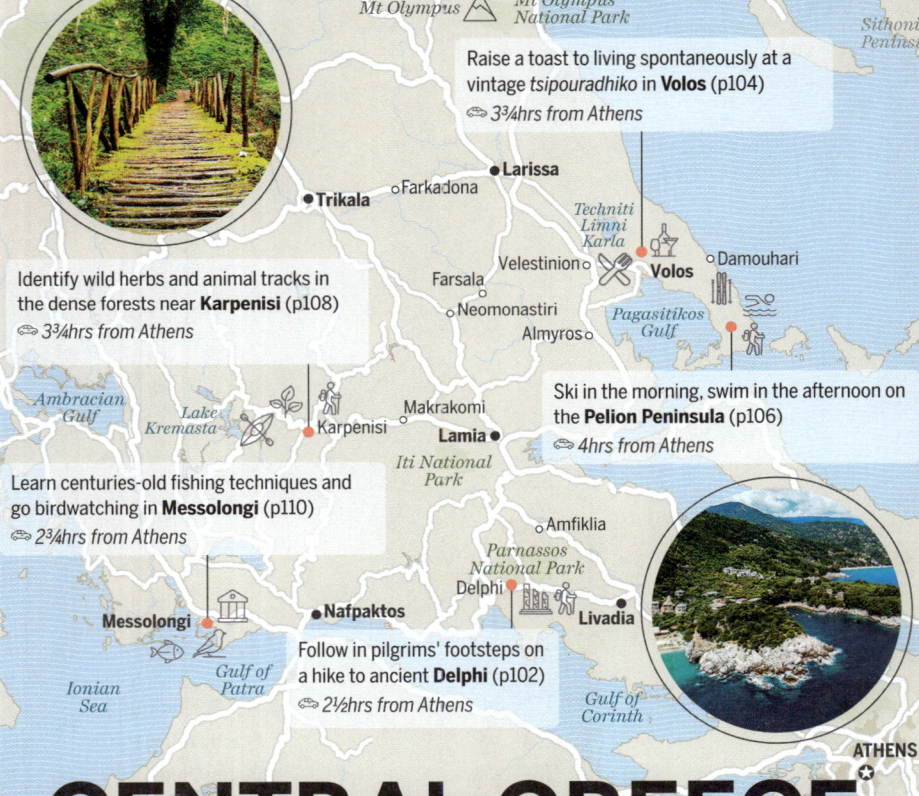

Raise a toast to living spontaneously at a vintage *tsipouradhiko* in **Volos** (p104)
🚗 3¾hrs from Athens

Identify wild herbs and animal tracks in the dense forests near **Karpenisi** (p108)
🚗 3¾hrs from Athens

Ski in the morning, swim in the afternoon on the **Pelion Peninsula** (p106)
🚗 4hrs from Athens

Learn centuries-old fishing techniques and go birdwatching in **Messolongi** (p110)
🚗 2¾hrs from Athens

Follow in pilgrims' footsteps on a hike to ancient **Delphi** (p102)
🚗 2½hrs from Athens

CENTRAL GREECE
Trip Builder

Central Greece's UNESCO World Heritage Sites of Meteora and Delphi are must-sees. But venture beyond these ancient marvels to discover bird-filled wetland habitats, spirit-fuelled eating and drinking rituals, river trekking, winding mountain trails, beaches the equal of any in Greece and more.

FROM LEFT: TSAGOS/SHUTTERSTOCK ©, CHAVDAR LUNGOV/SHUTTERSTOCK ©
PREVIOUS SPREAD: SERGII FIGURNYI/SHUTTERSTOCK ©

Practicalities

ARRIVING
Athens International Airport Express buses from central terminals connect with the extensive KTEL intercity bus network, reaching Pelion and Messolongi.

Volos Airport KTEL intercity buses run from airport to Volos. Regular routes operate between Volos and Pelion's villages.

MONEY

You can pay by card pretty much anywhere, but bring some cash just in case. ATMs are harder to come by in villages.

FIND YOUR WAY

GPS works fairly well in most towns and villages. Mapping apps can be unreliable in more remote areas.

WHERE TO STAY

Place	Pro/Con
Delphi	Mountain views and easy access to ancient site. Town and accommodation on the plain side.
Pelion Peninsula	B&Bs in traditional mansions. Inconvenient without a car.
Karpenisi	Snug guesthouses in pretty villages. The capital has lost character.
Volos	Inviting waterfront, vibrant nightlife. City hustle and bustle.

EATING & DRINKING
The region's fare is meat-focused – this is where spit-roasting originated. Chargrilled lamb chops are found everywhere, though locals favour chewier mutton. In Pelion, try *spetsofaï* (stewed pork sausages and peppers); in Karpenisi, wild-boar *stifadho* is often on the menu. In Thessaly, veggie-based dishes are plentiful. Also sample feta and other cheeses like Arahova's *formaela*.

Best fish Dimitroukas, Messolongi (p115)

Must-try chargrilled meats Any *tsipouradhiko*, Volos (p115)

GETTING AROUND

Car The best way to explore the region. Be prepared for road tolls, particularly between Athens and Volos.

Bus The KTEL intercity network is reliable. Buy tickets at bus terminals or online.

Train Services are limited and less convenient. Buy tickets at stations or online (*hellenictrain.gr*).

JAN–MAR
Ski and snowboard season in Karpenisi and Arahova.

APR–JUN
Warm, sunny days and mountains filled with wildflowers.

JUL–SEP
Peak season for ancient sites, swimming and festivals.

OCT–DEC
Ideal for hiking and intimate fireside escapes.

15 Delphi Done **DIFFERENTLY**

ANTIQUITY | TREKKING | OLIVES

There's more than one way to get to know Delphi. Trek the archaic footpath that pilgrims once followed to reach the sacred religious sanctuary in order to consult high priestess Pythia. Below the ancient site, a silvery sea of more than 1.5 million olive trees – some dating back 3000 years – spreads towards the sea, still producing fine olive oil.

How To

Getting here Delphi is a 2½-hour drive from Athens. Alternatively, take the train from Athens to Amfiklia followed by a 60-minute taxi ride to Delphi. KTEL intercity buses run regularly from Athens' Liossion bus terminal to Delphi.

When to go In spring, when wildflowers are abloom, or September through early November, when there are fewer visitors.

Local flavour Stock up on speciality goods like *hilopites* (fettucine-style pasta) at the nearby town of Arahova.

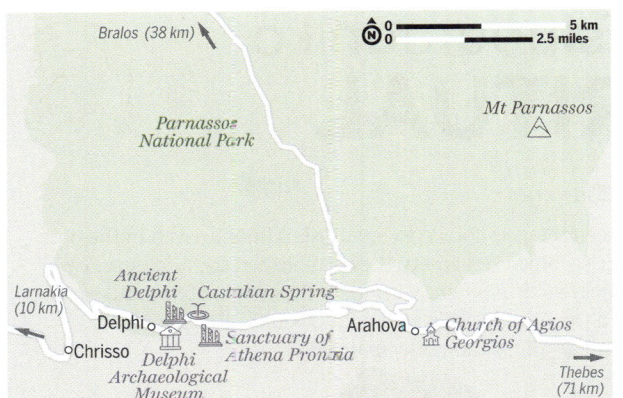

Left Ancient site at Delphi
Bottom left Mt Parnassos

Delve into the ruins Delphi is all about walking. Staying in town, you can walk to all the ancient sights and enjoy sweeping views along the way. Try to untangle the mystery of the **Sanctuary of Athena Pronaia** (*odysseus.culture.gr*), then sip from the sacred waters of the **Castalian Spring**. At both sites, you'll find a fraction of the crowds elsewhere. Then plunge into the core of **Ancient Delphi**, find a shady spot and read up on the extraordinary mysteries around the oracle and Pythia's ambiguous yet portentous pronouncements. Finally, ferret out your own favourite treasure in the **Delphi Archaeological Museum**.

Hike to the sites To get a sense of what it was like for pilgrims, rich and poor, to make the journey to Delphi, put yourself in their shoes. **Trekking Hellas** (*trekking.gr*) offers a four-and-a-half-hour, 8km guided hike along the ancient footpath. Departing from the alpine plateau of Livadi, at an altitude of 1200m, you'll trek the southern slopes of Mt Parnassos, passing through varying landscapes as you go from Alpine beauty to a classic Med landscape in surprisingly short order.

Get a guide Proud of her Delphic roots, **Penny Kolomvotsou** (*kpagona@hotmail.com*) relays her vast knowledge with enthusiasm. Athens-based **Greek Mythology Tours** (*greekmythologytours.com*) arranges day trips of Delphi designed for fans of Rick Riordan's *Percy Jackson and the Olympians* book and TV series.

Festival of Agios Georgios

In the nearby ski town of **Arahova**, a 12-minute drive east of Delphi, Greeks gather at cosy tavernas and chi-chi bars during snow season.

But few know of the annual **Panigiraki** feast that takes place at or after Orthodox Easter. With Homeric-era roots, this exuberant four-day celebration honours the village's patron St George.

Local men don fustanellas (knee-length pleated skirts) and women wear traditional *sigounia* (a sleeveless overcoat) and dance around the **Church of Agios Georgios** and in the streets, to the sound of the archaic *pipiza* (pipe) and *daouli* (tabor).

Hill races, discus throwing and wrestling count among its many sporting events.

16 Tsipouradhiko RITUAL

CULTURE | GASTRONOMY | DRINKING

In the early 1920s, Greek refugees forced to leave Asia Minor arrived in the port town of Volos. Proving that crisis breeds creativity, they established the *tsipouradhika* (small restaurants), serving fiery spirit *tsipouro* with mezedhes made of fish and seafood from the Pagasitikos Gulf and the Aegean. This revered sociocultural gastronomic tradition lives on at Volos' vintage joints and neo-*tsipouradhika*.

How To

Getting here/around Drive to Volos or take a KTEL intercity bus from Athens or Pelion Peninsula. Volos is easy to navigate on foot or by bicycle.

When to go Unless you don't mind the cold, short-sleeve season runs from April to October. July and August are busy.

Decipher an unwritten code Volos artist Alexandros Psychoulis reveals some of the mystery surrounding the *tsipouradhiko* in his book *Drinking Tsipouro in Volos*.

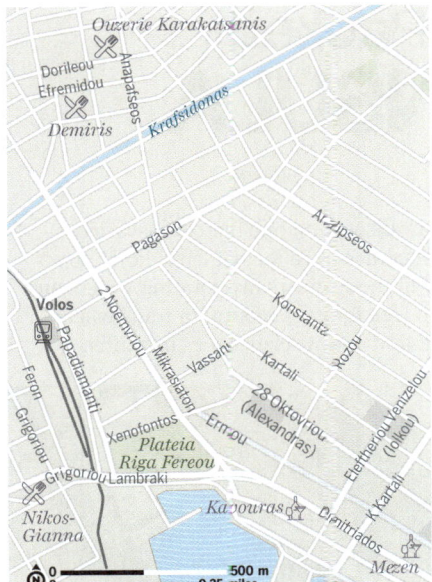

Left Making *tsipouro*
Bottom left Volos

 Tsipouradhiko's 10 Commandments

Thou shalt not peruse the menu. Let your server decide.

Thou shalt not covet meat. Fish and seafood are king.

Honour the holy spirit *tsipouro* (or *tsikoudia* or ouzo).

Thou shalt only decide on *tsipouro* with or without anise.

Thou shalt not take a sip without a bite of food.

Thou shalt not snub dishes, no matter how peculiar.

Thou shalt not eat, drink and run. Take it slow.

Thou shalt not monopolise mezedhes. It's meant to be shared.

Thou shalt only drink beer if it's your final round.

Thou shalt not refuse a complimentary *tsipouromeze*.

Recommended by Andreas Diakodimitris, *co-owner of Mezen* @an_diakodimitris

Gold school Venture to Volos' working-class Nea Ionia district, where the refugees brought their taste for unusual seafood to port workers. Pick from classics like **Demiris**, which has endured for more than four decades. Anise-infused *tsipouro* accompanies rarely found sea fig, native delicacy fried sea anemone and octopus ink sacs.

Vintage finds Another hive of authentic *tsipouradhika* can be found in the Palaia neighbourhood. Regulars, many of them local university professors, gather under mulberry trees at **Nikos-Gianna** for chargrilled octopus with *tsitsiravla* (pickled wild pistachio shoots) and fried skate with garlic dip. Down a backstreet, no-nonsense **Kavouras** has drawn a devout fanbase from politicians to plumbers for over 70 years. Smooth, well-rounded draft *tsipouro* is served with specialities such as monkfish liver and sun-dried horse mackerel.

Today's generation Chef Grigoris Helmis has been blazing a path since opening new-wave *tsipouradhiko* **Mezen** in 2013. Painstakingly selected *tsipouro* is paired with mezedhes in what only can be described as an ambrosial art form. Back in Nea Ionia, Pelion-born Timoleon Diamantis returned from Michelin-starred restaurants to revive much-loved **Ouzeri Karakatsanis**. The *MasterChef* winner takes inspiration from Mt Athos' monastic fare and prepares signature slow-food dishes like lemony cod with plums on a wood-fired hearth.

Action-Packed **PENINSULA**

SWIMMING | HIKING | SKIING

Swimming, touring and hiking – it all awaits you on one incredibly varied peninsula. Hard to believe, but it's true when it comes to Pelion, which is home to some 24 traditional villages. Immerse yourself in the Aegean's invigorating waters on splendid beaches fringing its eastern coast and trek forested mountain trails where mythical centaurs galloped. You can even dash down snow-clad slopes in winter.

How To

Getting here/around Fly into Volos or Athens. Driving is the best way to move around, but factor in sufficient travel time along winding roads.

When to go Year-round, or April to October for warm-weather activities and December to March for skiing and romantic getaways.

Wine down Book a wine tasting at Patistis (*patistis-wines.gr*) to sample terroir-forward organic vino, including unconventional labels like mandarin- and peach-scented Rodito Active, produced with the *roditis* grape varietal.

Left Mylopotamos
Bottom left Mountain village, Pelion

※ Festival Fun

Music Village unites a diverse array of global artists and music lovers in **Agios Lavrentios** village, where everyone is invited to be part of the creative process.

Held from August through early September, the festival features scheduled and spontaneous performances and workshops hosted in traditional homes, squares and forest clearings.

Agricultural producers, chefs and agritourism cooperatives count among members of the peninsula's flourishing gastronomic community who gather at the annual **Pelion Gastronomy Festival** held at **Karaiskos Farm**, usually in late September.

Watch cooking demonstrations, chat with farmers about their produce and sample traditional delicacies like spoon sweets but also local craft beer.

Swim the Aegean side The peninsula's finest beaches are found on the Aegean-washed eastern coast. Cool off in **Mylopotamos'** sapphire waters and dig your toes in tiny, multicoloured pebbles. Pelion's best-known swim spot sports a photogenic stone arch. Minuscule **Fakistra** may involve a steep trek but its turquoise waters are worth the effort. Get to this lovers' cove early to snag a spot beneath shrub-draped cliffs. Crowd-dodging locals prefer untamed **Kalamaki**, where flat pale-grey stones lead to crystal ne waters.

Trek between villages Throughout Pelion, a network of *kalderimia* (ancient cobblestoned paths) links villages, beaches, churches and plentiful springs. **True Adventure** offers a challenging but doable nine-day 168km-long hike on the **Long Pelion Trail**, through olive groves and maple, oak and beech forest to villages including **Makrinitsa** but also lesser-known **Lafkos**, plus **Damouhari** beach of *Mamma Mia!* fame.

Hop a cute choo-choo Dating to 1896, a narrow-gauge train line runs from Ano Lehonia, 12km east of Volos, to the cute mountain village of Milies in the centre of the peninsula. Today it's a tourist line that covers 20km of spectacular scenery in about 90 minutes. The train (*hellenictrain.gr*) rambles up and down hills, over old stone and metal trestles while offering great views. The schedule allows for a taverna lunch in Milies before returning. Although it now uses a diesel engine rather than steam, the train is still affectionately known as **Moutzouris** ('Sooty').

Cavorting in KARPENISI

NATURE | ADVENTURE | MOUNTAINS

Karpenisi may be a cosy winter escape for Greek city dwellers, but look beyond its serene stone-built villages at the foot of Mt Kaliakouda and Mt Velouchi and you'll find plenty of opportunities to chase adventure. Among the pulse-quickening pursuits on offer are canyoning, river trekking and rafting, while manmade Lake Kremasta remains virtually undiscovered and undeveloped.

How To

Getting here/around
Fly to Athens and drive to Karpenisi, as the area is best explored by car. Otherwise, KTEL intercity buses operate between Athens and Karpenisi.

When to go Throughout summer for the ongoing Forest Festival; October for the chestnut festival; November for the *tsipouro* festival; December to March for skiing on Mt Velouchi.

Karpenissi Trail Choose between four mountain trail races, including the tough 26km Kaliakouda Trail (*karpenissitrail.gr*).

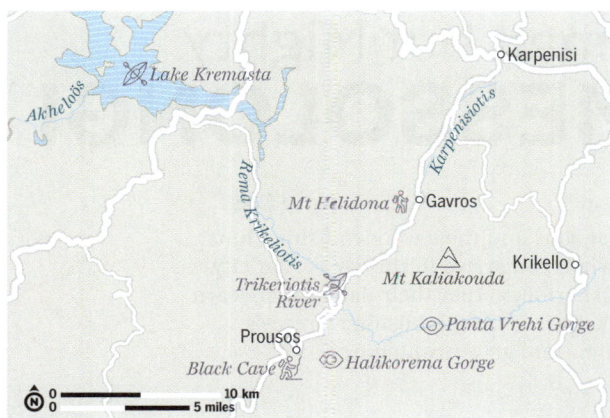

Left Lake Kremasta
Bottom left Krikeliotis River

Adventures on land Jump in a 4WD with a knowledgeable guide who will expertly navigate the lofty heights of **Mt Helidona**, passing through minute, single-digit-population villages and following gravel roads down to riverside beaches framed by sheer cliffs. Ramp up the adrenaline with a fir-forest hike across wooden bridges and past waterfalls to the **Black Cave**. From there, you'll traverse across a craggy vertical rockface following a via ferrata route consisting of steel fixtures that allow even inexperienced climbers to safely complete the course.

Water action If you're in Karpenisi between mid-May and September, don't miss seeing its biggest natural drawcard, **Panta Vrehi gorge**. Join a river trek through the **Krikeliotis River** to witness this marvel of nature. Springwater flowing from **Mt Kaliakouda** creates a curtain that resembles rain. Between December and May, the **Trikeriotis River** offers thrilling rafting experiences featuring technical turns, yet is suitable for families. More water fun can be had in red-limestone-lined **Halikorema Gorge**, which is ideal for easygoing canyoning. Rappel your way through four waterfalls reaching up to 10m high, then take a dip in natural pools.

Take to the lake Canoe the aquamarine waters and islets of artificial **Lake Kremasta**, which was formed from four rivers and by sinking 20 villages underwater in the mid 1960s as part of a hydroelectric project.

Book activities with **F-Zein Active** (active.com.gr) and **Trekking Hellas** (trekking.gr).

Forest Wandering

Mountain escort **Yannis Liaskonis** (@yannis liaskonis) knows Karpenisi's highly biodiverse forests like the back of his hand.

Follow his lead through a dense plane-tree forest along an unmarked fairytale-like trail between the villages of **Koryshades** and **Gorianades**.

He'll point out wild herbs like lemon balm, mint and snow-resistant thyme and, in early autumn, cyclamens.

Walking among Greek fir, horse chestnut, kermes oak, willow and hornbeam trees, you'll breathe in some of Europe's cleanest air.

At dusk, as you cross streams fit for drinking, keep your eyes peeled for shy roe deer but don't expect to spot their well-camouflaged predator, the Eurasian wolf.

19 Small but Mighty
MESSOLONGI

HISTORY | BIRDS | FISH

Messolongi's twin lagoons and their wooden fishing huts are what you first notice when you arrive in this small, flat city. Beyond discovering how fisherfolk gather their daily catch, learn about Messolongi's remarkable role in establishing Greece's independence, visit museums and go birdwatching.

Trip Notes

Getting here/around Fly into Athens and drive to Messolongi. Alternatively, take the KTEL intercity bus from Athens.

When to go April for the Exodus of Messolongi commemoration; May to June for Ai Simiou *panigyri* (festival); September for the fish festival; October to March for birdwatching.

Avian nation Nearly 300 endemic and migratory bird species, including flamingoes, avocets and curlews, pass through or reside in Messolongi, home to one of the Mediterranean's most significant wetland habitats.

Following Nature's Flow

Messolongi's fisherfolk utilise traditional aquaculture techniques inextricably linked with the seasons, fish breeding cycles and the unique lagoon habitat.

In spring, fish from the Gulf of Patras enter the shallow lagoons, where the sun fattens them. Find out more about these sustainable fishing methods on a fisher-led boat tour (messolonghiby locals.com).

05 **Aitoliko** islet hosts a museum dedicated to Greek painter and engraver Vasso Katraki. Politically and socially charged expressions of the human form constitute the majority of her riveting catalogue.

01 Visit the **Garden of Heroes** with a guide to learn about Messolongi's tragic yet decisive role in Greece's War of Independence. Greek and philhellene freedom fighters, including Lord Byron, are immortalised.

02 At the **History and Art Museum** (odysseus.culture.gr), moving artworks like François-Émile de Lansac's *Episode of the Siege of Missolonghi* (1828) convey the immeasurable courage of the city's 'free besieged'.

04 Cycle to **Tourlida** islet (pictured left) and cool off at a Gulf of Patras beach. At the Salt Museum (saltmuseum.gr), find out how Messolongi's precious 'white gold' is produced and see salt pans.

03 Drive around **Klisova Lagoon** at sunset to see traditional fisher's huts and boats in their best light but also Dalmatian pelicans and other species from the observatory. Soothing mudbaths also await.

Gulf of Patras

FROM TOP: GIANNIS PAPANIKOS/SHUTTERSTOCK ©, RINI KOOLS/SHUTTERSTOCK©

Escape to the Country

YOUNG GREEKS SHUN THE BIG SMOKE

Throughout central Greece, a palpable energy emanates from its vast fertile ground. New generations with innovative ideas are taking over family businesses while safeguarding centuries-old traditions. Above all, they're making a conscious decision to return to or stay rooted in their ancestral lands.

Standing beside a traditional fisher's hut above glimmering Klisova Lagoon, Alexandras Panagiotopoulos speaks passionately about his native Messolongi's potential to draw sustainability-minded travellers. 'We're not interested in mass tourism, though. We want to keep it small-scale so as to protect the environment. When we talk about responsible tourism, we want those who visit to become a part of our day-to-day lives,' he says.

Following university studies in Athens, Alexandras returned to Messolongi. In 2018, he and his partner, ex-Thessaloniki architect Kyra Papanikolaou, founded non-profit **Messolonghi by Locals** (*messolonghibylocals.com*) whose welcoming hub doubles as a tourism information centre. Their goals are multifold, including the development of historical, cultural and environmental tourism in this intriguing corner of the country. They consider community participation and mobilisation to be equally crucial. Among other initiatives, the organisation runs programmes for local schoolkids, educating them about fishing traditions, wetland habitats and wildlife.

Alexandros and Kyra count among growing numbers of young Greeks finding positive reasons to stay in, return to or relocate to the region, following a severe brain drain during Greece's decade-long economic crisis. Their chief motive: achieving a better quality of life.

Some, like Nikos Kontopanos, want to build on a successful family business. Together with his brother Panagiotis, Nikos is gradually taking over the reins at **Saloon Park** (*saloonpark.gr*), a dude ranch and fun park founded by his father below Karpenisi's Mt Velouchi. 'There are opportunities for work here as long as you have drive and enjoy being in nature. I love

Left Aitoliko
Centre Mt Parnassos
Right Fishing near Aitoliko

this environment and the animals. I don't need anything else,' he says. Others have no connection to the location where they've resettled. In the cosmopolitan ski town of Arahova, near Delphi, French-Greek industrial designer Eleni Prablanc crossed skis with future husband, Giorgos Korodimos, on the slopes of Mt Parnassos. In 2015, they founded a Delphi branch of pioneering Greek operator **Trekking Hellas** (trekking.gr). 'I love the fact that I can be snowshoeing on Mt Parnassos one day and trekking an ancient footpath pilgrims took to Delphi the next,' says Eleni, underlining their commitment to leaving no trace.

> 'We're not interested in mass tourism. We want to keep it small-scale.'

Giorgos, who grew up roving the mountains around Arahova with his shepherd grandparents, has never considered leaving his birthplace. An experienced mountaineer, he is happiest when rock climbing, downhill skiing and guiding visitors on hikes through stone-built villages and up alpine summits.

The young parents and their two children embrace local folk customs such as the annual Panigiraki feast celebrating St George and commemorating the 1826 Battle of Arahova. Reflecting a burgeoning interest among Arahova's youth to preserve traditions on the brink of oblivion, Giorgos hand-sews his fustanella (traditional skirt) for the event. 'During the crisis, Arahova received much fewer visitors from Athens and Thessaloniki, our two main markets,' he says. 'Many of us had to find a way to keep busy. This proved an opportunity to revive traditions like loom weaving. While cultivating a newfound respect for these near-forgotten arts, we realised it's something we really enjoy.'

✗ Local Know-How

Farm-to-fork Gather vegetables at **Karaiskos Farm** and learn how to prepare village-style spinach and feta pie from scratch with chef Dimitris Varalis, who gave up Mykonos' fat tips to head cooking lessons at the Pelion agritourism venture.

Ancient superfood At age 12, Paris Andreou Leontios planted the seed for what has evolved into a successful family-run business. Based in Arahova, **5 Raches** organically cultivates archaic *lathouri* (grass pea), high in protein and fibre, at an altitude of 1200m.

Oracle insider Certified guide **Georgia Hasioti** (delphi-guide.gr) is an energetic and enthusiastic guide for Delphi who knows secret shady spots for longer talks.

Listings

BEST OF THE REST

Meteora's High Points

Moni Megalou Meteorou
In 1340, St Athanasios scaled Meteora's highest rock and described a feeling of *meteoron* (levitation). View precious 9th-century manuscripts, rare Byzantine icons and a mid-16th-century kitchen at one of Greece's most revered monasteries.

Moni Agias Varvaras Rousanou
Perched atop a steep pinnacle and accessed via a high narrow wooden bridge, the less-visited 16th-century monastery covers the entire surface of a 484m-tall narrow rock pillar. Don't miss the post-Byzantine frescoes.

Outdoor Adventures

Meteora Photo Expedition
Meteora Photo Tour ventures to out-of-the-way spots that capture the colossal rock columns and monasteries in their best light. The new angles on the improbable beauty here always astound.

Pelion by Sea
The adjoining beach towns of Horto and Milina front the sheltered waters of the Pagasitikos Gulf at the south end of the peninsula. Rent sea kayaks and SUPs and face the daily task of choosing a mellow patch of sand to call your own.

Velouchi Snow Centre
Situated on Mt Tymfristos, north of Karpenisi, skiers at all levels can choose between 16 slopes, including free-ride pistes and black runs. There's a snowboard park, five lifts and kids' carousel.

Lake Plastira
Adrenaline experts Tavropos Activities lead guided MTB and e-bike rides around the lake and further afield. Alternatively, hire a canoe, waterbike or stand-up paddleboard and cool off with a swim afterwards.

Panigyria Revelry

Domnista
This village near Karpenisi hosts a rousing three-day autumnal toast to *tsipouro,* central Greece's favourite firewater, with plenty of traditional song and dance that lasts until late.

Ai Simiou
In Messolongi, local men don folk clothing and celebrate this deeply symbolic, tradition-rich *panigyri* with fervour and devoutness over four days in May or June.

Meat & Fish Specialities

Kaplanis Taverna   €€
Famished skiers gather by the fireplace at this family-run spot in Arahova for *sarmadhes* (dolmadhes made with cabbage), fried courgette

Moni Megalou Meteorou

flowers and soul-warming cockerel casserole with *hilopites* (fettucine-style pasta).

Stou Psiloú €

Logs burning in the fireplace, meats roasting on the grill, live music on the terrace and patrons quaffing ouzo all mean fun nights in Zagora high on the Pelion Peninsula.

Agios Athanasios Tavern €€

Swaying willow tree views and soft jazz accompanies huge, juicy pork chops and garlicky eggplant dip, setting this otherwise traditional taverna in Megalo Horio apart from others in the Karpenisi area.

Dimitroukas €€

Situated in downtown Messolongi, this fish taverna serves lagoon-fresh delicacies like salt-cured *mexinari* (grey mullet), *lizda* (gilthead sea bream) and butterflied flathead mullet with aromatic, locally produced Trikene ouzo.

Agios Athanasios Tavern €

Juicy pork chops and garlicky eggplant are just some of the highlights setting this traditional taverna apart. Huge yard and terrace with views in Megalo Horio near Karpenisi.

✖ Refined Restaurants

Cardamo Oinomageireio €€

Bypass the humdrum choices on Makrinitsa's busy main square for this hidden gem with sublime views and food to match. A refined menu with seasonal choices. Book ahead for lunch.

O Bebelis €€

Local speciality *kelemnia* (onions stuffed with mince, rice, tomato and herbs) and slow-braised pork shank are classics at this longtime Galaxidi favourite. Don't miss the mini folklore 'museum' upstairs.

Lake Plastira

Taverna Aggelika €€

Sample masterfully grilled fresh fish like *gofari* (bluefish) and seasonal *vlita* (greens) at this Pelion Peninsula favourite. It's perched at the southern end of Mylopotamos Beach; watch the moonlight over the Aegean.

Meteora's Wineries

Tsililis Distillery & Estate

Book a wine tasting at this family-run winery near prehistoric Theopetra Cave, close to Meteora. You'll want to try its award-winning red made from native *limniona* grape and fine *tsipouro*, a potent clear spirit.

Meteoro Winery

The Tsinas family might be new to winemaking but their Cabernet Sauvignon–Syrah is phenomenally good. Pick up a bottle or two from the winery, located in Megarchi near Meteora, to take home.

Liakou Winery

Near Kalambaka, sample fruity Asproparis, named after a protected vulture local to Meteora and produced from indigenous *malagouzia* varietal.

PELOPONNESE

HIKING | ARCHAEOLOGY | NATURE

- ▶ **Trip Builder** (p118)
- ▶ **Practicalities** (p119)
- ▶ **Kalavryta Rail Journey** (p120)
- ▶ **Following Literary Footsteps** (p122)
- ▶ **Admiring Arkadia** (p124)
- ▶ **Olive Oil, Lunch & More** (p128)
- ▶ **Meander Through the Mani** (p130)
- ▶ **Fortresses & Ancient Sites of the Peloponnese** (p132)
- ▶ **Listings** (p134)

PELOPONNESE
Trip Builder

Swim, hike and taste local delights. Rub shoulders with past legends in ancient sites. Discover a beach cove and read a page of Patrick Leigh Fermor. Wander castle ruins. Seek crowds. Find isolation. The Peloponnese offers everything an island does, and a lot more.

Meander up the dramatic Vouraïkos Gorge on the **cog railway** (ododontos) (p120)
🚗 2hrs from Nafplio

Hike to the monasteries and charming mountaintop villages of **Arkadia** (p124)
🚗 1½hrs from Nafplio

Soak up the facts about olive oil in beautiful **Messinia** (p129)
🚗 30mins from Kalamata

Discover the wild and rugged region of the **Mani** (p130)
🚗 1hr (plus) from Kalamata

Follow in author Patrick Leigh Fermor's footsteps in **Kardamyli** (p122)
🚗 1hr from Kalamata

ABOVE: ANDRONOS HARIS/SHUTTERSTOCK ©
PREVIOUS SPREAD: ALBERTO LOYO/SHUTTERSTOCK ©

Practicalities

ARRIVING
Athens International Airport, Eleftherios Venizelos, has both bus and metro connections, including to the Kifissos KTEL Bus Station in Athens. Kifissos KTEL is the departure point for buses (tickets cost from €13) to Nafplio and the region. Car hire is available at the airport.

MONEY
Most places accept credit cards and Apple Pay. Take some euros for mountain villages that may not.

CONNECT
Decent wi-fi connections exist in most places to stay and many restaurants and cafes.

WHERE TO STAY

Place	Pro/Con
Nafplio	Widest selection of accommodation and amenities. Good public transport. Convenient.
Kalamata	Good motorway connection from Athens. Larger city, but excellent jumping-off point to Mani.
Kalavryta	A haul to get here but has mountain air and serenity.

EATING & DRINKING
The Peloponnese is blessed with excellent meats (from mountain goats and sheep), seafood (from fishing villages along the coastline), olives (don't miss the olive tour; p128) and wines (particularly around Nemea). Vegetables, such as the aubergines of Leonidio, are of excellent quality and collecting horta (wild greens) is part of the region's culture. Kalamata has many historic speciality food shops.

Best regional dining Athinoli (p135)

Must-try Arkadian cuisine Zerzova (p135)

GETTING AROUND

Car A car is the most convenient way to access remote locales. Roads vary from massive motorways with tolls to narrow, village laneways.

Bus Subregional KTEL buses are a convenient way to get around much of the Peloponnese. Many buses from Athens go via the Corinth Isthmus KTEL bus station; in some cases, change here for other regional buses.

JAN–MAR Free of crowds; you can mingle easily with locals.	**APR–JUN** Springtime brings wildflowers and fewer visitors.	**JUL–SEP** Summer; crowds but a buzzy atmosphere.	**OCT–DEC** Cooler weather and major sights still open.

20 Kalavryta Rail JOURNEY

RAILWAY | GORGES | HISTORIC VILLAGES

Experience the stunning mountainous landscapes of the northern Peloponnesian Achaïa region as you chug through the Vouraïkos Gorge (and seven curving tunnels) on a vintage cog railway journey – a steep-grade railway with a toothed-rack rail (*odontotos* in Greek) – between the towns of Diakofto and Kalavryta. The latter is home to the incredibly sobering Museum of the Kalavryta Holocaust.

How to

Getting here/around
The railway journey starts from Diakofto and runs for 22km through the mountainous landscape with several small stops along the way, before ending in Kalavryta.

When to go It's recommended year-round.

(Note, closures do occur; check ahead.)

Budget The train costs around €9.50. For €24.80, the Kalavryta CityPass discount card covers a return train trip, plus the Cave of the Lakes, the Kalavryta Holocaust Museum and Kalavryta Ski Centre.

The Journey

One of the unmissable journeys is aboard the tiny train running along the vintage rack-and-pinion (cog) railway between **Diakofto**, a seaside town and small port on the north coast of the Peloponnese, and the alpine village of **Kalavryta**.

The route This remarkably scenic ride heads through the dramatic **Vouraïkos Gorge** and climbs over 700m in 22.5km. The line switches back and forth under a leafy canopy of plane trees, clinging to a narrow ledge overhanging the rushing rapids below, and passing through seven curving tunnels along the way.

Tickets You can buy tickets at Diakofto and Kalavryta train stations and in advance at *hellenictrain.gr* (€9.50). For information, call Diakofto railway on 2691 043206 or Kalavryta railway on 2692 023050.

Nearby sites From the small village of **Kato Zahlorou** (one of the stops), you can take an exhilarating hike to **Moni Mega Spileo**, a monastery built on the slopes of a steep hillside. The area is covered with cave systems and lakes, and a ski centre at nearby **Mt Helmos** is a popular winter destination.

Hike down Hiking the 22km from Kalavryta to Diakofto takes around five hours and follows the rail route. Train drivers give plenty of warning (there's no room in the tunnels for a train to pass) but it's safest to check the train schedule first.

Engineering Feat

Built between 1889 and 1895, the railway was a remarkable feat of engineering for its time with only a handful of equivalents in the world (most notably in the Swiss Alps). Between 2007 and 2009 the entire rails and cog sections were replaced, as well as the former carriages. The original steam engines can still be seen outside the Diakofto station.

Left The train between Diakofto and Kalavryta
Bottom left Moni Mega Spileo

21 Following Literary FOOTSTEPS

NATURE | COASTLINE | LITERATURE

Whether or not you've heard of British travel writer Patrick Leigh Fermor – author of *Mani: Travels in the Southern Peloponnese* – following in his footsteps is a joy. Leigh Fermor was so captivated by the region that he settled in Kardamyli until his death in 2011. Visiting his beautiful home is one thing. Walking in the very gorge and surrounding mountains he wrote about is quite another.

How to

Getting here/around
Daily buses run between Kalamata and Kardamyli; once here, there are excellent hiking and e-biking opportunities.

When to go Spring to autumn is the ideal time for weather conditions and wildflowers; the small village is also open for business.

Don't miss Contact 2407 Outdoor Experience (*2407m.com*) to arrange a guided hike or e-bike adventure. If you want to go it alone, it sells the excellent map, *Exo Mani 1:22000 Hiking Trails* (Anavasi).

Far left Kardamyli Below left Patrick Leigh Fermor Greece travel books

The writer Larger-than-life Patrick Leigh Fermor (1915–2011), a Hellenophile and engaging writer lived just outside **Kardamyli** for much of his later life with his wife Joan. A scholar and soldier (in the Cretan resistance during WWII), he is known largely for his travel book on the region, *Mani: Travels in the Southern Peloponnese*.

His home Designed by architect Nikos Hatzimichalis and completed in the 1960s, the **Patrick Leigh Fermor house** exudes literary air: lovely rooms lined with books, shaded nooks and Islamic influences, a Mediterranean garden and a pergola. There's even artworks by Greek artists, among the many visitors he welcomed to his house. Visitors can enter twice a week by appointment (once a week between June and September). Reserve at benaki.org and follow the links to the house. The one-hour visit costs €5. Between June and September you can rent the entire house, a smaller guest cottage or a studio in a shared garden. Prices start at €500 *(minimum three-night stay; ariahotels.gr)*.

His walks If you are inspired by Leigh Fermor's artistic space, explore his inspiration in the surrounds; hiking is superb around Kardamyli and an extensive network of colour-coded walking trails crisscross the mountains that hem this beautiful seaside village. Given the steep terrain, most of the hikes around here are medium to strenuous. Head off with **2407 Outdoor Experience** or tackle them alone (with care).

The Best Self-Guided Hikes Around Kardamyli

Yiannis Avrameas – owner of 2407 Outdoor Experience *(2407m.com)*

Kalamitsi–Proastio
(Easy) The most accessible route follows an old marked path. This 40-minute uphill walk (one-way) is good for families with children. Views abound.

Kardamyli–Petrovouni–Agia Sofia–Kardamyli
(Medium) Two-hour round trip on historic paths through villages, crossing a path Sparta built over 2500 years ago. It heads to the Byzantine church of Agia Sofia and back through the old town of Kardamyli.

Vyros Gorge (Challenging) Beautiful, 3½ hour tour from Kardamyli through the Vyros Gorge via two monasteries and back to Kardamyli via Agia Sofia.

Admiring ARKADIA

WILDFLOWERS | HIKING | MONASTERIES

Comprising bucolic landscapes and home to the fabled Pan (of human body with goat legs), this mountain area has forests, wildflowers and spectacular gorges. Roads wind through valleys and villages serving up excellent cuisine and historic sights. Hiking opportunities abound through the Lousios Gorge and Menalon Trail.

How to

Getting here/around
A car is required to explore this area and gives flexibility to visit sites. If walking, village taxis and some accommodation will drop/collect you at trailheads.

When to go Spring is the perfect time to experience the wildflowers and good weather for hiking.

Cuisine Village dishes – featuring mountain goat, mutton and rooster – are fabulous here. Ask locals for tips on tavernas that are beyond the settlements, too.

Village Ventures

Head on a driving tour that links the historic villages of **Andritsena**, Stemnitsa, Dimitsana and Karitena. All are built from stone, with tiny squares and canopies of plane trees. It's worth wandering through each to discover their sights. In Andritsena, don't miss the **Nikolopoulos Andritsena Library**. In **Karitena** stand atop the 13th-century Frankish castle that's perched on a massive rock. And in the striking village of **Stemnitsa** (pictured) peek into the Byzantine churches (ask around for the keys).

The medieval village of **Dimitsana** (pictured) is a great place to enjoy a local meal of *hilopites* (noodles) and rooster stew. That is, after you've visited Dimitsana's **Public Library and Museum of the Greek School** and the **Open-Air Water Power Museum**. It's the perfect

Temple of Epicurean Apollo

Situated 14km from Andritsena, on an isolated mountain, the World Heritage–listed **Vasses** is one of Greece's best-preserved sites. It consists of the **Temple of Epicurean Apollo** (420 BCE), a striking temple designed by Iktinos, architect of the Parthenon, and built by the inhabitants of nearby Figalia.

Top left Dimitsana **Left** Stemnitsa
Above Temple of Epicurean Apollo

departure point for the hike along the Lousios Gorge.

Walk Through Time & Nature

One of the most beautiful walks in the Peloponnese, the **Lousios Gorge** is a pretty ravine covered with a canopy of walnut and oak trees and a gushing stream below. As well as birds and beautiful natural surrounds, several monasteries – the 16th-century **Prodromos Monastery** and the 'new and 'old' **Filosofou Monasteries** – dot this route.

If you're not walking this section as part of the **Menalon Trail**, you can experience the hike in several ways: first, you can park (or be dropped) at **Ancient Gortys**, a set of ruins, and walk to the monasteries and back along the same route. Second, you can be dropped by village taxi at Ancient Gortys and walk one way along the gorge to Dimitsana or Stemnitsa (note: this route heads uphill, especially on entry into the villages). The third is by driving; the monasteries are near the road network.

My Three Secrets of Arkadia

Local trails Many villages have circular trails in their vicinity. Different colours denote each walk's difficulty. Signs in the village provide directions.

Horse riding in the forest Departing from Elati and following the Mylaonpas River, a circular route on horseback takes you through the forest. Beautiful!

Emialon Monastery Few know of the Emialon Monastery, the sixth monastery along the Lousios Gorge. It's still a working monastery (the monks produce herbs and conduct workshops) and it's accessible from near the Open-Air Water Power Museum in Dimitsana.

■ Recommended By *Nena Grintzia*, *Stemnitsa local, owner Mpelleiko B&B (mpelleiko.gr)*

If walking, with visits to the monasteries en route, allow at least five hours.

Power Through Water

Dimitsana's **Open-Air Water Power Museum** provides an entertaining romp through the region's pre-industrial past. It occupies a complex 2km south of town (signposted and with good parking), where a spring-fed stream once supplied power for a succession of mills spread down the hillside. The lush grounds are alive with rushing water powering a fully operational fulling mill, flour mill and gunpowder mill (the last having provided ammunition during the Greek War of Independence). The tannery is equally fascinating, and videos and demonstrations bring the often complex procedures alive.

Munch on Mountain Cuisine

Located in **Markou**, 10km south of Dimitsana, **Zerzova** is one of Arkadia's best restaurants. It sources sustainable products; the owners collect wild herbs, cultivate produce and succeed in recreating the tastes and aromas of their childhood. Check ahead for opening hours (these change) and expect a changing menu. The setting, overlooking a gorge, is heavenly, too.

Far left Emialon Monastery
Left Open-Air Water Power Museum

23 Olive Oil, Lunch & MORE

CULTURE | CUISINE | LEARNING

One of the best tours in the Peloponnese, this experience with **The Olive Routes** *(theoliveroutes.com)* covers everything olive. It's run by a passionate guide and professional olive oil taster, a fifth-generation family member of the 100-year-old mill. You can choose your combination of activities, which include olive groves, olive mills, a cooking class, a tasting workshop and a delicious food pairing.

How to

Getting here/around
The action takes place in Androusa, 22km northwest of Kalamata; you'll need your own transport to get here. Tours sometimes meet at the historic castle in Androusa.

When to go Advance reservations are necessary; tours are offered throughout the year.

How to organise See *theoliveroutes.com*; tours start at around €50 depending on the activities you choose.

Left Olive Orchard, Sparta
Far Left Vineyard, Peloponnese
Below left Olives, Messinia

This fun, informative olive oil experience can be tailored to your wishes. Throw in a cooking class, just visit the olive oil mills, or add in a visit to **Androusa Castle**, the village's 13th-century fortress that looks over the Messinian plains that are covered in olive groves. Lunch – a highlight – should not be missed.

Guide Dimitra is a professional olive oil taster and a member of a family of fifth-generation olive oil producers. She runs through the history of the area (think the castle) before you wander through the village to the contemporary, working olive mill. After learning about oil-making processes, you head to the original, **historic mill**. Here, in a brief but thorough tasting class, you learn how to differentiate your good oil from your bad. Lunch includes regional plates that pair different types of oils.

If local food products interest you, it's also worth doing a walking tour of Kalamata with **Kalamata Tours**. Owner/guide Sofie takes you to historic (and very atmospheric) historic shops of central Kalamata that make and sell everything from local sausages and smoked meats to *pasteli* (honey-and-sesame bars). You also visit the local food market that sells piles of fruits and vegetables and, of course, olives. Along the way you'll understand the context of regional cuisine.

(i) **Kalamata Olives**

Kalamata gives its name to the prized Kalamata olive, a plump, purple-black variety that is found in delicatessens around the world and is also grown extensively (although not exclusively) in neighbouring Lakonia. The region's reliable winter rains and hot summers make for perfect olive-growing conditions. The tree leaves of the Kalamata olive are twice the size of other varieties and a darker shade of green. Unlike other varieties, Kalamata olives can't be picked green. They ripen in late November and must be hand-picked to avoid bruising. You can buy and sample these famous olives at the markets in Kalamata.

24 Meander Through THE MANI

COAST | TOWERS | SCENERY

The Mani is a wild, rugged region, with dramatic craggy cliffs, coastal coves and tiny villages that nestle amid olive groves. Dotted throughout, abandoned stone towers emerge from the arid landscape. The various driving routes are fabulous – take your time.

Trip Notes

Getting here/around You'll need a car to explore this region. Decent bases include Areopoli and Gerolimenas.

When to go Spring is the perfect time, when the rugged cliffs and mountains pop with colourfulf wildflowers.

Map A useful map to the region is *Mani 1:30.000* published by Anavasi.

Hidden surprises As well as towers, hundreds of (less obvious) tiny Byzantine churches dot this area; peek inside for a fresco frenzy.

Manic Maniots and Their Towers

Dotted around the Mani, scores of stone towers (pictured) – solitary and in clusters – rise eerily from the landscape. From the 17th century until the 19th century, the region was ruled by clans that fought constantly over resources. These towers were family fortresses. Strict rules of engagement included the destruction of the rivals' towers and male members of their families.

Fortresses & Ancient Sites of the
PELOPONNESE

01 Mystras
A former Byzantine capital, this fortified city is a compelling set of medieval ruins spread over a steep mountainside and surrounded by verdant olive trees.

02 Palamidi Fortress, Nafplio
One of the biggest and best-preserved Venetian fortresses in Greece with views across Nafplio and the Argolic Gulf.

03 Ancient Olympia
A sanctuary to Zeus and the birthplace of the Olympic Games, where the Olympic flame is still lit.

04 Ancient Corinth
The streets of Ancient Corinth were once trodden by the likes of Greek traveller Pausanias and St Paul. Superb remains evoke a sense of life during Roman times.

05 Ancient Messini
This remote and sprawling ancient city was founded in 371 BCE after a Theban general defeated Sparta, freeing the Messinians from almost 350 years of Spartan rule.

06 Ancient Nemea
The original venue for the Nemean Games (one of the Panhellenic Games), held in honour of Zeus.

07 Nestor's Palace
The best preserved of all Mycenaean palaces. Homer described it as the court of the hero Nestor, who took part in the voyage of the Argonauts.

08 Ancient Mycenae
The most powerful kingdom in Greece for four centuries was also home to Agamemnon, ruler of the Greeks during the Trojan War.

09 Theatre of Epidavros
The best preserved of all ancient Greek theatres, with phenomenal acoustics. It's located near the site where pilgrims worshipped Asclepius, god of medicine.

10 Kastro, Methoni
One of the largest castles in the Mediterranean and surrounded on three sides by the sea, lending stunning vistas. The entrance is via a 14-arch stone bridge.

Listings

BEST OF THE REST

 ### Outdoor Thrills

Trekking Hellas
The professional folk in Kalavryta offer a range of canoeing, cycling, walking and other outdoor fun around the gorgeous Mt Helmos.

2407 Outdoor Adventures
Discover Kardamyli and its gorge-filled surrounds on an e-bike or guided walking tour. You explore both the mountains and the coast.

Menalon Trail
Do-it-yourself adventure awaits. Hike sections of the stunningly beautiful Menalon Trail and stay at Arkadian villages along the way.

 ### Museum Mania

Museum of the Kalavryta Holocaust
A moving tribute to the male residents of Kalavryta who were slaughtered on 13 December 1943 by the German army, the museum is housed in the schoolhouse where the women and children were imprisoned.

Victoria Karelias Collection of Traditional Greek Costumes
Established and donated by passionate collector, Victoria Karelias, the beautifully curated exhibits showcase male and female folk dress from the 18th to 20th centuries.

Archaeological Museum of Ancient Olympia
This museum features finds from the archaeological site of Olympia; visit it in conjunction with the ruins to put the site into perspective.

Archaeological Museum of Patra
This fabulous museum showcases regional objects, including Mycenaean ceramics and Roman mosaics. It's arranged across three themed halls: Private Life, Public Life and Cemeteries.

Ancient Corinth Museum
The site's excellent museum contains finds from Corinth. Prized pieces are two *kouros* (male statues of the Archaic period) that were stolen and retrieved along with finds from the nearby Sanctuary of Asklepios, including small 'body part' shaped votive offerings.

Ancient Mycenae Museum
Exhibits here initiate visitors into the mysteries of Mycenae's construction, its various incarnations and its excavation from 1841 onwards. It showcases written tablets in Linear B script.

Museum of the Olive & Greek Olive Oil
This beautifully designed museum initiates you into the mysteries of the olive from its initial appearance in the Mediterranean to the present.

 ### Picturesque Villages

Kosmas
A delightful hilltop village accessed via the scenic Leonidio-to-Monemvasia inland circuit. Massive plane trees shade a square and tavernas

Gythio

Gythio
A lovely seaside strip that lines a small port, this is a great spot for a seafood feast at one of the tavernas. Look for lines of hanging squid outside.

Stemnitsa and Dimitsana
These two historic mountain villages in the region of Arkadia are worth an hour for beautiful stone houses, churches, clock towers and traditional cafes.

Kardamyli
Backed by gorges and cliffs, this is one of the most beautiful villages in the Mani. V sit Byzantine ruins, waterfront tavernas and small coves.

Gerolimenas
An atmospheric village to spend the night if you like historic (boutique) hotels, excellent seafood and waking up to lapping ocean water.

Leonidio
Popular with climbers, beautiful Leonidio is dramatically located at the mouth of the Badron Gorge. The tiny Plateia 25 Martiou is an archetypal, unspoilt, whitewashed village square.

Tasty Tours

Cooking with Suzanna
This hands-on experience has you in the kitchen of Hotel Pelops, Olympia, where your host, Australian-Greek Suzanna, will guide you through preparing three courses of Greek cuisine.

Food Tours Kalamata
Run by Kalamata Tours, the food tour explores the best of Kalamata's traditional foodie spots and the local market, with plenty of bites of regional delights and information along the way.

Nafplio Bio-Farms
Visit a small organic farm near Nafplio, help whip up local goodies, and sit with a family at their Greek table to share in the delicious, local bounty.

Olive Oil Tour
The Olive Oil Routes runs one of the region's best tours: learn about olives, olive oil and tastings in an interactive tour and workshop (followed by a delicious lunch).

Best Bites

Zerzova €€
Located in the village of Markou, near Dimitsana, the owners here source, prepare and serve nothing but local delights on a whatever-is-available menu.

Aspasia €€
This former souvlaki joint in Stavri was restored into a wonderful casual-fine dining experience featuring Greek fusion treats. The dynamic menu changes daily depending on what local produce is available.

Drosopigi €€
Located on the hill above Skoutari, Drosopigi is set to do big things (with a new chef from Santorini) in a laid-back environment. High-quality offerings with a view.

Athinoli €€€
The English spelling of 'Athivoli', there's nothing confusing about the area's best cuisine: Greek, with a contemporary twist. In Agia Pareskevi, near Monemvasia.

Notre Maison €€€
A family runs a tight ship here; this adds a smart factor to an already-chic seaside strip in Gialova. Good service and higher end Greek seafood and 'standard' favourites. In Gialova, near Pylos.

Kourmas €€€
It's a sum-of-the-parts experience at Limeni's Kourmas: water almost laps at your feet, seafood almost jumps onto your plate. This is a dreamy locale for some of the region's best, most simply prepared, seafood. A winner.

25 Saronic Gulf ESCAPE

COMMUNITY | HISTORY | SWIMMING

▬▬ The Saronic Gulf Islands dot the waters nearest Athens and offer a fast track to Greek island life. As with all Greek islands, each has an individual feel and culture, so you can hop between classical heritage, celebrity-studded harbours, exquisite architecture and remote escapism.

How to

Getting here/around
Frequent conventional and fast ferries from Piraeus serve these islands. Allow 30 minutes (Aegina) to three hours (Spetses). Skip the car – all the towns are best on foot, and some prohibit vehicles. Exception: to explore Aegina widely, it's best to hire wheels.

When to go
Late spring and early autumn, to avoid busy summer but still have great weather.

Ice-cream stop
Get homemade goat's-milk ice cream at Flora's in Hydra.

From Ancient History to Azure Seas

Beyond its bustling port, **Aegina** has the seductive, easygoing character of a typical Greek island. Added bonuses are prestigious ancient sites such as the splendid 500 BCE **Temple of Aphaia**, celebrating a local goddess of pre-Hellenic times, and the magical Byzantine **Paleohora** ruins. Weekending Athenians spice up the mix of laid-back locals, creating lively waterfront life.

Tiny **Angistri** lies a few kilometres off the west coast of Aegina and, out of high season, its mellow pine-clad lanes and azure coves make a brilliant day trip or, even better, a longer escape. Dirt paths through the pine trees lead to beaches like the broad, pebbly and clothing-optional **Chalikiada Beach** with crystalline waters.

Seafaring Champions

Hydra's and Spetses' history as maritime powerhouses and their important roles in the War of Independence are significant even today, celebrated annually in Hydra's **Miaoulia Festival** (June) and Spetses' **Armata** (September). It's a blast to come for days of celebrations culminating in fireworks and explosive staged battles in the harbour.

Top left and right Aegina
Bottom left Temple of Aphaia

Car-Free Island Showstopper

Whether you sail or ferry into **Hydra**, the sparkling boat-filled **harbour** and the bright light striking the tiers of carefully preserved stone houses make for a scene you'll never forget. Breathtaking Hydra is one of the few Greek islands that is free of wheeled vehicles. No cars or scooters – just tiny marble-cobbled lanes, donkeys, rocks and sea. Artists (Brice Marden, Nikos Chatzikyriakos-Ghikas, Panayiotis Tetsis), musicians (Leonard Cohen, David Gilmour), actors and celebrities (Melina Mercouri, Sophia Loren) have all been drawn to Hydra over the years. In addition to the island's exquisitely preserved stone architecture, divine rural paths and clear, deep waters, you can find a good cappuccino along the harbour which is great for people-watching.

If you're an outdoors type, don't forget the island's idyllic coastal paths and hidden swimming bays. Another unbeatable experience is the long haul up to **Moni Profiti Ilia**. The

Where to See Hydra Arts & History

Faneromeni Harbourside monastery complex with 17th-century Kimisis Tis Theotokou Cathedral.

Lazaros Koundouriotis Historical Mansion Handsome ochre-coloured *arhontiko* (stone mansion) of the Greek war hero. Exquisite 18th-century architecture, furnishings, outfits and art exhibition.

Studio of Panayiotis Tetsis Home and atelier of one of Greece's best painters, with paints and paintings intact, plus perfectly preserved shop.

Historical Archives Museum of Hydra Portraits and naval artefacts, plus well-curated art and cultural exhibitions and summer concerts.

Deste Foundation Small former slaughterhouse with a high-season exhibit of top-name international art.

■ Recommended by Dimitris Fousekis, *local artist and illustrator* dimitrisfousekis.com

Far left
Historical Archives Museum of Hydra
Below Xylokeriza Beach, Spetses

wonderful monastery complex contains beautiful icons and boasts endless, dramatic views.

Historic Haven with a Ring of Beaches

Spetses stands proudly a few kilometres from the mainland Peloponnese, but there is a stronger sense of carefree island Greece here than in other Saronic Gulf destinations. The lively, historical old town is the only village on the island. The rest, ringed by a simple road, is rolling hills, pine forests and aquamarine-clear pebble coves. With a rich naval history, it is still incredibly popular with yachties, and its vibrant culture attracts artists, intellectuals and lovers of a good island party. The mansion of Spetses' famous daughter, the 19th-century seagoing commander Laskarina Bouboulina, has been converted into **Bouboulina's Museum**.

From the main **Dapia Harbour**, lined with shops and cafes, and passing the church of **Moni Agios Nikolaos**, you'll arrive at the attractive **Palio Limani** (Old Harbour) yacht anchorage and more bars and restaurants.

Hire a bike or scooter, or hop on the bus or summertime caïque to get to tiny, pretty **Xylokeriza Beach** or popular, long and pebbly **Agia Paraskevi** and the sandier **Agii Anargyri**. At the north end of Anargyri, you can follow a small path to submerged, swimmable **Bekiris Cave**.

IONIAN ISLANDS

NATURE | HISTORY | GASTRONOMY

- ▶ **Trip Builder** (p142)
- ▶ **Practicalities** (p143)
- ▶ **An Ionian Sailing Adventure** (p144)
- ▶ **Country Life on Corfu** (p146)
- ▶ **A Window onto Italy** (p148)
- ▶ **Corfu Town Secrets** (p150)
- ▶ **Eating All Over Corfu** (p154)
- ▶ **A Smashing Easter** (p156)
- ▶ **Listings** (p158)

IONIAN ISLANDS
Trip Builder

Stroll the honey-hued twisting alleys of Corfu's Venetian-influenced **Old Town** (p148)
⛴ 1¼hrs from Igoumenitsa

Visit hidden vineyards for a taste of the Ionians' best wine in **southern Corfu** (p146)
🚗 1¼hrs from Corfu Town

Take a dip in Greece's best waters and snorkel off the coast of **Antipaxi** (p145)
⛴ 15mins from Paxi

Dine with locals at their favourite harbourside taverna on **Lefkada** (p144)
⛴ 1¾hrs from Kefallonia

Hike deep into the olive groves and to the pristine beaches of **Kefallonia** (p159)
⛴ 1¾hrs from Lefkada

It's no secret that the Ionians, greener and more lush than the rest of the Greek islands, are a haven for nature lovers. From elegant Venetian old towns and aquamarine waters frequented by dolphins to hidden vineyards, charming farmstays and immersive culinary retreats, you'll find it all in the 'emerald' isles.

FROM TOP: BALATE DORIN/SHUTTERSTOCK ©,
YAU MING LOW/SHUTTERSTOCK ©
PREVIOUS SPREAD: BALATE DORIN/SHUTTERSTOCK ©

Practicalities

ARRIVING

Ioannis Kapodistrias Airport Taxis connect to Corfu Town (€23) and Gouvia Marina (€40).

Ferries From Albania, connect with Corfu Town via Saranda. From Italy, connect in Igoumenitsa, which offers lines to Corfu, Paxi and Kefallonia.

FIND YOUR WAY

Most towns are easily navigated on foot, but GPS might find backstreets tricky. Sailors: use the Windy and Navionics apps.

MONEY

ATMs are widely available in towns and larger villages. Many places accept contactless cards and digital wallets.

WHERE TO STAY

Place	Pro/Con
Corfu Old Town	Lively place to stay, with centuries-old Venetian apartments.
Gaios, Paxi	Self-catering apartments on the waterfront.
Kefallonia	Beautiful stone villas and reasonably priced apartments near beaches.
Lefkada	Boutique hotels, all-inclusives and self-catering apartments at reasonable prices.

EATING & DRINKING

The Ionians' regional dishes show influences from Italy. *Pastitsadha* (slow-cooked meat in a tomato sauce), along with *bourdeto* (spicy fish casserole) and *tsigareli* (wild greens in a spicy sauce) are just a few of the must-try dishes inspired by the Venetian rulers six centuries ago.

Must-try seafood Nautilus, Bay of Garitsa (p153)

Best wine Pontiglio Winery, southern Corfu (p155)

GETTING AROUND

Sailing Yachts, catamarans and sailing boats can be chartered with a captain or without (if you have a licence) from Corfu's Gouvia Marina (€200 to €800 per day).

Ferry Between Corfu, Kefallonia and Paxi (ferryhopper.com); smaller boats service the smaller islands.

Car The best way to get around. Car-hire companies are at airports and ports.

MAR–MAY The islands are in full bloom. Great hiking weather.	**JUN–SEP** Summer season in full swing. Beaches and tavernas fill up.	**OCT–NOV** Cooler weather and olive harvest. Bargain rates.	**DEC–FEB** Drizzly and wet. Corfu Town still buzzes with activity.

TOP: ARTUR.NYK/SHUTTERSTOCK ©
BOTTOM: MELIDIS A/SHUTTERSTOCK ©

IONIAN ISLANDS FIND YOUR FEET

26 An Ionian Sailing ADVENTURE

BEACH | SWIMMING | SEAFOOD

Diehard sailors will tell you that you haven't truly seen the Ionians unless you've explored them by boat. Thanks to their unique topography and plenty of mountainous, green zones, these gorgeous islands have stretches of coastline that aren't easily reached by land. Prepare your sea legs – the dolphins, turtles and secret beaches await.

Trip Notes

Getting around The best way to island-hop is on a chartered sailboat. Use *sailogy.com* to find the right boat for you, or head straight to the Sunsail or PlainSailing offices in Corfu's Gouvia Marina (pictured above).

When to go The Ionian Sea generally offers smooth sailing conditions from late April until late September.

Top tip Stop off at tiny islands Ereikousa and Othoni for empty, white-sand beaches, great hiking and caves that demand exploration with a snorkel or paddleboard.

A Stop in Lefkada

If you're coming into Lefkada Town harbour on a boat, you have to drop by **Frini Sto Molo** taverna for lunch or dinner. It's a favourite with the locals and has excellent seafood dishes. Then, if you have time, sunset from **Exanthia** village with a drink at **Rachi** is a must.

Recommended by photographer Sandra Semburg
@sandrasemburg

01 The crystal waters of Corfu's **Paleokastritsa** are a great place to take the plunge when the midday sun is high. Catch the sunset from Angelokastro, a 13th-century Byzantine fortress.

02 Stop off at Paxi's **Gaïos Marina** for a Greek coffee and a stroll past pretty Venetian buildings, then sail on to Erimitis Beach, a stretch of wild coastline created by the falling cliffs that tower above.

03 Antipaxi is known for having the best swimming water in all of Greece. Throw down the anchor at **Voutoumi Beach** for swimming-pool-like water.

04 Impossible to reach without a 4WD or a boat, Ithaki's **Marmakas Beach** is lined with eucalyptus trees and looks out onto the small island of Agios Nikolaos, home to the chapel of St Nicholas.

05 Drop into electric-blue waters at the **Papanikolis Cave** on Meganisi, named after a WWII submarine. It's here that the submarine would hide during the war, undetected between patrols.

FROM TOP: MILOS VUCICEVIC/SHUTTERSTOCK ©
SERBIANONTHEROAD/SHUTTERSTOCK ©

27 Country Life on CORFU

HIKING | FARMSTAYS | NATURE

Benefiting from high precipitation in the winter months, Corfu is so lush that it can feel tropical in summer. Fertile ground and centuries of olive cultivation give the island an agricultural edge, with plenty of honey, olive oil and wine produced locally. Step inland, away from the beaches and onto winding dirt paths leading into olive groves, for a taste of the country life.

How to

Getting around Corfu's intercity bus network is operated by Green Buses (ktelkerkyras.gr) with services to major beaches and communities. For greater flexibility, though, it's best to rent a vehicle.

When to go
Wildflower-flecked meadows bloom in spring, with the best months for outdoor activities being April and May, just as the winter rains clear and before the heat really kicks in.

Zesty kumquat Corfu is famous for its kumquat fruit. Try the local kumquat liqueur or jam, which make great souvenirs.

Hike it Lace up for the **Corfu Trail**, a 180km hiking route that runs from the monastery of **Arkoudilas** in the south through dense forest, olive groves and onto wild, cliff-lined beaches, up to the mountain village of **Liapades** and the dramatic summit of **Mt Pantokrator** (906m), the island's highest peak. Visit thecorfutrail.com to tackle it solo; small, family-run **Aperghi Travel** handles tours and accommodation for walkers.

Live like a farmer Tucked into an olive grove only a short distance from Corfu Town, **Dr Kavvadia's Organic Farm** offers stays in its bright, modernist apartments and a chance to get immersed in agricultural lifestyle. Depending on the season, you can help out with the olive harvest in October, sow and pick organic vegetables in the garden or collect your own eggs from the hens each morning.

Lakeside activities Take a drive in the south of the island towards **Lake Korission** for horse riding around the cinematic dunes of **Issos Beach** with the **Corfu Horse Riding Centre**, or turn off the main road down a gravel path for **Bioporos Organic Farm**, where you can stay and keep the family donkey company. Completely enveloped by nature, Bioporos offers beekeeping experiences and organic cosmetics workshops. Through the olive groves and down a winding path on the farm is Bioporos' very own corner of Lake Korission, complete with rowing boat.

Far left Corfu Trail
Bottom left Corfu beaches

🥾 A Coastal Hike

Hike to the secret beach of **Akoli**, on the northeastern coast of Corfu. It's beautiful – the wild olive trees give ample shade to shelter from the sun. It's been a safe haven for activists to meet, organise and start action against tourist development in the region because it's a symbol of pristine beauty on the island.

It's rarely frequented by others in the spring months, and dolphins can often be spotted from the beach here off season.

Recommended by
Xenia Tombrou, local environmentalist @xenia313

A Window onto Italy

CORFU'S VENETIAN LEGACY LIVES ON

Corfu's proximity to its neighbours is not the only reason the island feels more akin to Italy than Greece. From singular Easter traditions and its characteristic rose- and gold-toned Old Town colour palette to the food that makes this island one of Greece's best for gastronomy, Corfu has the Venetians to thank for it all.

Left Corfu Town
Centre Mt Pantokrator
Right Old Perithia

On a clear day, Corfu is visible from Puglia's Santa Maria di Leuca. The island's proximity to Italy made it a strategic entry point to the east, first Byzantium and then the Ottoman Empire. Not actually falling under Greek rule until the 19th century, Greece's most western isle first came under Venetian influence in the 1200s. Even before then, Corfu was captured by the Sicilians twice over the course of a 200-year period and was jostled between Sicily and Venice until the late 1300s when the Corfiots themselves asked that Venice take over. The island was in the Venetians' hands from then until the late 18th century.

Under Venetian rule, Corfu's economy flourished. The island's oldest settlement, Old Perithia on the foothills of Mt Pantokrator, still holds onto the vestiges of its Venetian past – the crumbling mansion homes built in the 14th century by Venetian merchants stand testament to the wealth that was poured into the island from across the Ionians. By the mid 1700s, Kythira, Antikythira, Kefallonia and Lekfada also became colonies of Venice, with the main industry in the Ionians focused on the export of produce grown on the islands.

Corfu's dense olive groves can be accredited to the Venetians, who brought olive cultivation to the island, making its distinct and bitter Lianolia variety of olive oil Vatican-worthy produce. By the 16th century, it was Corfu that supplied olive oil to the Vatican.

To defend Corfu, their colonies and the blossoming industry there, the Venetians completed Palaio Frourio (Old Fort) in the 1540s and Neo Frourio (New Fort) a couple of decades later. Between these two examples of Venetian engineering,

Corfu Town began to take shape. In the same style as Ragusa in Sicily (also conquered by the Venetians), multistorey buildings began to crop up tightly around central gathering points, the *plateia* (squares), which developed organically around cisterns and wells. Off the *plateia* ran narrow cobblestone alleyways, which the Corfiots still call *kantounia*. This all exists today – one example is the charming Plateia Dimaercheiou, with the *kantounia* leading off towards the very heart of town and the Church of Agios Spyridon, the patron saint of Corfu.

> Greece's most western isle first came under Venetian influence in the 1200s.

Apart from architecture and industry, the Venetians brought a culture of learning and music to the island. Corfu's first newspaper was printed in Italian and the Academy of Modern Greece opened under Venetian rule. Opera also found its way into the consciousness of the Corfiots, laying the foundations for the island's affinity to music that is still flourishing today, with its philharmonic orchestra being the most highly esteemed in Greece.

In villages across the island, signs of the Venetian reign remain – some locals are completely oblivious that the dishes they're accustomed to (*stifadho, pastitsadha, bianco* and *bourdeto*) were originally brought to Corfu by their Italian neighbours. Language, too, still hints at the Corfiots' Italian heritage. In Corfu, to wake up early is to get up *'A buon ora'*, while grandmothers are referred to as *Nonna* in some parts of the island. Italian is so woven through the Corfiots' daily life that some are not even aware of it.

Corfu under Napoleon

After the fall of the Republic of Venice in the late 1700s, Napoleon ensured that the French were next to step in to take control of the Ionians.

Vestiges of Corfu's brief French rule can be seen in the grand, photogenic esplanade in the heart of Corfu Town.

Built between 1807 and 1814, the Liston – with its distinct arcades that nod to the elegant Parisian architecture of the period at Rue de Rivoli – was built by French architect Ferdinand de Lesseps.

At the time, the aristocratic families of Corfu were the only people permitted access to the Liston, now Corfu's best people-watching spot.

28 Corfu Town SECRETS

LOCAL LIFE | SHOPPING | CUISINE

Historic and elegant, UNESCO-listed Corfu Town hides many secrets down its winding narrow lanes. Seek out the less touristy side of the Venetian-influenced Old Town, from shaded gardens to family-run tavernas, local designers and traditional workshops, and rub shoulders with Corfiots rather than the day-cruise crowds.

How to

Getting around Corfu's main airport is walking distance to the Old Town. Take a taxi or local bus 15, or stroll into town; once you're there, the narrow streets – many of them pedestrianised – demand to be explored on foot.

When to go Locals avoid the town in July and August because of the heat and influx of visitors. Go in April, May, September and October to get the best of the weather and avoid the crowds.

What's on Corfu Town has a lively cultural life; check sources like *enimerosi.com* or *mykerkyra.com* for upcoming events.

The Old Fort or the New Fort?

Corfu's Venetian-built 14th-century **Palaio Frourio** sits on the water and can be spotted as you fly into the island. What visitors often overlook is the **Neo Frourio** (New Fort, built in the 1570s – so not as new as you might think), tucked behind the *laiki* (central market). Dank tunnels and passages wind through the walls, leading to ramparts offering unrivalled vistas.

Wander the Kantounia

Corfiot for 'narrow alleyway', the *kantounia* of the Old Town were extolled by Greek singer Rena Vlahopoulou in her 1972 song 'Kerkyra, Kerkyra', dedicated to the island and its highlights. Taking a turn down one of these alleys – the washing strung high above your head, swallows flitting between the buildings – leads to Corfu's own world, one in which old men

Dream of Saponification

Step into Greece's oldest soap factory, **Patounis**, and discover the tradition of olive soap making. Since the 1850s, the Patounis family has been perfecting their time-honoured, chemical-free method in their workshop down Ioannou Theotoki street. Want a closer look? Book a tour at *patounis.gr*, then stock up on the handcrafted soaps in the little store in front.

Top left Souvenir shops, Corfu
Bottom left and top right Palaio Frourio

play backgammon in shaded squares and students fill the air with the chords of their late-night bouzouki sessions. The *kantounia* are many and demand an exploration. Even locals can get lost here.

Escape for a Lunchtime Dip

Come summer, Corfu Town can be a swelteringly hot experience. If you're missing your own yacht, why not follow the locals to their favourite swimming spots and avoid the crowded heart of town? At the end of the Bay of Garitsa, the **Anemomilos Windmill** marks the spot where Corfu Town's old-timers cool off with a dip. A 15-minute stroll south takes you to the **Mon Repos Estate**, birthplace of the late Prince Philip of Greece (husband to Queen Elizabeth II). The estate's sprawling gardens are shaded by cypress trees leading to **Kardaki Beach**, where the long stone jetty reaches into inviting blue-green waters, fringed by dense foliage.

Coffee like a Corfiot

One of the great delights enjoyed by both locals and visitors to Corfu Town is to sit in a charming cafe and people-watch while nursing a coffee. Whether it's a short, silty Greek number or an ice-cold 'Freddo Cappuccino', it's best enjoyed in the shade and can take upwards of an hour to drink. A stylish place to hang out is **Josephine** under the Liston arcade. **Coconella** and **Saltino** are also atmospheric spots. Take some Greek coffee home from the family-run **Markosian**, a 100-year-old *kafekopteio* (coffee roastery) that feels like stepping back in time on entry.

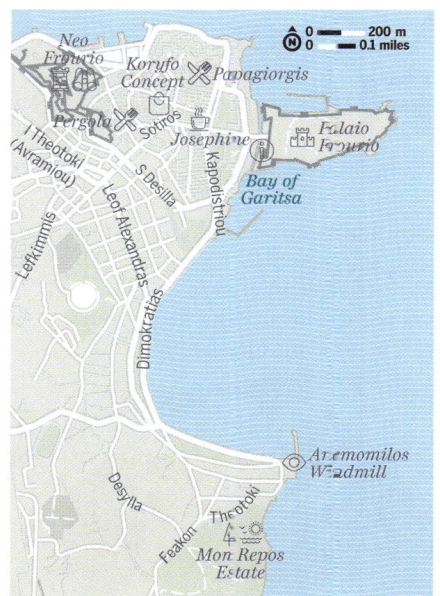

Where the Locals Eat

At the height of summer, escape the crowds and enjoy a fresh sea breeze with your ouzo and mezes at **Nautilus** in the Bay of Garitsa, or dip into possibly the island's best *taramosalata* (a thick purée of fish roe and potato) at **Poseidonio** in the dappled shade of eucalyptus trees. In the heart of town, **Pergola** is the taverna of choice for locals, with plenty of hearty, home-cooked dishes like the island's famous *stifado* (stew). For gelato, the century-old, family-run **Papagiorgis** is really the only place Corfiots will go; the chocolate kumquat or wild strawberry sorbet are best sellers.

Shop Greek Designers

One thing Corfu Town is not lacking in is shopping – but how to sift through all the souvenir stores and actually get to the good stuff? Visit Corfiot designer Marianna Kastrinos' **Koryfo Concept**, tucked away behind a main thoroughfare, for Corfu-inspired jewellery, prints and loose linens. Other boutiques with distinct items by Greek designers you'll actually want to take home are **Muses** and **La Poupee**.

Far left Mon Repos Estate
Left Anemomilos Windmill

29 Eating All Over CORFU

CUISINE | WINE | CULTURE

Thanks to the distinctive blend of cultural influences stemming from the periods of Venetian, French and British rule, Corfu's gastronomy is a standout and offers tastes and treats that are quite distinctive compared to other regions of Greece. Meet the local producers to experience the best of the food on the island, from classic Greek specialities to fresh seafood and Italian flavours.

🍴 How to

Getting around Hire a car and hit up Corfu's culinary heroes, from local chefs to artisan food producers. Make pit stops that turn into tasty adventures, taking your sweet time to savour both the sights and the bites.

When to go Producers offer tours year-round, but it's best to aim for May, June and September. They'll have more time for you outside the harvest seasons, and cooking classes outdoors are much more enjoyable when the heat of the summer isn't in full force.

Cook with the experts Visit a Greek grandmother in her village home and make a traditional Greek coffee together, then spend a week foraging wild mountain herbs and cooking local dishes with Corfiot food writer Anastasia Miari on her **Flavours of Corfu** (matriarcheats.com) retreat. Or head to the centuries-old vineyard **Ambelonas** where Vasiliki Karounou, author of *Corfiot Cuisine*, does step-by-step cooking demonstrations followed by a feast.

Meet the producers The island's fertile land is one reason Corfu is known for its gastronomy. In the south of the island, **Pontiglio Winery** offers tours and tastings at the small, family-run vineyard that was set up in the years following the economic crisis and now provides wine for the island's best restaurants. Visit the **Governor** olive mill for a hike deep into its olive groves and a special tasting featuring unusual flavour combinations of its unique olive oil that boasts cancer-fighting properties.

Best bites For fresh seafood on the water, head to **Toulas** in Agni Bay and plump for a *bianco* (fish stew in a zingy lemon salsa). Further down the island, in the heart of Corfu's Old Town, the **Venetian Well** takes traditional recipes and serves them with an elegant twist in a pretty courtyard around a 500-year-old Venetian well. Visit Nikos Bellos' **Klimataria** in the fishing village of **Benitses** for the best octopus *pastitsadha* and juicy tomatoes you'll find on Corfu.

Left Sofrito slow-braised beef
Bottom left Governor olive oil

 Thank the Neighbours

The Corfiots have the Venetians to thank for their rich, spice-filled cuisine. The *stifadho* – from the Italian *stufato* – is a slow-cooked tomato stew featuring rabbit, beef or octopus and an injection of spices that can be accredited to Corfu's location on the spice trail. Cinnamon, spicy paprika, nutmeg and cloves have been known to feature in a *stifadho*, but each local will prepare it differently, some swearing by just a spicy paprika and others throwing it all in there.

30 A Smashing EASTER

FESTIVAL | CULTURE | HISTORY

During Orthodox Easter weekend, Greeks from all over the country flock to Corfu's Old Town to experience the ritual pot-smashing celebration. With origins in the Venetian era, this quirky custom symbolises the First Resurrection of Christ and is believed to ward off evil.

How to

Getting around Arrive ahead of events, and if driving, park clear of the Old Town and walk. This is the busiest weekend of the year and you don't want to be looking for parking while the action is taking place.

When to go Greek Orthodox Easter is usually observed on different dates from the Easter celebrated in Western countries. The main events take place from Friday to Monday of the Easter weekend across the island.

Traditional Easter foods Try *magiritsa* (lamb soup) and *tsoureki*, a sweet braided bread flavoured with mastic and *mahlepi* (wild cherry bark)..

Far left Philharmonic orchestra
Bottom left Throwing clay pots
Above left Carrying the Epitaph

Follow the band On the evening of Good Friday, join the procession of the Epitaphios, representing the funeral bier of Jesus Christ. The Epitaphios, adorned with wildflowers, is carried by Greek Orthodox priests through the grand esplanades, accompanied by philharmonic orchestras playing solemn tunes. Locals light candles and burn frankincense along the procession, which ends with the Epitaph of the Mitropolis – a symbolic representation of Christ's burial – at the **Liston arcade** at 10pm.

Pot smashing Watch your head at 11am on Holy Saturday – that's when locals start throwing pots from their balconies. A classic place to watch this spectacle is at the Liston arcade. Thousands gather to look up at the Venetian balconies bedecked in red sashes, where giant clay amphorae – known as *botides* or *canates* – painted crimson red and filled with water, teeter precariously on the edge. When the clock strikes 11am, the vessels – some taller and wider than the men pushing them – are dropped from the balconies, smashing into pieces only steps from the crowds below. When it's over, pick up a piece for good luck and enjoy the atmosphere as the orchestras burst into joyful tunes.

Fireworks and feasting In the evening of Holy Saturday, make your way to a church or the bandstand in the park opposite the Palaio Frourio for the final Resurrection Mass. Everyone carries a candle, creating a magnificent light display. Come midnight, fireworks fill the skies to celebrate the resurrection of Christ and to mark the end of 40 days of fasting. Locals then return home for a midnight feast with the family or head to the town's clubs and bars to party until the early hours of the morning.

What's Behind It?

The story goes that the Ancient Greeks would toss out their old clay pots once spring came to make way for new seeds planted in brand-new pots.

Later, around the 16th century, the colonising Venetians would mark the New Year in Corfu by tossing out all of their old belongings in a dramatic (if not wasteful) spring clean.

The Corfiots are then said to have adopted the tradition for their biggest religious holiday, Orthodox Easter.

Local priests say the crashing of the pots symbolises the earthquake-like tremors that were felt as Christ was resurrected.

Listings

BEST OF THE REST

 Best Bites

Tassia, Kefallonia €€€
Harbourfront dining in Fiskardo's oldest (since 1972) restaurant, run by well-known Kefallonian chef Tassia Dendrinou.

Rachi, Lefkada €€€
Eye-candy sea views compete with sophisticated feasts at this romantic terrace restaurant high up in the mountain village of Exanthia.

Elia, Corfu €€
Cliff-top taverna above breathtaking Myrtiotissa Beach serves an enticing menu of Corfiot specialities with garden-fresh ingredients.

Old Perithia Taverna, Corfu €€
Oozing rustic ambience with a view of Mt Pantrokrator, this timeless jewel's Corfiot soul food has been a crowd-puller since 1863.

Taverna Kouloura, Corfu €€
Enjoy the best catch of the day in a tiny fishing bay that looks out onto Albania.

Bars with Character

Josephine, Corfu Town €€
The best spot to people-watch over a cocktail from within the Liston's Parisian-style arcades in Corfu Town.

7th Heaven, Corfu €€
Perched atop the limestone cliffs near Peroulades, this open-air bar wows with a skywalk, swings, flirty vibes and energetic beats.

La Grotta, Corfu €€
Tucked into a cliffside cove above Paleokastritsa's turquoise waters, this scene-stealing bar serves up a party complete with diving board.

Erimitis, Paxi €€
Clever cocktails and great Greek wines pair with panoramic views over coastal cliffs from an expansive deck.

 Picturesque Villages

Kioni, Ithaki
An idyllic haven of mustard-and-cream Venetian houses that line a pretty harbour you can sail straight into.

Assos, Kefallonia
A picture-perfect confection of Italianate honey-hued houses embracing a crescent-shaped cove sheltered by a romantic peninsula.

Old Perithia, Corfu
Corfu's oldest settlement has ramshackle stone houses tucked into the foothills of majestic Mt Pantokrator.

Liapades, Corfu
Bougainvillaea winds around bright, whitewashed houses close to one of the island's best beaches.

Kioni, Ithaki

Argyrades, Corfu

Walk to Agios Ioannis church at the heart of the village for panoramic views over the south of the island.

Beaches to Seek Out

Petani Beach, Kefallonia

Locally adored serviced patch of white sand and pebble on the Paliki Peninsula, blissful enough to entice a jaded mermaid.

Chouchoulio, Corfu

Pebble-strewn and tucked into a quiet bay with a charming seafood taverna just a stroll away.

Megali Petra, Lefkada

Pristine beach with electric-blue waters that are dotted with impressive rock formations.

Egremni Beach

Shockingly pretty cliff-flanked 2.5km-long crowd-free band of white pebbles, but access involves walking and stairs (or arrive by boat).

Feeling Cultured

Achilleion Palace, Corfu Town

Sissi's summer retreat served as a film set of the James Bond film *For Your Eyes Only* and offers sweeping coastal views from its sculpture-studded gardens.

White House, Corfu

More a living museum with a restaurant dropped into a pretty bay, this was once home to famous British author Lawrence Durrell, who regularly hosted his equally famous brother Gerald.

Angelokastro, Corfu

The ramparts of this impregnable hilltop Byzantine fortress remain largely intact, and the views back to Paleokastritsa are unforgettable.

Black moray eel

Mon Repos Estate, Corfu Town

Birthplace of the late Prince Philip of Greece, hidden amid a forest of cypress trees and moments away from a favourite swimming spot of Corfu Town locals.

Outdoor Thrills

Kefallonia

Take the path from Antisamos to Koutsoupia with Outdoor Kefallonia for a paradisiacal beach reached along a verdant coastal road. The long-established operator offers all manner of trips throughout the island.

Ithaki

A superb half-day walk begins and ends in the village of Stavros, the centre of hiking activity on Ithaki. Along the way, it takes in a museum, historic sites, pretty woodlands, airy viewpoints and high goat pastures.

Lefkada

Specialising in learn-to-windsurf packages, Club Vassiliki also offers board hire, private lessons and a wide range of other activities from diving to mountain biking.

Paxi

With clear visibility and diverse habitats, Paxi offers some great diving. Paxos Oasi Sub offers try dives, snorkelling safaris and PADI open-water courses.

CRETE

SCENERY | HISTORY | CUISINE

- **Trip Builder** (p162)
- **Practicalities** (p164)
- **Unmissable Hania** (p166)
- **Ancient Knossos** (p168)
- **Exploring Gorges** (p170)
- **Alluring Beaches** (p172)
- **Enchanting Rethymno** (p174)
- **Mountain Villages** (p176)
- **Foods of Crete** (p178)
- **Mysterious Minoans** (p180)
- **Listings** (p182)

Laze away your days on **Falasarna Beach** where sunsets dazzle (p173)
🚗 1hr from Hania

Enjoy evocative **Hania**, a city of sensational sights and good food (p166)
🚌 1¼hrs from Rethymno

Get lost in the labyrinthine, Renaissance-era lanes of historic **Rethymno** (p174)
🚌 1¼hrs from Hania

Revel in the pink sands and turquoise water of **Elafonisi Beach** (p173)
🚗 1½hrs from Hania

Start in the mountains and trek to the sea through **Samaria Gorge** (p170)
🚗 1½hrs from Hania

Wander **Argyroupoli**, an ancient mountain village built atop Roman ruins (p177)
🚗 30mins from Rethymno

Get lost in the **Amari Valley** and its quilt of unspoilt villages (p177)
🚗 1hr from Rethymno

CRETE
Trip Builder

Crete is a long island that packs a country's worth of highlights within its craggy shores. From the immersive charm of its Venetian cities and the wonders of Knossos to its soaring mountains and bounty of beaches, it's a traveller's feast.

Explore Crete's top collection of Minoan artefacts at the **Heraklion Archaeological Museum** (p168).
🚌 1½hrs from Rethymno

Watch out for falling dates at the palm-shaded **Vaï Beach** (p173).
🚗 2½hrs from Iraklio

Rub shoulders with the Minoans at the **Palace of Knossos** (p168).
🚗 15mins from Iraklio

Practicalities

ARRIVING

Airports Crete's two airports are in Iraklio and Hania. The former is convenient for travel in the east and the latter for the west. Both have plenty of car-rental agencies (keep in mind that local Crete-based firms can be cheaper than international brands) and local bus services to their respective city centres. If using a taxi to reach the city centre, check the posted fixed price and get the driver to agree first.

HOW MUCH FOR A

Coffee
€2

Souvlaki
€3

Fresh fish
€15 or more

GETTING AROUND

Car The best way for exploring Crete's large and varied countryside. It gives you the flexibility to try any mountain-pass road that attracts you. Note that some very remote beaches will require a 4WD.

Bus Crete has an efficient network of buses that connect all the main cities and towns. On more remote routes they may only run two or three times per day, so opportunities for complex outings are limited.

Ferry The great joy of the southwest coast, frequent ferries in summer (less often at other times) provide a scenic and enjoyable way to travel between beach towns and are essential for car-free towns.

WHEN TO GO

JAN–MAR
Cold and blustery; much is closed.

APR–JUN
Warming weather, wildflowers; widespread openings after Orthodox Easter.

JUL–SEP
High temperatures, prices and crowds. September is beautiful and less crowded.

OCT–DEC
After October, Crete turns inward for winter.

EATING & DRINKING

Cretan cuisine evolved from the abundance of local produce, coupled with enormous ingenuity. You'll find a wonderful array of Cretan specialities, such as the dozens of wonderful cheeses produced primarily from goat's and sheep's milk or a combination of the two. Another part of the magic of Cretan cuisine is the ingredients gathered from hillsides and around villages. The fresh bounty includes all types of fruit and vegetables. And don't miss the range of grilled meats served in village tavernas across the mountains and the fresh seafood in coastal towns.

Best seafood taverna Taverna Knossos, Rethymno (p182)

Must-try baked goods Kirkór, Iraklio

CONNECT & FIND YOUR WAY

Wi-fi Places to stay, cafes and some port areas have fast and free wi-fi.

Navigation Map apps sometimes don't offer accurate or smart choices for smaller roads, especially in rural areas. A large paper map is very useful. Download Crete mapping data to your app for regions with no mobile service.

WATCH THE SEASONS

Check what's fresh when, as the best Cretan cuisine uses seasonal ingredients. Summertime farmers markets are a joy to wander.

WHERE TO STAY

Crete is an affordable place to stay. Book as far ahead as possible to score good deals in peak season, and note that selection is limited from November to March.

Town	Pro/Con
Hania	Crete's most appealing city. It can fill up in summer.
Rethymno	Plenty of Venetian magic. Best for only two or three nights.
Iraklio	Close to the busiest airport. Less interesting for sightseeing.
Matala	Major beach town near ruins. Crowded in summer.
Agios Nikolaos	Beaches and good nightlife. Isolated in the island's east.
Paleohora	Close to many beaches and on a ferry route, but somewhat remote.

MONEY

Nearly all places to eat and shops take cards (some even eschew cash). Even in high season, Crete's costs are moderate compared to Western Europe. Book accommodation and rental cars well ahead to save money.

31 Unmissable HANIA

HISTORY | WATERFRONT | FOOD

Hania is Crete's most evocative city, with its pretty Venetian quarter crisscrossed by narrow lanes and culminating at a magnificent harbour. Examples of Venetian and Turkish architecture abound, which makes the old town a superb place to walk around and explore. Many visitors settle back in a cafe with a view, and restaurants that showcase the full range of Cretan food are aplenty.

How to

Getting around Everywhere worth getting to in Hania is easily reachable on foot.

When to go In summer Hania is thronged and steamy. In April, May, September and October everything is open and crowds are manageable.

Buying local food Hania revels in its reputation for serving some of Crete's best food; the Saturday market boasts top produce and scores of food vendors. Drandaki Bakery still uses a woodfired oven.

There are few places where Hania's historic charm and grandeur are more palpable than in the centuries-old **Venetian Harbour**. It's lined with pastel-coloured buildings that punctuate a maze of narrow lanes filled with shops and tavernas. The eastern side of the harbour is dominated by the domed **Mosque of Kioutsouk Hasan**, now an exhibition hall. The waterfront curves onto the 14th-century breakwater, which is over 500m long. Clamber over the huge blocks of stone as you take in captivating views back to the old town, out to sea and the iconic **lighthouse**.

Hania's massive fortifications, built by the Venetians to protect the city from marauding pirates and invading Turks, are impressive. Known as **Topanas**, this is one of Hania's most appealing neighbourhoods. Best preserved is the western wall, running from the **Firkas Fortress** to the **Schiavo Bastion**. Follow lanes to the top of the bastions for sweeping views down into the moat, which was recently restored with a park along the base. The hulking Firkas Fortress is also home to the interesting **Maritime Museum of Crete**.

The collection of the **Archaeological Museum of Chania** is as striking as the recently opened building. Treasures from across Crete are displayed in light-filled galleries, with signage offering details. Artefacts from Neolithic to Roman times fill the main floor.

Far left Venetian Harbour
Bottom left Fresh seafood, Crete

Best Places to Eat in Hania

To Maridaki A modern seafood *mezedhopoleio* (restaurant specialising in mezedhes) that's usually packed. Excellent locally sourced fare.

Kouzina epe This stylish cafe serves a creative mix of modern options and blackboard-listed daily specials.

Thalassino Ageri A delicious fish taverna among the vestiges of Hania's old tanneries near the new Archaeological Museum building.

Christostomos Tucked away from the crowds behind the harbour; popular with residents and visitors for its classic Cretan cuisine.

Marina Sailing Club Wonderful views and fewer crowds at the eastern end of the historic harbour near the breakwater.

32 Ancient KNOSSOS

PALACE | MINOANS | ART

Knossos was the capital of the mythical Minoan empire more than 4000 years ago. An extraordinary wealth of frescoes, sculptures, relics, jewellery and structures lay buried under the soil here until the site's excavation in the early 20th century. Combining a visit to this unmissable ancient marvel with a spin around the excellent archaeological museum in nearby Iraklio is highly recommended.

How to

Getting here Knossos is only 5km south of Iraklio. It is served by city buses.

When to go From May to September Knossos is open into the evening. Dusk here is evocative. In the winter months, you may have vast swaths of the sight to yourself.

Top tip See original frescoes (many on-site ones are replicas) and other treasures plus a scale model of the palace at the Heraklion Archaeological Museum.

Far left Throne Room
Bottom left South Propyla on
Above left King's Megaron

A spin around the partially and imaginatively reconstructed **Palace of Knossos** delivers an eye-opening glimpse into the remarkably sophisticated society of the Minoans, who dominated the Mediterranean some 4000 years ago.

From the ticket booth, follow the marked trail to the **North Entrance** where the Charging Bull fresco gives you a first taste of Minoan artistry. Continue to the **Central Court** and join the queue to glimpse the mystical **Throne Room**, which probably hosted religious rituals. Turn right as you exit and follow the stairs up to the so-called **Piano Nobile**, where replicas of the palace's most famous artworks conveniently cluster in the Fresco Gallery. Circle back and descend to the **South Propylaion**, beautifully decorated with the Cup Bearer fresco.

Make your way back to the Central Court and head to the palace's eastern wing to admire the architecture of the **Grand Staircase** that led to what might have been the royal family's private quarters. For a closer look at some rooms, walk to the south end of the courtyard, stopping for a peek at the **Prince of the Lilies fresco**, and head down to the lower floor. A highlight here is the **Queen's Megaron**, playfully adorned with a fresco of frolicking dolphins. Stay on the lower level and make your way to the **West Magazines** with giant pithoi, huge clay jars used for storage.

ⓘ Enjoying Knossos

Beat the crowds and avoid the heat by getting to Knossos before 10am when tour buses start arriving, or late in the afternoon when it's cooler and the golden light is good for photos. Budget a couple of hours to do the place justice.

Optional guided tours last about 1½ hours and most are in English, though other languages are available. You can arrange private or group tours.

Eating options in and around the site are uninspiring. Bring a picnic, or save your appetite – and thirst – for the many wineries in the nearby **Iraklio Wine Country**, where winemaking dates back to Minoan times.

33 Exploring GORGES

WILD | OUTDOORS | HIKING

Don't miss the scores of superb hikes in Crete, including many on the crenellated southern coast. Gorges abound here and offer fascinating glimpses into life through the aeons, with ancient churches, crude caves harbouring the ghosts of hermits, often-lush foliage and stark, geologic beauty. The Samaria Gorge is the most famous of these walks, or you can try other excellent and less-crowded choices.

How to

Getting here The gorge walks are one-way, so you'll need to arrange transport in one direction to or from your car. (Some tour companies arrange the pick-up and drop-off practicalities.)

When to go In spring, the gorges are lined with wildflowers and green grasses, and in autumn the leaves change colours. In summer it can get blistering.

Top tip Bring plenty of water; sturdy shoes are essential as paths are often rough.

Far left Samaria Gorge
Bottom left Imbros Gorge

Samaria Gorge Often referred to as Crete's only national park, **Samaria Gorge National Park** is the well-organised home to its namesake gorge, one of the most popular sights on the island. From the park entrance in the hillside village of **Xyloskalo**, an 18km trail descends through sheer cliff faces down to the Mediterranean. Along the way you'll pass through 500m-high rock faces that are at times only 3m apart. The route is dotted with holy sites.

Imbros Gorge The 8km walk through Imbros Gorge is much recommended for its natural beauty and lack of crowds. An old mule path is bracketed by 300m-high walls lined with fig and almond trees, cypresses and oaks. At one point the sheer cliff faces are only 2m apart. Another highlight is an arch of stone over the path. The route begins in the tiny village of **Imbros** and finishes at **Komitades**.

Aradena Gorge The 3.5km trail into this gorge begins just before the squeaky **Vardinogiannis Bridge**, which also draws bungee-jumpers. After the first 800m, the uncrowded trail reaches the early Byzantine **Church of Agios Ioannis**. Follow the route through the fairly lush landscape to the endpoint, idyllic **Marmara Beach**. This is one of the best of the isolated beaches on Crete's southwest coast and is lapped by water that seems an almost impossibly vibrant teal in colour.

 Hiking Samaria Gorge

Day trips to the gorge are heavily marketed to tourists across Crete. All start at the park entrance and include pickups from major tourist areas such as Hania or from nearby coastal towns such as Sougia or Hora Sfakion, both about a 40-minute ferry ride from the walk's finish point at the car-free seaside village of **Agia Roumeli**.

The gorge (samaria-gorge.gr) is open for hiking from May to October. It can be cold and wet at the trailhead. Stay alert for kri-kri, a mountain goat that's native to Crete. At the trail's end, few can resist a dip in the water at Agia Roumeli.

34 Alluring BEACHES

SWIMMING | FUN | NATURE

Beaches of every flavour line Crete's 1046km of coastline. Many are far from developed areas so you can enjoy a remote holiday on the sand. No matter your mood, there is a beach for you – if you want your own little cove where you can take it all off, you can, or join the action at one of the taverna-lined party beaches.

How to

Getting here The most popular of Crete's beaches are easily served by car or bus. For others, you'll need your own vehicle. Reaching even more isolated ones requires a 4WD.

When to go June to September are the best months as the water is warm.

Ferries Many beaches along the southwest coast are linked by scheduled ferries, which offer a relaxing way to travel while enjoying the beautiful scenery.

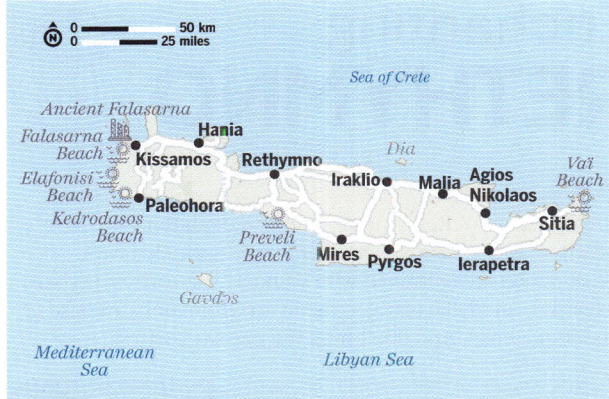

Far left Falasarna Beach
Bottom left Elafonisi Beach

 More Wonderful Beaches

Balos Go tropical on this sultry and incredibly photogenic lagoon-like sandy beach.

Preveli Beach Crete's 'other' famous palm beach, at the confluence of river and sea amid cave-combed cliffs.

Agios Pavlos For crowd-free suntanning, head to the massive sand dunes spilling into this isolated southern-coast beach.

Xerokambos Find solitude and natural beauty along the dozen or so beaches stretching for 4.5km in Crete's last frontier, the remote southeastern region.

Matala The original hippie beach from the '70s still dazzles with its cave-pock-marked cliffs and you can escape the mobs at nearby quiet strands.

Gavdos Island The southernmost spot in Europe exudes a sense of happy isolation and has wonderful, untrodden beaches.

Elafonisi Beach Sparkling white sand with a pinkish hue makes Elafonisi a standout in a nation of islands where pebbly, grey beaches are common. Its shallow, azure waters surround an islet just offshore that is an easy walk. Cliffs, dunes and semi-secluded coves are highlights here. Beat the summer crowds by walking 2km east to **Kedrodasos Beach**. Otherwise, climb the dunes on the islet for panoramic views of this entire magical spot.

Falasarna Beach Sunsets dazzle throughout the year at this very long beach, which faces directly west across azure water. Waves here are regularly the largest in Crete as sets of rollers crash into the sand from the open Mediterranean, which draws people ready to ride them, whether on a board or freestyle. Tavernas, cafes, modest hotels and gear-rental stands line the shore in summer; olive trees and greenhouses form the backdrop. An easy 2km walk along a dirt path takes you to **Ancient Falasarna**, an archaeological site dating to the 4th century BCE.

Vaï Beach Try to catch falling dates from the largest indigenous palm forest in Europe on this beach at the far northeastern end of Crete. The beach here is small but perfectly framed by turquoise waters lapping at the edges of the inlet. Trails lead to cliffside walks, vista points and more secluded beaches.

35 Enchanting RETHYMNO

HISTORY | WALKING | FOOD

Wandering the labyrinthine lanes of Rethymno's historic old quarter is a highlight of Crete. Charismatic Renaissance-era Venetian buildings sprinkled with exotic features from the Turkish period are enlivened with wonderful surprises: perhaps a romantic flower-filled courtyard or an idyllic plaza, a cafe in an Ottoman bathhouse or a Venetian mansion turned boutique hotel. And don't miss the massive fortress.

How to

Getting around/around Rethymno is entirely walkable, and that is the best way to explore this age-old city. There are good bus connections to the airports in Iraklio and Hania.

When to go Many of the best tavernas, restaurants and shops close from November to March. Conversely, in winter you can savour Rethymno's charms without being jostled.

Avoid the crowds Quiet lanes worth a stroll include Minoos, Neophytou Patealarou, Patriarchou Grigoriou and Vivylaki.

Far left Venetian Harbour
Bottom left Fortezza

Can you say 'Rethymno' with a pirate voice? Try your best as you gaze out to sea from the 15th-century **Fortezza**, the vast fortress built to protect the port from marauding pirates and invading Turks. The old town's tangle of streets off the **Venetian Harbour** are delightful. Although small enough not to get too lost, they still allow you to be swallowed up by the past – and you can always stop for a drink at an atmospheric cafe. Wander the maze of old stone lanes, which are shaded by canopies of flowers and accented by old buildings with wooden balconies and the occasional minaret.

Seek out the tiny **Agios Spyridon Church**, built into the cliff below the fortress. You'll be dazzled by the cacophony of gilded treasures, ancient icons and colourful artwork. Major Venetian sites include the **Loggia**, a restored 16th-century landmark that originally served as a meeting house for Venetian nobility. Just west, join the scores of selfie-takers posing in front of the ornate **Rimondi Fountain**. Originally, animals drank from the smaller of the three basins fed by water flowing from lions' heads.

At the **Archaeological Museum of Rethymno**, don't miss the bronze lamp from the 1st century BCE depicting Dionysus riding a panther, exquisite hand-painted Minoan ceramics and a 9000-year-old limestone deity statue.

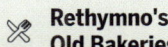
Rethymno's Old Bakeries

Among the many fine restaurants in Rethymno are two bakeries that preserve old traditions.

Run by one of the last traditional filo masters, the eponymous **Yiorgos Hatziparaskos** bakery still makes superfine pastry by hand. Enter through a Venetian doorway and watch the spectacle when they whirl the dough into a giant bubble before stretching it over a huge table.

Hidden away in an alley, **Spanoioakis** bakery is famous for its bread shaped like dinosaurs and flamingos, as well as *kouloures* – a lacquered, intricately decorated (but inedible) bread. Each design is symbolic: pomegranates bring luck; trees, longevity; and rings, an eternal bond.

36 Mountain VILLAGES

COUNTRYSIDE | REMOTE | VIEWS

Crete's mountain villages are the cradles of the island's culture. Hardscrabble and self-reliance are two characteristics proudly embraced by Cretans and for centuries were essential for survival amid the craggy peaks. Today, the villages offer stunning views, an enthusiastic welcome and meals featuring wood-grilled meats in cosy tavernas. In the mountains of western Crete, you'll find winding roads linking top villages.

How to

Getting here Some villages are along bus routes but there may be limited service, which makes village-hopping hard. Rent a vehicle for a day or two of blissful exploration.

When to go May to September are the months with the best weather and the widest choices for eating and shopping. In winter you can join residents hunkered down near wood fires.

Join the crowd On Sunday afternoons, tavernas fill with festive families.

Far left Rethymno
Bottom left Kritsa

The **Amari Valley**, not far from Rethymno, is a quilt of tranquil villages punctuated by Byzantine churches and framed by olive groves and orchards amid mountainous grandeur. Highlights include **Meronas** and its 14th-century **Church of Maria**, with beautiful frescoes and lavish royal-blue altar vestments. **Thronos** is a tidy one-taverna kind of hamlet, perched on a hillside. The **Agia Panagia** (Church of the Assumption) boasts extraordinary, if faded, 14th-century frescoes. The valley's namesake, **Amari**, has an enchanting medley of Venetian buildings and a square framed with cafes and overflowing flowerpots. Climb the 19th-century bell tower to share beautiful views with the pigeons.

In the hills above **Paleohora**, you'll discover some of western Crete's most scenic and least visited mountain hamlets: the **Innahorion villages** (the name is derived from Enneia Horia, meaning 'nine villages'). Spread along the route connecting the main Paleohora road with the west coast and Falasarna, each of the villages beckons you with views, beauty and good food. This lush, quiet area is renowned for its chestnuts and olives and you won't want for opportunities to purchase olive oil, honey, dried herbs and raki.

Top Innahorion villages include **Azogires** and its sylvan valley with waterfalls and caves you can visit. **Elos** is the region's largest town and the centre of the chestnut trade. The hamlet of **Pappadiana** has a single cute cafe with good coffee. Enjoy superlative sea views at barely there **Amygdalokefali**.

 Other Villages Not to Miss

Argyroupoli Devour trout while surrounded by rushing natural springs in this ancient mountain village.

Hora Sfakion This whimsical southern port boasts larger-than-life characters, a long, colourful history and delightful ferry rides.

Kritsa Clinging to the Dikti mountains, Kritsa offers fine shopping, an atmospheric old town and a church with amazing Byzantine frescoes.

Mohlos Minoan antiquity meets seashore vibes at this village with many fine tavernas.

Myrthios On clear days you can spot Africa from this whitewashed village high above the Libyan Sea.

Theriso Recharge your batteries at this historically significant mountain village in thick forest south of Hania.

Foods of CRETE

01 Rusks
Crunchy *paximadia* (rusks) are hard, dry crackers used in the famous *dakos*, a salad with tomatoes, olive oil and creamy cheese.

02 Kalitsounia
Cretan stuffed cheese pies start with hand-made filo-pastry dough, often formed into tiny cups. There are myriad variations.

03 Olive oil
Crete remains an important olive-growing area, producing the largest quantity of extra virgin olive oil in Greece. Many brands are acclaimed.

04 Gamopilafo
This rice dish is a deluxe risotto prepared in a rich meat broth and *stakovoutiro* (butter created from boiled fresh goat's milk).

05 Hohlioi (snails)
Collected after rainfall and prepared in dozens

of interesting ways: try *hohlioi bourbouristoi* (simmered in wine or vinegar and rosemary).

06 Horta
For centuries Cretans have been gathering and boiling *horta* (wild greens) for salads, pies and stews.

07 Sfakianes pites
From the Sfakia region, fine pancake-like sweets with a light cheese filling, served with honey and a dash of raki.

08 Wood-grilled meats
Cretans have their own barbecue style called *ofto* or *antikristo,* in which chunks of meat are slow-roasted upright around hot coals.

09 Hirina apakia
It's a multiday process to create this delicious smoked pork. The marinated meat is smoked over a fire stoked with local herbs.

10 Cretan cheese
Many kinds of cheese are produced across the island, including *anthotiro* (buttery white cheese) and *yaourti,* a tangy sheep's-milk yoghurt..

Mysterious Minoans

AN ANCIENT CIVILISATION LONG BEFORE CLASSICAL GREECE

More mystery than reality, the Minoans left extraordinary palaces and artefacts now found at archaeological sites and museums across Crete. What is known is that from roughly 3000 to 1100 BCE, they had a rich culture, as seen in surviving mosaics, sculptures, pottery and jewellery. Evidence suggests that they believed in gender equality, peaceful relations and scientific achievement.

Pictured Frescoes, Palace of Knossos

A Sophisticated Culture

Speculation shrouds the Minoans – we don't even know what they called themselves, 'Minoan' being the term given by British archaeologist Sir Arthur Evans in honour of the possibly mythical King Minos.

Evidence uncovered in Crete's grand palaces indicates they were a peaceful, sophisticated, well-organised and prosperous civilisation with robust international trade, highly developed agriculture, splendid architecture and art, and seemingly equal status for men and women. Women apparently enjoyed a great degree of freedom and autonomy. Minoan art shows women participating in games, hunting, and public and religious festivals.

Their exquisite artistry in pottery and jewellery survives to this day. Richly coloured frescoes, such as those at Knossos, portray landscapes abundant in animals and birds, marine scenes teeming with fish and octopuses, and banquets, games and rituals.

Axes & Bulls

The double-axe symbol that appears in frescoes and on Knossos palace walls was a sacred symbol for the Minoans. Other religious symbols that frequently appear in Minoan art include the mythical gryphon and figures with a human body and an animal head. The Minoans appear to have worshipped the dead and believed in an afterlife.

The bull was another potent Minoan symbol. The peculiar Minoan sport of bull-leaping, where acrobatic thrill-seekers seize the charging bull's horns and leap over its back, is depicted in frescoes, pottery and sculptures.

First in Pre-Greek Letters

In Crete, Minoan painting is virtually the only form of Greek painting to have survived. Large-scale sculptures have disappeared in natural disasters like the tsunami that swept from Thira (Santorini) in 1450 BCE. Minoan art inspired the invading Mycenaeans; its influence spread to Santorini and beyond.

> Minoan art shows women participating in games, hunting, and public and religious festivals.

At the same time, the Minoans' inscrutable written hieroglyph system, Linear A, provides another indication of a culture that was very advanced. The most significant example of this writing is on the 3600-year-old terracotta tablet known as the Phaestos Disk, which has been the object of much speculation since it was discovered in 1908. The disk, about 16cm in diameter, consists of an Early Minoan pictographic script made up of 242 'words' written in a continuous spiral. It has never been deciphered.

We know more about Linear B, a script written on clay tablets that lay undisturbed until they were unearthed at Knossos. The decipherment of this script by English architect Michael Ventris in 1952 provided the first tangible evidence that the Greek language had a recorded history longer than scholars had previously believed. The language was an archaic form of Greek 500 years older than the Ionic Greek of Homer. The Knossos clay tablets are mainly inventories and records of commercial transactions, dating from the 14th to the 13th centuries BCE. They give a glimpse of a fairly complex, well-organised civilisation.

📖 Minos: Man or Myth?

Minos, the legendary ruler of Crete, was the son of Zeus and Europa and attained the Cretan throne, aided by Poseidon. Or maybe not.

Homer describes him and his land in the '*Odyssey*': 'Out on the dark blue sea there lies a rich and lovely land called Crete that is densely populated and boasts 90 cities... One of the 90 cities is called Knossos and there for nine years, King Minos ruled and enjoyed the friendship of the mighty.'

His mythical heritage aside, whether Minos even existed is open to much debate and is yet another – and key – Minoan mystery.

Listings

BEST OF THE REST

 Crete's Tastes

Kalderimi €€
A traditional taverna in Topanas, Hania's most characterful neighbourhood, that's always busy. Here you'll find Cretan standards such as *hirina apakia* (marinated, smoked pork) cooked with a creative flair.

To Stachi €€
Stelios Michelakis and his family grow almost everything used in their excellent vegan and vegetarian taverna on their farm near Hania. He arrives each day at 5am to start baking the delectable whole-grain bread.

Taverna Knossos €€
Amid a sea of mediocrity lining Rethymno's old port is this absolute delight. The hard-working Stavroulaki family will feed you well – bounteous platters of fresh seafood come in waves from the kitchen.

Peskesi €€
Culinary magic forged from family-farm ingredients and served amid relaxed sophistication in a candlelit Venetian mansion in Iraklio. Enjoy the intimate surroundings within the atmospheric stone walls.

Vegera €
Located in a sun-yellow building, Vegera is a Zaros institution and is presided over by the vivacious Vivi, who turns farm-fresh local produce into memorable dishes based on traditional recipes.

Ferryman €€
Try not to devour but rather savour next-level Cretan meals at the seafront tavern of Yiannis Baxevanis, a Greek celebrity chef. The simple, fresh fare is beautifully presented. In swank Eloundra.

 Local Goods

Botano
Step into this aromatic shop and a melange of Cretan mountain herbs hits your nose. This top purveyor of organic dried herbs, teas and spices is in the village of Listaros.

Workshop Worry
What? Me worry? Vangelis Tsoupakis strings your cares into iconic Cretan worry beads at his Rethymno workshop. Also makes rosaries, prayer beads etc. Does custom orders as well. Great browsing.

Sifis Stavroulakis
Beautiful naturalistic jewellery made in this Hania workshop takes on floral and human forms. The small shopfront is on a lane with other interesting higher-end stores.

 Outdoor Thrills

Eco Events
This excellent Rethymno-based Cretan

Hiking in Crete

tour company specialises in small-group English-language tours that get you in touch with land, people and culture.

Mountaineering Club of Rethymno
An excellent resource for advice on treks in western Crete including up into the nearby peaks – Crete's highest. They also lead and organise climbing adventures.

Chania Boat
Rents out small powerboats from Loutro that you can use to explore the ravishing coast. There's no licence needed to pilot your way to little coves with untrodden pockets of beach.

Stay Wet Diving Center
Organises dive trips in the warm offshore waters and gives lessons right on the perfect beach cove at Agia Pelgia.

Vamos Village Tourist Office
Crammed with regional information, arranges all sorts of fascinating walking tours of the region's cultural and natural attractions.

Gone Surfing Crete Windsurfing & Wingfoiling Center
Excellent Palekastro-based operator at Kouremenos Beach, Crete's best place for catching air. Peak season runs from mid-June to mid-September. Book well ahead.

Historical Vibes

Heraklion Archaeological Museum
Unmissable but not overwhelming. Snake goddesses, bull leapers and the Prince of the Lilies are among the intriguing characters you'll encounter in the world's premier museum of the Minoan culture.

Spinalonga Island
Once a Venetian and Turkish stronghold, the fortress remains as does the island's recent notorious past. It's an ideal day trip with a

Gortyna

spectacular walk around its perimeter boasting stellar views.

Phaestos
Crete's second-largest Minoan palace has grand views of the Libyan Sea. After Knossos, come here for the big-sky panorama of the olive-tree-studded Messara Plain and the more intimate hillside ruins.

Moni Arkadiou
The 16th-century monastery has deep significance for the Cretans. Hundreds of cornered locals massacred both themselves and invading Turks, making it a stark and potent symbol of the island's soul.

Etz Hayyim Synagogue
Hania has Crete's only remaining synagogue, which was badly damaged in WWII and reopened only in 1999. It sports a mikvah (ritual bath), tombs of rabbis and a memorial to the local Jews killed by the Nazis.

Gortyna
This mesmerising archaeological site figures prominently in the myth of Zeus and Europa. It's been inhabited since the Neolithic period but capped its career as capital of Roman Crete in the 1st century BCE.

CYCLADES

BEACHES | RUINS | FOOD & WINE

- **Trip Builder** (p186)
- **Practicalities** (p188)
- **Volcanic Santorini** (p190)
- **Beach-Hopping Milos** (p192)
- **Taste of Sifnos** (p194)
- **Treasures of Tinos** (p196)
- **Uninhibited on Mykonos** (p198)
- **Adventures on Land & Sea** (p200)
- **Magic Mountains & Beaches** (p202)
- **Get Away from It All** (p204)
- **Ancient Art from the Cyclades** (p206)
- **Wines of the Islands** (p208)
- **Listings** (p210)

Tour marble villages and gorgeous dovecote valleys on **Tinos** (p196)
🚢 *35mins from Mykonos*

Admire natural beauty with delicious Cycladic cuisine on **Sifnos** (p194)
🚢 *2½hrs from Piraeus*

CYCLADES
Trip Builder

On a quest to find the Greek islands of your dreams? Start here. Sun-drenched outcrops of rock, anchored in azure seas and peppered with vibrant snow-white villages, stellar archaeological sites and blue-domed churches – this is Greece straight from central casting.

Sun yourself on the stone cliffs of volcanic **Milos** (p192)
🚢 *2hrs from Santorini*

Practicalities

ARRIVING

Santorini or Mykonos Flights from Athens and European cities. Fly in and ferry to other islands. Be aware that ferries are packed in high season and some are pricey – book ahead.

Paros, Syros, Naxos or Milos Flights from Athens and connections to onward ferries, with Paros, Syros and Naxos offering the most choice.

Ferry ports All islands are served by ferries from one or more mainland ports: Piraeus, Rafina and Lavrio. Some connect to Crete.

HOW MUCH FOR A

Gyros
€5

Craft beer
€5

Sunbed
€10–€25

GETTING AROUND

Ferry The key to sculpting an itinerary through the islands is knowing which ferries go where – and when. Peak services run in July and August. In winter, services are reduced or nonexistent on some routes. Check *ferries.gr*, then see ferry locations in real time at *vesselfinder.com*. Many islands have both conventional (slower) and high-speed ferries – check trip duration when booking.

Car On the islands, cars, scooters and buzzing ATVs are the easiest way to get around and are reasonably priced outside high season, though larger islands have buses (super crowded in summer), and most have small boats to beaches.

Walking Towns and tiny islands are perfect for walking. All islands have hiking trails.

WHEN TO GO

FEB–APR
Cool, sunny days, perfect for hiking.

MAY–JUN, SEP–OCT
Gorgeous swims and walks, with gentler weather.

JUL–AUG
Peak high season: crowds, party life, baking temperatures.

NOV–JAN
Windswept winter with serenity, but many services close.

EATING & DRINKING

The Cyclades are home to excellent regional cuisines, and each island boasts different traditions with local cheese, herbs and sweets. Some excel in everything, like Tinos and Amorgos. Don't miss the chance for a long seafront-taverna lunch – a parade of dips, salads and seafood. Fancier islands like Mykonos, Santorini, and, increasingly, Paros, Syros and Koufonisia, have sophisticated high-end restaurants. Sometimes the best food isn't in the most stupendous location, so delve into small villages and backstreets. Book ahead on crowded islands in high season.

Best cake Sifnos' *melopita* (honey-cinnamon custard cake) at To Steki (p210)

Must-try Shrimp *saganaki* with local cheese at Santorini's To Krinaki (p210)

CONNECT & FIND YOUR WAY

Wi-fi Free in most hotels and available in many restaurants.

Navigation Mobile signal gets spotty outside towns, and local print maps are of varying quality. It's easy to get lost on unmarked back roads and trails without a proper offline resource. Terrain (terrainmaps.gr) maps are invaluable for getting off the beaten track and exploring on foot or wheels.

WHERE TO STAY

Summer season is highest-priced and busiest – always book ahead. Shoulder season is about 20% less expensive, and in winter many lodgings on the islands close.

Island	Pro/Con
Santorini and Mykonos	Heart of the action (particularly Fira and Oia on the former and Mykonos Town on the latter), but pricey and crowded.
Paros and Naxos	Large, interesting islands with a broad range of lodgings. They get hectic in summer.
Amorgos, Small Cyclades and Serifos	Quiet islands with gorgeous nature. Sleepier outside high season when services close.
Tinos and Syros	Interesting small islands central for island-hopping, though they lack world-famous sights.

ARRIVAL PICK-UP

Many hotels and rent-a-car outfits will send someone to pick you up from the ferry or airport. When booking, check if port/airport transfer is included.

MONEY

Carry €100 or €200 for places that don't take cards. To save money, visit during low season (exact months are a bit different on each island) and stick to less touristy islands.

37 Volcanic SANTORINI

LANDSCAPE | WINE | RUINS

Approaching Santorini (also called Thira) from the water, it's hard not to be awed by the sheer cliffs soaring above a turquoise sea, by the fact that you're sailing in an immense crater of a drowned volcano and that high above the main villages of Fira and Oia are a snowdrift of white Cycladic houses. The feeling is almost supernatural.

How to

Getting around Though having your own wheels is the easiest way to explore, traffic in high season (May to October) is a menace. One-way streets encircle Fira and Oia, and roads are jammed with racing transfer vans and inexperienced drivers on scooters and ATVs.

When to go Plan for the fact that Santorini is expensive and crowded. Visit in low season (November to April); avoid July and August.

Foodie tip Best small villages with excellent restaurants are Finikia, Pyrgos and Megalohori.

Far left Oia
Bottom left Fira coast

Caldera rim Santorini's main town of **Fira** is a booming place where the caldera edge is layered with swish cave hotels, infinity pools and restaurants. On the caldera's northern tip **Oia** sparkles, built on a steep slope with many of its white dwellings hewn into the volcanic rock. The stunning walk from Fira to Oia (three hours, 9.1km) traces the rim of the caldera via Imerovigli and Skaros Rock. If you time it right, you can reach Oia for its world-famous sunset.

Pick the colour of your beach Two of the best qualities of Santorini's beaches are their dramatic cliffs and how the different volcanic sands and pebbles play on the water's colours. Choose between **Red (Kokkini) Beach** with its impressive red cliffs, the sheltered cove of **White (Aspri) Beach** – named for the colour of its cliffs, not its sand – or **Black (Mesa Pigadia) Beach**. Although, truth be told, the majority of Santorini's beaches are beautifully black.

Incredible ruins Vertiginously positioned on a mountaintop above Kamari and Perissa, the magnificently sited and elaborate town of **Ancient Thira** was first settled by the Dorians in the 9th century BCE and remains a massive maze of Hellenistic, Roman and Byzantine ruins. Nearby, explore the ancient Minoan city of **Ancient Akrotiri**, unearthed in 1967 from deep beneath volcanic ash caused by a catastrophic eruption in 1613 BCE.

 Top Santorini Wineries

Estate Argyros Terrific, internationally renowned *asyrtiko* (Greek white wine variety), Nykteri (*asyrtiko* made at night) and *mavrotragano* (full-bodied red), plus exceptional Vinsanto (dessert wine) in a gorgeous vineyard with mountain and sea views.

Hatzidakis Winery Santorini's only organic winery, run by the family of a Cretan oenologist.

Art Space The island's smallest winery, combined with an interesting art gallery.

Gaia Winery Seafront with delish *asyrtiko* and reds from its other winery in Nemea.

Vassaltis Winery Modern winery with peaceful sea views.

38 Beach-Hopping MILOS

BEACHES | VILLAGES | ANCIENT ART

Volcanic Milos arches around a central caldera and is ringed with dramatic coastal landscapes of colourful, surreal rock formations. The island's dozens of beaches (supposedly the most of any Cycladic island) have something for any mood – or weather pattern. The built-up portion of Milos covers a small part of the island; Plaka is the crowning village, ideally suited for wandering on foot.

How to

Getting here/around Ferry service is frequent and there's an airport. You'll need to rent a vehicle to visit most beaches; a 4WD or ATV is required to reach the rugged ones.

When to go Summer is best as the water is warmest.

Go really remote The tiny neighbouring island of Polyaigos is uninhabited. Its top beach, Ammura, is a semi-popular stop for day-trippers who luxuriate in the idyllic water.

Far left Sarakiniko
Bottom left Plaka

Splendid Beaches

Milos and its offshore islets have more than 70 beaches garnished with different-coloured sands and stone. It's always possible to find a sheltered beach, no matter which way the wind is blowing.

Provatos is bookended by glowering headlands and boasts a long swath of golden sand. One of Milos' best, it has a few tavernas and watersports rentals.

Plathiena sits at the end of a valley beyond Plaka to the north. Pebble-strewn and sandy, the beach is exceptionally pretty, with craggy limestone formations at each end plus a summertime beach bar.

Firopotamos is quiet and framed by a little cove lined with craggy limestone cliffs and *syrmata* (traditional fishers' huts).

Sarakiniko features meringue-like rock formations and caves. The sandy beach is tiny but there's a deep channel that's perfect for swimming, and room to spread out on the rocks.

Mandrakia is a cute fishing harbour with small shingle beaches on either side. It also has one of the island's top lunch spots.

Timeless Villages

Plaka embodies the Cycladic ideal with its white houses and labyrinthine lanes perched along the edge of an escarpment. The courtyard of **Panagia Korfiatissa** church offers spectacular sunset views.

Klima is a waterfront fishing village that offers the best example of Milos' *syrmata*.

 The Home of Venus de Milo

Clinging to a lonely patch of hillside amid olive trees, a large Roman-era theatre entertained the citizens of Ancient Melos from the 1st to the 4th century CE. It was rediscovered in 1735. Only 85 years later, a farmer stumbled upon a statue that was immediately taekn by French archaeologists.

Taken to the Louvre and named *Venus de Milo*, this artefact remains a sensation. Meanwhile, you can see a Venus replica at Plaka's **Archaeological Museum of Melos**. A campaign to repatriate the statue *(takeaphrodite home.gr)* has the slogan: 'She's not missing her arms, she's missing her home.'

39 Taste of SIFNOS

WATERFRONTS | STROLLING | CUISINE

Sifnos is a feast, both literally and figuratively. Whitewashed villages, anchored by the capital Apollonia sit like pearls on a string along the crest of the island. The changing light kisses the landscape that has beguiling vistas. Known first for food, Sifnos has excellent places to eat, which celebrate the island's bounty.

How to

Getting there/around Sifnos is a ferry hub. Roads stretch down to beachy bays, with Apollonia as the head. Distances are short.

Stay in the port The ferry port of Kamares is appealing beyond its utility. There are waterfront cafes, tavernas, shops, tiny churches and a beautiful large beach.

Go hiking Sifnos is laced by trails and the roads are (mostly) quiet enough to make walking a pleasure, enabling you to feel for the fabric of the island.

Exceptional Kastro

Dramatically positioned on a crag with sheer drops to the crystalline waters below, **Kastro** is Sifnos' most atmospheric and magical settlement.

It's a sleepy place where cats snooze the day away on stoops. A handful of alleys curve around the hilltop perch, passing through tunnels formed by ancient houses and emerging onto terraces with stunning views of the coast and across the Aegean to Paros. A couple of tavernas have verdant views inland across terraced hillsides. Like a diamond on a ring, the **Church of the Seven Martyrs** sits on a rocky promontory surrounded by surging blue water right below Kastro.

Far left Church of the Seven Martyrs
Above Apollonia

Apollonia Labyrinthine and church-studded, the island's main town comes alive in high season with the well-dressed promenading along buzzing Odos Prokou, better known as the **Steno** (meaning 'narrow') because of its slenderness. From Apollonia, the string of white houses continues north into the conjoined village of **Ano Petali** and then to **Artemonas**, with its terraced olive groves, mansions and blue-domed churches. By day, there are upscale food vendors and stylish shops selling designer clothes and expensive handmade knick-knacks. By night, fine restaurants and bars come alive for a great nightlife. Away from the Steno bustle, follow your nose to traditional tavernas serving island specialities like *revithada,* the savoury chickpea stew for which every family has its own treasured recipe.

Faros The beach hamlet of Faros is an appealing traditional village, with fishing and pleasure boats intermingling in the harbour. The main beach is a mix of sand and pebbles atop which taverna tables and sunbathers compete for space. It's worth taking a short walk along a curving path past a clutch of tavernas to the west beach, which is serene. Only a short hike from here around a knoll is the beautiful, azure **Chrysopigi Beach**, home to two excellent tavernas.

Vathy On the southwest coast, this relaxed resort village is on an almost circular and sheltered bay of aquamarine beauty. The beach is wide and shaded in parts, although the string of slightly upscale cafes, tavernas and shops is built right up to the water's edge. This is a good town for fresh seafood.

40 Treasures OF TINOS

VILLAGES | FOOD | VISTAS

Tinos beguiles with a mix of tradition, intrigue, divinity and the region's best food. Within Greece, it's known for a Greek Orthodox pilgrimage site in the port and main town of Hora. Across Tinos, the countryside is a wonderland of natural beauty, dotted with more than 50 marble-ornamented villages found in hidden bays, on terraced hillsides and atop misty mountains.

How to

Getting there/around
Tinos is a ferry hub. The closest airport is at nearby Mykonos. Buses from Hora serve the larger villages.

Sampling the food Local cooks, many running their own family tavernas, draw on the local produce (cheeses, sausages, tomatoes, wild artichokes, honey and more) for extraordinary culinary creations.

There she blows Tinos is known for its winds. Staying off exposed ridgelines is a good idea.

Far left Volax
Bottom left Pyrgos

The interior of Tinos is a glorious mix of broad terraced hillsides, mountaintops crowned with crags, and more than 50 unspoilt villages with fascinating architecture. From one whitewashed hamlet, others can be seen in the distance.

The centre of the island's marble industry is the intriguing, church-dotted village of **Pyrgos**, one of the prettiest in the Cyclades. Narrow lanes accented in marble wind towards a little square lined with cafes that looks like a film set.

Just north of Hora, beautiful **Ktikados** perches in a hanging valley, with a good taverna and a skyline punctuated by a blue-domed church with an elegant campanile. **Kampos** sits atop a scenic hill surrounded by fields.

Don't miss **Tarabados**, a maze of small streets, blue-shuttered houses and marble sculptures. Excellent signage details local history. The surrounding breezy valleys are lined with dove-cotes and watched over by Tinos' prominent landmark, the rocky peak of **Exobourgo**.

A minor detour takes you to ethereal **Agapi**, a pretty village set in a lush valley of dovecotes. It lives up to its name (meaning 'love' in Greek). Nearby, **Volax** sits at the heart of an amphi-theatre of low hills festooned with hundreds of enormous and incongruous multicoloured boulders

The main road runs high along the northwest coast and the views towards Syros are exhilarating. Lovely **Kardiani** perches on a steep cliff slope.

Making a Pilgrimage

The large **Church of the Annunciation** rising behind Hora's centre is one of the most significant Orthodox pilgrimage sites in Greece.

Built in 1830 using marble from the island's Panormos quarries, the church lies within a pleasant courtyard.

Its most important sacred object is the icon of Our Lady of Tinos, uncovered in 1823 in the ruins of a chapel beneath the current church after a nun, now St Pelagia, received visions from the Virgin instructing her where to find it.

The icon's image is now almost completely obscured by jewels.

41 Uninhibited on MYKONOS

BEACHES | BARS | PARTIES

Mykonos is one of the top party destinations on the planet. Yes, it's a playground for people who travel with entourages. But it's not just the dissolute mega-rich – much of the island's energy comes from its enormous popularity with gay men, who party with abandon. All visitors revel in the exquisite restaurants, rollicking bars and salubrious beach clubs.

How to

Getting there/around
Ferries from across the Aegean call on Mykonos throughout the day. The airport is busy. Many people rent cars, but there's not far to drive. Buses and boats serve the party beaches.

When to go From May to September the island hops.

Get on Mykonos time
The clichéd schedule for visitors is close to reality: breakfast at 4pm, lunch at 6.30pm, dinner at 11pm and party till dawn.

Far left Tavern in Hora
Bottom left Elia

 Unmissable Ancient Delos

The Cyclades fulfil their collective name (*kyklos* means 'circle') by encircling the sacred island of Delos. The mythical birthplace of twins Apollo and Artemis, splendid **Ancient Delos** was a shrine turned treasury and commercial centre.

This UNESCO World Heritage Site is one of the most important archaeological sites in Greece. Cast your imagination wide to transform the sprawling ruin into the magnificent city it once was – it's not difficult to picture Ancient Delos in all its original splendour.

Just 5km long and 1300m wide, Delos offers a soothing contrast to Mykonos, from where it's easily reached on a short ferry ride.

Hora (aka Mykonos town) is a maze of narrow lanes and whitewashed buildings, all watched over by the island's iconic windmills. Tiny flower-bedecked churches jostle with luxe boutiques for a 'Greek-island village by central casting' scenario. Vast numbers of humble visitors join the catwalk cast of wannabe influencers, celebrity-spotters, party boys and the dazed and hungover squeezing past the clubs, cafes and bars.

The beaches on Mykonos' south coast are among the most rollicking in the Mediterranean. Stylish clubs, all-day party bars, loungers jammed together and moods from snotty to promiscuous create an unmatched scene.

Platys Gialos is one of Mykonos' most popular beaches – you may need to step on someone to reach the water. It's ideal for making new friends. Tip: pay to park your car, as the tiny lanes are clogged with fuming visitors trying to find a free space.

Paradise is completely lined with hopping beach bars like **Tropicana** and tight rows of loungers and umbrellas. The partying barely pauses during the morning hours.

Super Paradise is flashy, trashy and great for people-watching. The action is split between the glitzy and expensive **JackieO' Beach Club** and the Super Paradise beach bar.

Elia is backed by a large resort, and rows of loungers jam the sand. It's especially popular with gay men. Head further west for the nudist area and an intimate cove.

42 Adventures on LAND & SEA

HARBOURS | BEACHES | WATERSPORTS

The large, fertile island of Paros is redolent of herbs, tinkles with the sound of goat bells and remains lustrous in the shifting lights from dawn to dusk. With a zippy ring road circling its central mountain and connecting the beaches and villages, it's a favourite for families. And with its brisk *meltemi* (dry northerly wind) and a channel to Antiparos, it's world-famous for windsurfing and kitesurfing.

How to

Getting there/around
Paros has an airport served by Athens and a well-connected ferry port. Smaller car ferries run from Paros to Antiparos. Realistically, it's important to have your own wheels on Paros.

What's on Paros has a rich cultural life year-round. Find out what's up at *parosweb.com* and *friendsofparos.com*.

Most famous residents Antiparos attracts the glitterati, perhaps lured by homeowners Tom Hanks and Rita Wilson? Or maybe it's just the beauty!

Pretty harbour towns For its petite size, **Parikia**, the port town where the ferries arrive, packs a wallop. Its labyrinthine Old Town contains the **Panagia Ekatontapyliani** (Our Lady of the Hundred Doors) church dating from 326 CE. It's one of the finest churches in the Cyclades, with superb columns of Parian marble and a carved iconostasis. The incredibly Insta-worthy village of **Naoussa** has gradually turned from a quiet fishing village into an increasingly stylish resort and visitor magnet. Boats bob in its harbour, perched on the shores of the large **Plastira Bay** and guarded by crumbling remains of a 15th-century Venetian kastro (castle). Both towns' charming whitewashed lanes are filled with boutiques, restaurants and sparkling chapels draped in blossoms.

Beaches, sea and ruins The beauty of Paros' ring road is that it takes you to most any beach you'd like. But don't forget the glorious, tiny **Antiparos** across the channel, where the quiet countryside is rimmed by luminescent cerulean waters. There, **Captain Sargos Boat Trips** goes to the archaeological site of **Despotiko** on its own uninhabited islet, including time to swim off the island's spectacular beach and cruise through sea caves.

Take to the air Paros' west coast, around **Pounta**, is the hub for top watersports: a long shallow-water shoreline and perfect side-shore wind conditions make it ideal for all skill levels of kiteboarder or windsurfer. **Paros Kite** or **Force7 Surf Centre** (the latter on the east coast) will outfit you with all you need.

Far left Naoussa, Paros

 Craft Beer on Paros & Beyond

56 Isles, Paros Sample crisp Aegean Witbier, Pilsner, IPA and lager made using local wheat and barley, at the taproom outside of Naoussa.

Ftelos Brewery, Santorini Swing in to Santorini's newest brewery for its range of beers named after the blue monkeys from the Akrotiri frescoes.

Mikònu Craft Beer, Mykonos This tiny brewery makes great IPAs, lagers and saisons, some barrel-aged.

Nissos Beer, Tinos A superb island to visit, it's also home to this brewery with top lager-style beers.

43 Magic Mountains & BEACHES

NATURE | VILLAGES | GRANDEUR

The largest and one of the most magnificent of the Cyclades, Naxos has wow factor from the moment you see the remains of the Temple of Apollo at the mouth of the harbour. Its main town backs a gorgeous waterfront with a web of steep cobbled alleys climbing to its hilltop *kastro*. Within easy reach are excellent beaches, fascinating mountain villages and inspiring ancient sites.

How to

Getting there/around Naxos has an airport served by Athens and a well-connected ferry port. It's important to have your own wheels to explore outside Hora.

Summer festivals Domus Festival and Naxos Festival hold cultural events in the *kastro*, Bazeos Tower and around the island.

Wildest artefacts Naxian marble is famous, and three *kouroi* (male statues of the Archaic period) can be found left where they fell in ancient marble quarries.

>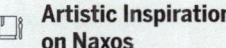
> ### Artistic Inspiration on Naxos
>
> **Archaeological Museum of Naxos** In my early days on the island they would kick me out for returning day after day to look at the Cycladic-era figures.
>
> **Temple of Demeter** When you walk the site, you feel the sheer beauty and power.
>
> **Bazeos Tower** The best place for a summer programme of theatre, art and music.
>
> **The landscapes of Naxos and its villages** I feel like I am inside the spaces; like they can gently hold me, not be outside of them looking in.
>
> *By Ingbert Brunk, sculptor of Naxian marble (ingbert-brunk.de)*

Left Temple of Apollo
Bottom left Plaka Beach

Brilliant beaches Beaches south of **Agios Georgios** (Hora's town beach) get quieter the further you go – idyllic places for a chilled-out beach stay. The closest, beautiful **Agios Prokopios**, lies in a sheltered bay to the south of **Cape Mougkri**. Broad sandy beaches, some with blindingly white sand like **Glyfada**, continue as far as **Agiasos**, passing the turquoise waters of the long, dreamy **Plaka Beach**.

Fortified town The main town of **Hora (Naxos Town)** feels different from other Cycladic island capitals. It's bigger and busier, for starters. Spend the afternoon climbing to its fortified Venetian **Kastro**. This was the seat of power for Marco Sanudo, the 13th-century Venetian who founded the town and made Naxos the heart of the Duchy of the Aegean. Then, have sunset cocktails or dinner at **Avaton 1739** with sweeping views of town and sea.

Mountain villages Naxos' lovely inland Tragaea region is a vast plain of olive groves and unspoilt villages high in the mountains, crowned with Byzantine churches and ringed by crumbling Venetian towers. The Cyclades' highest peak, **Mt Zeus** (1004m; also known as Mt Zas), dominates. **Apiranthos** seems to grow out of the stony flanks of Mt Fanari (883m). The village is known for its crafts, best seen at the **Women's Association of Traditional Art** (*paradosiakai fanta.gr*), where they also sell homemade sweets. Apiranthos' excellent tavernas include **Lefteris** for meat dishes, **Amorginos** for traditional fare with views, and **Bakalogatos** for mezedhes.

44 Get Away from IT ALL

BEACHES | WALKS | PEACE

A band of small islands scatters the seas between Folegandros and Amorgos, along with dozens of islets and rocks. They are surprisingly distinct from one another in character and terrain, with Koufonisia welcoming rural-chic swimmers, quiet Schinousa appealing to beach lovers, and Iraklia luring folks looking to slip off the radar. This is where to go to relax.

How to

Getting there/around In addition to occasional conventional and high-speed ferries, these islands are served by old-fashioned Small Cyclades Lines, great for open-deck island hopping. They are all easily walkable, and have taxis, buses or caïques.

When to go Outside the high-season months of July and August these islands get quiet, and services begin to close in September.

Fiercest wind The *meltemi* can howl from the north in summer throughout the Cyclades.

Far left Koufonisia
Bottom left Iraklia

Eat & Drink in the Small Cyclades

Mikres Cyclades, Koufonisia €€ Elegantly showcases the best of Cycladic produce.

Capetan Nikolas, Koufonisia €€ Cheerful seafood mainstay overlooking the harbour and sunset at Loutro.

Scholio, Koufonisia €€ Cosy cavern of a bar and late-night hangout, with a long list of cocktails.

Loza, Schinousa €€ For handmade pizza and traditional Greek dishes, plus delicate sweets.

Okto Adelphia, Schinousa €€ Generous portions of local produce shine at this family-run upper-level terrace in Hora.

Araklia, Iraklia €€ Sensational sea views and creative Cycladic fare in a lively atmosphere.

Avli, Donousa €€ There's a lot to love about this innovative little restaurant: the sea views, Donousa's best wine list, plus classy Aegean cuisine.

Glittering waters The smallest of the inhabited Cyclades, **Koufonisia** has slowly been transformed into a fashionable destination with prices to match, a beautiful place to unwind in contrast to the frenetic action of Mykonos and Santorini. Koufonisia's radiant white-sand beaches reflect through shockingly blue waters and include the main village's **Ammos Beach** and those along its southeast coast. A path continues to the north, skirting the headlands with dramatic, multihued rocky swimming coves, including the deep and clear **Piscina**, a swimming hole surrounded by rock and linked to the sea.

Beach bumming The undulating hills of small, laid-back **Schinousa** are a palimpsest of fields, ancient stone walls, Byzantine chapels and ruins of Venetian fortifications, reflecting the ebb and flow of many civilisations. During three centuries of Turkish rule, the island sheltered pirates from the Mani, but these days it attracts sunseekers looking for a slower pace of life. Walk its earthen roads to 16 exquisite beaches.

Drop out Sparsely inhabited (115 people!), **Iraklia** only shakes off its soporific air in July and August, when the cove-like harbour and village of **Agios Georgios** grows lively and yachts dot the island's sheltered **Livadi Bay**. Iraklia rewards hikers who explore its hills with secluded bays and thyme-scented solitude – there are five well-marked trails. In local restaurants, look out for Iraklian thyme honey, goat cheeses and fava.

Ancient Art from
THE CYCLADES

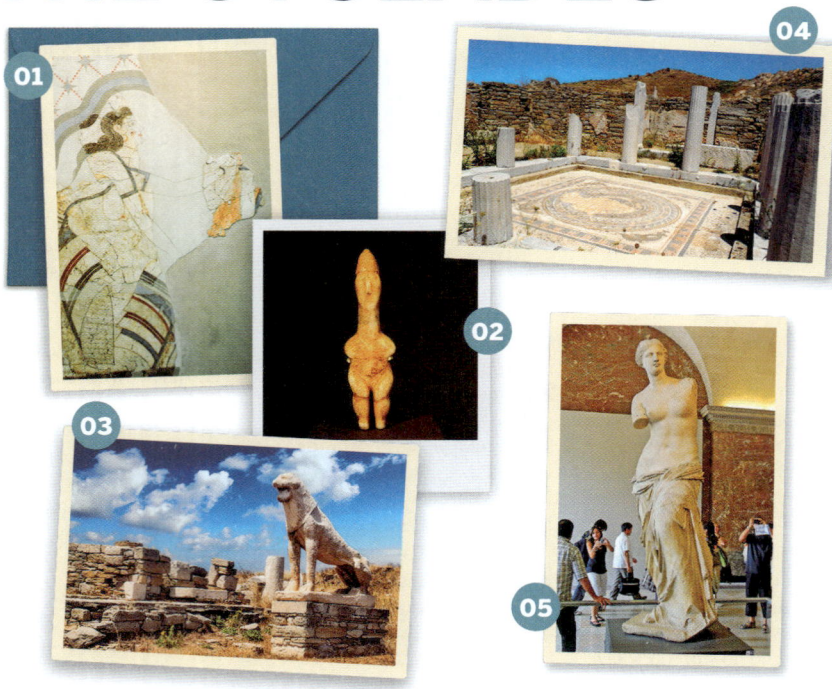

01 Akrotiri frescoes
Spectacular Minoan frescoes from the prehistoric settlement of Ancient Akrotiri on Santorini (Thira) were discovered protected under ashes from a 16th-century eruption.

02 Cycladic figurine
These mysterious minimalist marble statues dating from 3000 BCE to 2000 BCE inspired many 20th-century artists, such as Picasso and Modigliani.

03 Lions of Delos
The terrace facing the Sacred Lake at Ancient Delos was lined with nine to 19 (the number is unknown) stone lions, guarding the way.

04 Mosaic from the House of the Dolphins
One of Delos' grandest houses contained this well-preserved mosaic with youths riding dolphins in each corner.

05 Venus de Milo
That's Aphrodite to you! The island of Milos' most celebrated export, the *Venus de Milo* sculpture, is now far away after being taken away to the Louvre.

06 Golden ibex
This glowing pure-gold ibex from Akrotiri was hand-crafted in the 17th century BCE and now sparkles at the Museum of Prehistoric Thera.

07 Kouros of Naxos
One of Naxos' three fallen *kouroi* – marble statues of youths left in quarries, damaged and discarded millennia ago.

08 Nike of Samothrace
Winged *Nike* was discovered on the northeastern Aegean island of Samothraki, but she was crafted of Parian marble, like many masterpieces of her time.

09 Nike of Delos
A stylised contrast to her sister from Samothraki, the 570 BCE *Nike from Delos* was carved by a sculptor from Chios.

10 Mykonos vase
This giant 7th-century BCE pithos has one of the earliest depictions of the Trojan horse story from Homer's *Iliad*.

Wines of the Islands

ENJOY THE FRUITS OF AEGEAN VINEYARDS

Rich reds and bright whites, the wines of Greece have come a long way since they were quaffed on the knee of Dionysos. The Cyclades make some excellent wines, right up with those from other regions of Greece. Local cafes and tavernas always have a few examples ready to pour.

Santorini

Beyond caldera views, infinity pools and black-sand beaches, Santorini has become a magnet for oenophiles, drawn to the island by its reputation for excellent wine (p191). Santorini is blessed with a dry volcanic microclimate and wine culture here goes back millennia. The island's existing vines are Europe's oldest, impervious to the phylloxera bug that wiped out most of the continent's vines in the late 19th century. Grapes are grown close to the ground, in a *kouloura* (nest) of vines to make the most of the moisture and protect the grapes from fierce winds, while also inhibiting the spread of infestations and disease.

Santorini's most lauded wine is the crisp, dry white *asyrtiko*, as well as the amber-coloured, unfortified dessert wine known as Vinsanto (it must be made from at least 51% *asyrtiko*, plus *aidani* and *athiri* in order to qualify). Both wines are made from the heritage-protected, indigenous grape variety *asyrtiko*, as is Nykteri (*asyrtiko* made at night). *Asyrtiko* grapes are grown across the Cyclades, but the Santorini variety stands out in terms of unique flavour. You'll also come across *mavrotragano* (full-bodied red) and *mandilaria* (medium-bodied red).

Paros

Paros is a rich agricultural island, with much food – from olives to figs, citrus and potatoes – grown here, and the vineyards yield increasingly interesting wines.

Near Naoussa, pressing grapes since 1910, the Moraitis family has it down to a fine art. Sidle up to the Moraitis Winery bar for a taste. Their bestseller is the Paros White,

Left and right Santorini vineyards
Centre Chrysoloras Winery, Serifos

made with the island's indigenous grape, *monemvasia*, also used to make the Malvasia dessert wine. They also have Moraitis Vinothéque in Naoussa proper.

The new kid on the block is Domaine Myrsini in the south of the island, where a Nantes native and her husband have just started pressing their own Parian wine. They can give tastings outside the harvest season (August when they are busy pulling in the grapes).

> Santorini is blessed with a dry volcanic microclimate and wine culture here goes back millennia.

Other Islands

In the hills above Platys Gialos on arid and rocky Serifos, Chrysoloras Winery is now making some good organic whites. It uses grapes that are right at home in the Cyclades: *serifiotiko, mandilaria, monemvasia* and *asyrtiko*.

In Arnados on Tinos, Ballis Tinos Winery creates wines in a medieval style using grapes from the surrounding vineyards. Famous for all manner of food, Tinos is lusher than many Cycladic islands, so grapes that like it wet do well here.

On Naxos, visit Saint Anna Winery in a lush, olive-grove-draped valley with lovely historic walking paths between Ano and Kato Potamia villages.

Milos isn't known only for its ring of beaches – it also has a growing wine reputation thanks to Kostantakis Cave Winery. A relative newcomer, it has rescued vineyards that had been neglected for 40 years. Its wines age in naturally formed caves near the beach town of Pollonia.

Greek Grape Varieties

Greece's wine industry benefits from some age-old indigenous varietals with unique character. The contemporary generation of winemakers is producing great, award-winning wines from Greece's premier wine regions, including the Cyclades.

Greek white varieties include *moschofilero, asyrtiko, athiri, roditis, robola* and *savatiano*. The most popular reds include *xinomavro, agiorgitiko* and *kotsifali*.

Retsina (white wine flavoured with the resin of pine trees) became popular in the 1960s and is what many visitors associate with Greek wine, given its prevalence in Greek restaurants worldwide. It's something of an acquired taste but some winemakers produce a smoother, modern version.

Listings

BEST OF THE REST

Seafront Tavernas

Armeni €€

With the seashore at your table, this gem of a taverna is worth the steep descent from Santorini's Oia to sup at the altar of seafood with a short, brilliantly executed menu.

Halaris Ouzerie €

Harbourfront in Paros' Piso Livadi, this seafood-taverna-cum-*ouzerie* is ideal for small plates of creative seafood and salads for the quintessential long lunch.

Captain Pipino's €

A highlight of a day at Antiparos' beaches is lunch at Captain Pipino's. You may need to wait for a table at this gloriously old-school fish taverna with panoramas of uninhabited Despotiko island.

To Steki €€

Excellent traditional taverna on Sifnos' Platys Gialos waterfront, with tables on a tree-shaded stone terrace.

Medusa Taverna €€

In the fishing harbour of Mandrakia on Milos, village ladies cook at this fabulous taverna. The views are killer, so arrive early to be sure of getting a table.

Village Eats & Plateia Cafes

Symposium €

Parikia in Paros contains inviting village cafes, but none so much as Symposium. Under a massive bougainvillea, it serves delicious light meals with jazz and classical music.

Tereza €€

This renowned lunch stop is hidden amid the maze of lanes in pint-size Myrsini. Once a tiny old market, it now serves stupendous lunches.

To Krinaki €€

Slip away from Santorini's caldera edge to the traditional hamlet of Finikia, where chef Elvis sources and combines local produce to delicious effect at this sweet, small restaurant.

Doukato €€

Reserve a table at this always-jammed former monastery on Naxos, now a courtyard filled with happy eaters of specialities like *kalogeras* (beef, eggplant and cheese).

O Rokos Myrsini €€

Perfect taverna meals on a terrace amid trees in Volax on Tinos. Follow a cobblestoned lane to the entrance and enjoy fine hillside views.

Hidden Beaches

Pori Beach

Koufonisia's broad scoop of Pori Bay is a gorgeous swirl of blues and a favourite yachtie

Cove on Milos

anchorage. Alongside the Ksylompatis Sea Caves, it's around the corner from Piscina, a literal swimming hole in the cliffs.

Firiplaka

On Milos, Firiplaka has a stunning cliff-backed setting with a hodgepodge of dirt parking areas above a series of tiny coves. The larger main beach is covered by loungers from a stylish club.

Hawaii Beach

This wee baylet on Naxos' west coast is aptly named for its iridescent cerulean waters and is backed by tawny rock formations and cliffs.

Fokos Beach

This Mykonos beach is never busy and attracts a laid-back crowd all summer. A short jaunt around the headland to the east, Mersini is easily the quietest beach on Mykonos.

 Active Outings

Atlantis Oia

Santorini's underwater topography is no less spectacular than the land above. At antis Oia, a member of Cousteau Divers with a stellar record in marine conservation, will take you there.

G3 Boats

In Paros, this outfit is run by affable Georgios, who will take you zooming across the water to Antiparos' sea caves, a deserted island with ancient ruins or even to Mykonos.

Naxos Kitelife

One of three excellent operators in Naxos' windsurfing capital, Mikri Vigla, it will train or outfit you for kitesurfing and kite foiling.

 Monasteries & Museums

Museum of Prehistoric Thera

This standout museum in Fira, Santorini, houses extraordinary finds excavated from

Panagia Paraportiani

Ancient Akrotiri. Examine the wealth of Minoan frescoes and the glowing gold ibex figurine dating from the 17th century BCE.

Panagia Paraportiani

Mykonos' landmark whitewashed church looks like it's grown organically from the rock. Built between the 15th and 17th centuries, it's one of 70 Hora churches hiding in plain sight.

Museum of Marble Crafts

A short walk uphill from the village of Pyrgos on Tinos, this outstanding, modern complex creatively explains the island's centuries of marble quarrying and sculpting techniques.

Sanctuary of Poseidon & Amphitrite

On Tinos, this ancient site offers an engrossing look at the classical Greek era. From the 4th century BCE to the 3rd century CE, this was a major religious sanctuary.

Moni Chrysopigi

Perched on an islet off Sifnos and connected to the shore by a stone footbridge, this whitewashed monastery with divine sea views is considered the protector of the island.

DODECANESE

FAR-FLUNG | SPLENDOROUS | TIMELESS

- ▶ **Trip Builder** (p214)
- ▶ **Practicalities** (p216)
- ▶ **Stroll Medieval Alleys** (p218)
- ▶ **Breathtaking Harbour** (p220)
- ▶ **The Greenest Island** (p222)
- ▶ **Nisyros' Volcanic Beauty** (p224)
- ▶ **Ancient Remains & Beaches** (p226)
- ▶ **Astypalea's Beauty** (p228)
- ▶ **Cliffs & Quiet Beaches** (p230)
- ▶ **Listings** (p232)

Eat, hike and sunbathe on beautiful **Astypalea** (p228)
✈ 1hr flight from Kos

Step into the steaming crater of the magnificent volcano on **Nisyros** (p224)
⛴ 1hr from Kos

DODECANESE
Trip Builder

Want to get away from it all? Come to the Dodecanese – their timeless charm, natural beauty, historic ruins, tranquil beaches and distant islands epitomise old Greece. Expect a focus on sustainability, impressive historic remains and great gastronomy.

- See where Hippocrates taught medicine under the plane tree on **Kos** (p227)
  🚶 7mins from Kos Town port

- Dock in one of the world's prettiest harbours on **Symi** (p220)
  ⚓ 1hr from Rhodes

- Wander through the cobbled alleyways and Byzantine arches of **Rhodes Old Town** (p219)
  🚗 20mins from Diagoras Airport

- Get down to some serious hiking, bird-watching and nature loving on **Tilos** (p222)
  ⚓ 2hrs from Rhodes

- Dive in the bluest cave on **Kastellorizo**
  ✈ 1hr flight from Rhodes

- Take in the breathtaking scenery from the **Acropolis of Lindos** (p232)
  🚗 45mins from Rhodes Town

FROM LEFT: LEOKS/SHUTTERSTOCK ©, NEJDET DUZEN/SHUTTERSTOCK ©, SAIKO3P/SHUTTERSTOCK ©, KATVIC/SHUTTERSTOCK © PREVIOUS SPREAD: ECSTK22/SHUTTERSTOCK ©

Practicalities

ARRIVING

Rhodes and Kos Flights from Athens and European cities. Fly in and continue to other islands. Be aware that ferries are packed in high season and some are pricey – book ahead.

Ferry ports Athens' Piraeus port serves the main islands by ferry. Journey times can be up to 12 hours; onward trips to smaller islands might require a change. Marmaris and Bodrum in Türkiyehave services to Rhodes and Kos.

HOW MUCH FOR A

Souvlaki
€3

Greek salad from €10

Sunbed
€10-€20

GETTING AROUND

Boat The best way to travel between all the Dodecanese islands is by ferry or catamaran. Tickets can be bought online from the main companies or at the harbours. Note that ferry services can be pretty sporadic, especially in July and August when the *meltemi* (dry northerly wind) blows heavily in the Aegean Sea.

Car The best way to see the islands once there is to hire a car. Public transport services can be few and far between. Driving is a great way to explore hidden coves and visit out-of-the-way places.

Air Some of the smaller islands have domestic airports, making connecting by plane possible.

WHEN TO GO

FEB–APR
Cool, sunny days, perfect for hiking.

MAY–JUN, SEP–OCT
Gorgeous swims and walks, with gentler weather.

JUL–AUG
Hottest months; very busy. *meltemi* blows from July.

NOV–JAN
Windswept winter with serenity, but many services close.

EATING & DRINKING

Each island in the Dodecanese has its own specialities stemming from traditional practices and rich cultural heritage that combine to make a unique regional cuisine. Expect delicacies such as the *pitaroudia* (chickpea fritters) found in Rhodes.

Symi's famous baby prawns are a delicacy – just squeeze on some fresh lemon and tuck in.

Karpathos, a more agricultural island, produces its own *makarounes* – homemade pasta served with sautéed onions and various sheep and goat milk cheeses, the most typical of which is called *myzithra*.

Best Symi prawns Pantelis (p232)

Rhodes Town's best taverna food Paradosiako Kafeneio I Symi (p232)

CONNECT & FIND YOUR WAY

Wi-fi All good hotels, cafes and restaurants offer free wi-fi. Some bigger islands have free wi-fi at ports and airports. In roaming your phone might be prone to alternating between a Greek and Turkish mobile service due to proximity to Türkiye.

Navigation Google Maps is useful when driving to remote beaches and villages or walking through the narrow streets of the old towns.

WHERE TO STAY

These islands offer a range of accommodation – whether you're island-hopping or staying put, there are options from budget to boutique. Prices are determined by season, irrespective of the accommodation option.

Island	Pro/Con
Rhodes and Kos	The two biggest islands both offer a choice of package-holiday hotels, family-run establishments and boutique hotels.
Symi	Neoclassical, pretty architecture makes Symi perfect for spending some time in gorgeous sleeping options.
Tilos	Simple, and some luxury accommodation, a stone's throw from the sea.
Nisyros	Quality accommodation encouraging longer stays.

ANCIENT SITES

The Dodecanese offer a plethora of historic and archaeological sites such as the Acropolis of Lindos on Rhodes and the Asklepieion on Kos.

MONEY

Most places accept cards and contactless payments. Carry some euros with you to buy street food or for small souvenirs. Seeking out restaurants away from the tourist strips is usually more affordable.

45 Stroll Medieval ALLEYS

DOMES | MINARETS | GARDENS

Ruled by the Knights of St John in the 14th century, medieval Rhodes Town has fortresses, gates and over 200 labyrinthine streets and cobbled alleyways. The Old Town throngs with activity, making it an atmospheric, living UNESCO World Heritage Site. Strolling the medieval walls and moat is an excellent way to see this historical wonder.

How to

Getting here Fly into Rhodes or arrive by ferry. The Old Town walls are easily reached on foot, but taxis and rental cars can drop you off outside any of the gates.

When to go The best times to visit are spring and autumn – the high summer months of July and August can be very hot and crowded.

Picnic time The moat is full of green grass and lovely trees and plants in spring and autumn, so bring a picnic and have it mid-walk.

Far left Palace of the Grand Master
Bottom left Old Town of Rhodes

Medieval time capsule Sealed behind a double ring of high walls and a deep moat, the beautiful **Old Town of Rhodes** is a UNESCO World Heritage Site. Lose yourself in this magical labyrinth and witness ruins and relics of the Classical, medieval, Byzantine, Ottoman and Italian eras, all entangled in a maze of charming, twisting, bougainvillea-laden lanes.

Ancient fortifications Rhodes' Old Town is rare in retaining its 500-year-old fortifications all but intact. On weekdays, visitors can grasp their sheer scale by walking a broad, grassy 1km stretch of the ramparts, from the **Palace of the Grand Master** to **St John's Gate**. There's no shade, but you get superb views of everything inside the Old Town; look out across the deep surrounding moat, and pass the massive, sealed-off **Bastion of St George**.

Bucolic moat Drop down at **St Anthony's Gate** and walk along the moat, exploring its spacious lawns and lush flowers. Look out for stacks of stone cannonballs, fired by Ottoman besiegers in 1480 and 1522. The moat was simply a defensive ditch, never filled with water. Now landscaped as a park, it's a great place to stroll or picnic – locals do yoga classes here and come to read and relax. It's accessible from a number of gates.

🏛 Rhodes in a Historical Nutshell

The Minoans and Mycenaeans established early outposts on Rhodes followed by the Dorians. Over the next centuries, Rhodes switched allegiances between Athens, Persia, Sparta and Alexander the Great; the island was assimilated into the Roman Empire in 70 CE, then into the Byzantine province of the Dodecanese. When the Crusaders seized Constantinople, it was granted independence. Later, the Genoese gained control followed by the Knights of St John, who ruled Rhodes for 213 years from 1309. They were ousted after two sieges by the Ottomans, before the Italians took control nearly four centuries later. In 1947, after 35 years of Italian occupation, Rhodes became part of Greece.

46 Breathtaking HARBOUR

BEACHES | ARCHITECTURE | GASTRONOMY

The island of Symi is so beautiful that just sailing into its harbour is an event. The first sight of its amphitheatre of pastel-coloured houses rising on all sides is unforgettable. It was the island's Italian rulers who, a century ago, established the neoclassical architectural style that has been the signature mark of Symi ever since.

How to

Getting here There are daily ferries to and from Rhodes and Kos.

When to go Summer is hot and crowded. September and October are less so, yet still warm enough to swim.

Water taxi The best way to see Symi's beaches is by a water taxi (€10 per person). You will find the little stand along the inner side of Gialos Harbour (plus one in Pedi) and with regular trips to the island's beaches. In high season there's at least one departure an hour, from 10am onwards, with the last boat back usually at 6pm.

Sailing in The first view of **Gialos Harbour** is unforgettable, with its neoclassical amphitheatre of colourful houses on all sides. Fishing boats sit on transparent waters, sponge sellers hawk their treasures, while an occasional Hollywood star arrives in a gleaming superyacht. The best thing to do in **Gialos** is to sit in one of the tavernas and cafes along the quayside, tasting the island's celebrated shrimps, followed by an exploration of the backstreets that brim with fruit stores, ice-cream parlours and bakeries. Head north along the seafront from the clock tower, away from the centre, and you're immediately in smaller **Harani Bay**. Traditionally a base for shipbuilding, it still holds assorted beached boats, along with its own crop of bars and tavernas.

Stunning beaches Once a village, now more of a yachting marina and low-key resort, **Pedi** sits immediately below **Horio**. **Agia Marina** to the north is a lagoon-like little bay, facing a chapel-topped islet across turquoise waters, which gets very crowded in summer. **Agios Nikolaos**, on the south side, is broader and sandier, with decent tree cover and idyllic swimming. Two large bays south of Pedi, **Nanou** and **Marathounda**, hold large beaches and tavernas and make great destinations for water-taxi day trips. Marathounda, backed by a lush valley and scattered with roaming goats, is especially recommended.

✕ Small Island, Big Bites

The renowned speciality in the kitchens of Symi are the *simiako garidaki*, Symi prawns: tiny shrimp prepared with some lemon and olive oil and eaten whole. Also try the *akoumia sumiaka*, literally the Simian doughnut. *Lachanondolmades* are similar to stuffed vine leaves but made with white cabbage leaves. *Misokofti* is a Symi variant of *mustalevria*, a Greek dessert that's made with a combination of *fragosyko* (prickly pear) pulp, cornstarch and sugar. It is usually served sprinkled with cinnamon and walnuts, almonds or pistachios.

Above left Symi
Below left Agia Marina

The Greenest ISLAND

MOUNTAINS | WILDFLOWERS | BEACHES

Tilos is the definition of slow travel, perfect for those who want peace, quiet, good food, swimming and hiking. Gorgeous meadows, mountains and valleys are criss-crossed with shepherds' paths, and there are many deserted beaches. The island is the first 'green' and zero-waste island in the Mediterranean, with entirely sustainable energy. It's a place to stay a while.

How to

Getting here/around
Tilos has no airport and only a minimal ferry service – it's two hours from Kos and Rhodes, and 14 hours from Athens.

When to go Spring and autumn for hiking, summer for beaches.

Hike and pie Hike to the fishing village of Agios Antonios, and pop into O Gialos for a rich Greek coffee and a *galaktoboureko* (a sort of custard pie).

Hiking This is the main reason that people come to Tilos. There are around 54km of trails, with varying degrees of marking. One well-maintained and very scenic 3km walk leads north from **Livadia** to **Lethra Beach**, an undeveloped pebble-and-sand cove with limited shade. A longer walk leads to the small, abandoned settlement of **Yera** and its accompanying beach at **Despoti Nero**.

Bird-watching More than 150 species of birds have been recorded on Tilos. Some are residential, some migratory. An estimated 46 species are threatened. Keep your eyes peeled for the Bonelli's eagle, Eleonora's falcon, long-legged buzzard, Sardinian warbler, scops owl and Mediterranean black shag.

Wealth of beaches Close to Livadia, there are some serviced beaches, but head to the northwest part of the island to reach the long, broad **Eristos Beach**, lapped by sapphire-hued waters and perfect for swimming. Generally deserted but for the odd local person line fishing, its greyish sands are fringed by tamarisk trees. **Kokkini Beach** to the south of the island is hidden in a small bay. Kokkini is Greek for the colour red, and the sand here is a reddish colour – hence the name – from the iron and other minerals. Further down is Lethra Beach, with gorgeous indigo waters. The rocky islet of **Vrachonisida Prasouda**, to the west of Tilos, has clear blue waters, ideal for long swims.

🌿 A Role Model for Sustainability

Tilos came to be known as the first 'green' island in the Mediterranean in 2019, and the first zero-waste island in the world in 2023 and has implemented a comprehensive waste management programme, Just Go Zero Tilos *(justgozero.com/en/tilos)*. Its residents use energy sourced exclusively from renewables, and they participate in a door-to-door collection system for the recycling plant. This way of living, combined with its hiking, bird-watching and beautiful beaches, make Tilos a role model for sustainable tourism.

Above left
Abandoned village, Tilos **Below left**
Sardinian warbler

48 Nisyros' Volcanic BEAUTY

VOLCANO | HIKING | GASTRONOMY

The charming volcano island of Nisyros is very much off the tourist radar, excepting the day-trippers from nearby Kos who come to witness the magnificent caldera. This lack of crowds – owing to the island's relative lack of beaches – makes it perfect for those seeking natural beauty, excellent food and soaring mountain views over terraced fields and wildflowers.

How to

Getting here/around
There are ferries from Kos twice a week. The journey takes about an hour. Public buses do a circuit around the island three times daily in summer; catch them at the port. You can rent cars and scooters at Manos K rentals in Mandraki.

When to go Spring and autumn are best for hiking.

Visiting the caldera
Try to get to the caldera before 11am, to avoid the busloads of day-trippers that arrive from Kos. The surface is soft and hot, so make sure you wear sturdy footwear.

Far left Stefanos crater
Below left Emborios

A hollow caldera This vast and otherworldly plain that was home to thousands of ancient farmers encloses several distinct craters at its southern end. A path descends into the largest crater, **Stefanos**, where you can examine the multi-coloured 100°C fumaroles, sometimes listen to their hissing and smell the sulphurous vapours. A track leads to the wilder craters of **Polyvotis** and **Alexandros**. Take great care here as it's unsupervised. Wear sturdy shoes.

Nisyros walking You can walk to the heart of the caldera in around 2½ hours from Mandraki. Hike directly beyond **Evangelistrias monastery**, or follow the longer track to its shallower southern side. A shorter volcanic jaunt starts behind the **volcano museum** and takes 45 minutes to reach the Stefanos crater. Take careful note of landmarks on your way down.

Beautiful villages Emborios is perched high on the jagged northern rim of the caldera, 9km up from Mandraki, and has some lovely stone houses and restaurants. The village of **Nikea** is 4km south along the crater's edge. No vehicles can penetrate this tight warren of dazzling white houses, so every visitor experiences the thrill of walking along the narrow lane from road's end to reach the tiny central square. Less a square than a circle, actually, it's among the most jaw-droppingly beautiful spots in the Dodecanese.

The Volcanic Acropolis of Paleokastro

Best reached by a lovely 20-minute hike through the fields, along a trail that starts southwest of the monastery, the astonishing Mycenaean-era acropolis of **Paleokastro** was founded 3000 years ago. Its restored cyclopean walls are a little newer, from the 4th century BCE – what looks like modern graffiti is in fact ancient dedications. Pass through the forbidding gateway and you can climb atop the massive blocks of volcanic rock for breathtaking views. Good explanatory signs in English are scattered throughout.

49 Ancient Remains & BEACHES

HISTORY | SAND | SWIMMING

Kos is an island ringed by some of the finest beaches in the Dodecanese, and visitors naturally gravitate towards these fine sandy stretches. Beyond beach bodies, Kos Town has ancient Greek ruins scattered at every turn, and a mighty medieval castle keeps watch over the harbour. Just a few kilometres west of Kos Town, the island retains considerable wilderness.

How to

Getting here Kos has an international airport with connections to many destinations.

When to go Summer and autumn are the best times to visit.

Bike to beaches You'll be tripping over bicycles for hire. Cycle lanes thread all through Kos Town, running along the waterfront to connect the town with Lambi to the north and Psalidi to the south.

Historic town Kos Town is a handsome harbour community squeezed amid an array of ancient ruins. Kos' magnificent 15th-century **Castle of the Knights** took about 130 years to build, meaning the architectural styles encompass several historic periods. North of the Ancient Agora is the lovely **Plateia Platanou** and the **Hippocrates' Plane Tree**, under which Hippocrates is said to have taught his pupils.

Ancient medicine The island's most important ancient site, **Asklepieion**, stands on a pine-covered hill 3km southwest of Kos Town, commanding lovely views across towards Türkiye. A religious sanctuary devoted to Asclepius, the god of healing, it was also a healing centre and a school of medicine. It was founded in the 3rd century BCE, according to legend by Hippocrates himself, the Kos-born 'father' of modern medicine.

Blissful beaches The nearest to Kos Town, **Lambi Beach** is a busy strip with a range of hotels and restaurants. South of Kos Town, hot mineral springs warm the sea at **Therma Loutra Beach**, but it tends to get very busy – go early in the morning for solitude. **Pserimos** island is only a few kilometres offshore and served by excursion boats from Marmari in summer. If you want a day or a week in the sun, with everything to hand, head for **Mastihari**. Hardly more than a village, this delightful old-fashioned beach resort holds everything you need.

ⓘ The Hippocratic Botanic Garden

A little-known place 1km before Asklepieion, the **Hippocratic Botanic Garden & International Hippocratic Foundation** may not be immediately impressive, but its collection is wonderful if you give it your attention. It houses a small text-heavy exhibition on Hippocrates, explaining the oath for doctors, plus ancient medical instruments – many are still used today. The highlight is the botanic garden, growing herbs and plants that were used in Hippocratic times. It is not a pruned and sculpted garden and this is intentional – its 'scrappy' nature is authentic.

Above left Castle of the Knights
Below left Therma Loutra Beach

50 Astypalea's BEAUTY

LANDSCAPES | SWIMMING | STYLE

The most Cycladic of Dodecanese islands, remote Astypalea is awe-strikingly beautiful with its incredible beaches and blue-and-white streets and houses. It is swathed in silky aquamarine waters, ridged by dramatic cliffs, far-flung, butterfly-shaped and richly rewarding for walkers, campers and history buffs. Mountainous meadows and rugged beaches are lapped by blue waters – this is the ultimate escape for island hunters.

How to

Getting here Astypalea has flights to and from Athens, Kos and Rhodes, as well as ferry connections.

When to go Astypalea is best visited in spring, summer and autumn. Hiking is best done outside of the hot months of July and August.

Vehicle sharing Astypalea has a vehicle-sharing service for electric cars, scooters and bicycles, as well as an on-demand electric bus service. You'll need to register on the astyMove app *(astypalea-sustainable-island.gr)*.

Far left Hora village Below left Livadi

Pretty villages Astypalea's main settlement, **Pera Gialos**, curves around an attractive bay. Visitors delight in the beauty of the old settlement of **Hora** looming above, its white houses spilling down the hillside beneath its impressive *kastro* (castle). Hora is a delightful maze to explore. Stroll around the hushed tangle of streets and climb up to the fort. Don't miss a visit to **Hora Library**, housed inside one of its windmills and with an excellent range of English and other foreign-language titles. Borrow, read and return before you leave.

An array of beaches Astypalea's most popular beach, **Livadi**, stands at the mouth of a lush valley in the first bay south of Hora. It's an easy 20-minute walk down from the old town. There are good restaurants, shops and cafes by the water. The slender isthmus that links Astypalea's two 'wings' holds some of the island's most popular beaches. **Steno Beach** is sandy, shady and conveniently shallow for kids. The road west of Livadi leads through mountainous meadows to several remote beaches. First along the way, reached on a brief detour, is the pretty, tree-shaded **Agios Konstantinos Beach** on the south side of Livadi Bay. Reach the splendid **Kaminakia** and **Vatses Beaches** by a dirt road in the far west.

◎ Vathy: Ancient Erotic Graffiti

Providing invaluable insight into the lives of Greece's earliest – archaic and classical – inhabitants, the discovery of ancient erotic graffiti on rock at remote **Vathy** was a real boon for archaeologists. Chiselled into the outcrops of dolomite limestone along the cape 2500 years ago, these blunt descriptions of sexual shenanigans show that homosexuality wasn't taboo at the time. Experts claim that whoever wrote the words in stone was quite skilful at writing, showing that literacy was available to ordinary people and not only the ruling classes at a time before the Athens Acropolis had been built.

51 Cliffs & Quiet BEACHES

MOUNTAINS | BEACHES | TAVERNAS

While its sponge-fishing heyday is long past, Kalymnos remains inextricably entwined with the sea. The island is characterised by its craggy cliffs and dramatic mountains that draw climbers from all over the world. The beautiful islet of Telendos is immediately offshore and has an array of quiet beaches and tavernas, making it an ideal place for a peaceful few days.

How to

Getting here/around
Kalymnos can be visited on a day trip from Kos, but staying at least one night is recommended. Frequent water taxis also connect Myrties with Telendos Islet year-round.

When to go Summertime is best for the beaches.

Local Kalymnos Learn about Kalymnos with a group of passionate young locals at Kalymnos Experience – they offer alternative local experiences.

Far left Rock climbing, Kalymnos
Below left Telendos

A **bewitching islet Telendos** sits like the perfect peak on the Aegean, just off the west coast of Kalymnos. Crowned by a mountainous ridge that soars 450m high, it's thought to have been set adrift from the rest of Kalymnos by an earthquake in 554 CE. It now makes a wonderful, vehicle-free destination for a day trip or longer stay. Head right to reach the ruins of the early Christian basilica of **Agios Vasilios** and a footpath that climbs to the similarly dilapidated basilica of **Palaiopanayia**. Head left, on the other hand, and you can either cross a slender ridge, rich in colourful oleander, to access windswept, fine-pebbled **Hohlakas Beach** or the nudist **Paradise Beach** beyond, a gloriously tranquil little swimming cove. Explore the islet's low-lying southern promontory, which holds some tiny early Christian tombs now inhabited by goats.

Get outdoorsy Steep crags, stark cliffs and daredevil overhangs have turned Kalymnos into Greece's premier destination for rock climbers. It now has more than 80 designated climbing sites, holding over 3500 marked routes. The enthusiastic local group in charge of **Kalymnos Experience** (kalymnosexperience.gr) provide an excellent way to get to know the island. They offer alternative local experiences such as nature walks, yoga, rock climbing and scuba diving. There are also herb walks in the mountains – and the recent addition of a vegan food bar!

A History of Sponge Diving

Kalymnos was for centuries the centre of the Greek sponge-diving industry. Local divers gathered their sponges from the seafloor by diving naked, connected to a rope with a large flat stone to help them sink. They reached depths of up to 30m, holding their breath for up to five minutes. In 1865, a diving suit, the *skafandro*, allowed divers to go deeper and for longer, and large fleets replaced individual boats. The danger to the divers was immense. Deaths and disability were commonplace. The industry collapsed after sponges were infected by pollution in the 1980s.

Listings

BEST OF THE REST

Historical Highlights

Acropolis of Lindos, Rhodes
Atop a steep cliff in the fishing village of Lindos (just over an hour's drive from Rhodes Old Town) sits the ancient Acropolis, dating back to the 4th century BCE. Wear sturdy shoes.

Monastery of the Apocalypse, Patmos
Enclosed within an 11th-century chapel, this is where St John is reputed to have rested his head and experienced the vision resulting in the Book of Revelations.

Monastery of St John the Theologian, Patmos
An immense 11th-century monastery-cum-fortress with a sumptuously frescoed chapel, fronted by marble columns taken from an ancient temple.

Archaeological Museum, Rhodes Town
Visitors are treated to exquisite ancient pieces at the magnificent 15th-century Knights' Hospital that holds Rhodes' archaeology museum.

Balmiest Beaches

Pedi, Symi
Sitting below Horio, Pedi has two beachesto either side of the bay, with clear waters.

Agios Theologos Beach, Kos
On the west coast of Kos and backed by meadow bluffs carpeted in olive groves, this beach feels far removed from the resort bustle.

St Paul's Bay, Lindos, Rhodes
Spend a day on this quiet, sandy beach nestled in Lindos and home to the small St Paul's Chapel. With sunbeds and umbrellas, it's perfect for families.

Kaminakia, Astypalea
Bookended by granite boulders, Kaminakia is Astypalea's best altar to sun-worshipping, with water so clear you can see the pebbles through the turquoise.

Terrific Tavernas

4 Rodies €€
Eat perfectly prepared Rhodian dishes in the garden of this family-run restaurant.

Paradosiako Kafeneio I Symi €€
Rhodes' cutest terrace and some of the best seafood you're likely to taste. Plus loads of cats.

Pantelis €€
Gialos best restaurant – the huge dishes are so full of flavour, you'll be back several times. Try the *gigantes* beans and the octopus.

Tholos €€
Possibly the most romantic restaurant in the Dodecanese: view the sunset from the waterfront tables, and order the famous Symi prawns.

Monastery of St John the Theologian

Almyriki €€

Our favourite, Almyriki sits on a terrace by the water and has a menu of seafood, salads and vegetables – try the baked aubergine and fava.

Issikas €€

Mandraki's best restaurant is on the waterfront, serving a simple menu of local specialities cooked to perfection. Try the baked goat.

Aegean Tavern €€€

An upmarket experience in a stylish building on Kalymnos that juts over the water overlooking Telendos. Locals love the fresh seafood catch.

Outdoor Activities

Kalymnos Experience

Get down to some local experiences such as herb-gathering walks, rock climbing and diving.

Cycle to Beaches in Kos

Hire a bicycle in Kos Town and bike to the long sandy stretch of beach in the north of the island; it's endless and uncrowded.

Hike Astypalea

Sunday mornings, at 10am, hike with the Pardalo Katsiki club – turn up by the windmills in Hora and get a chance to be guided around Astypalea's incredible landscapes.

Walk Across Tilos

There are around 54km of trails, with varying degrees of marking. Some might find the website (*tilostrails.com*) useful, with brief outlines and a grading of each walk, from easy to challenging.

St Paul's Bay

Cutest Cafes

Oxos

The most magical cafe in the Dodecanese is on Nisyros, on a little square at the far end of the harbour, nestled below the monastery and under tamarisk trees overlooking the sea.

Mevlana

This gorgeous Rhodes Town cafe has belonged to the same family for the past 200 years – slurp on a hot Turkish coffee and suck on a shisha.

Kafeneio Oi Myloi

Coffee, drinks and food, and late night partying in Astypalea's refurbished *kafeneio* (cafe).

Bagia Cafe

Popular, great value and friendly, Tilos' Bagia sits in the middle of everything, serving breakfasts and Greek pies.

Archipelagos

Incredible homemade cakes, teas and terrace views of the slopes of Astypalea's Hora.

Law Court Cafe

Facing Hippocrates' plane tree in Kos Town, this cafe feels remote from the tourist scene.

53 Drinking Ouzo
ON LESVOS

CULTURE | CUISINE | SOCIAL LIFE

While no drink is more synonymous with Greece than ouzo, on the northeastern Aegean island of Lesvos (Mytilini) it's much more – an expression of land, lifestyle and a rich cultural heritage that reflects a deep connection to Asia Minor.

How to

Getting here/around
Daily flights connect Mytilini Town with Athens. Ferries leave from Athens and the northern ports of Thessaloniki and Kavala. It's a large island; buses go to most places, but it's best to hire a car to get around.

How much? Ouzo with a couple of simple mezedhes costs little more than a cocktail or two.

Pack some binoculars
Between permanent avian residents and migrating visitors, more than 300 species can be spotted among Lesvos' diverse biotopes (*lesvosbirds.gr*).

Ouzo & Lesvos

Ouzo may be ubiquitous all over Greece, but the North Aegean is its heartland. Lesvos has 17 distilleries and a total of 44 different labels, among them some of the most popular bottles in Greece and abroad. But its story goes much deeper than that: ouzo reveals the island's soul.

Related to arak and raki, ouzo is part of the cultural heritage of Lesvos, an island populated by the descendants of Greek refugees from Asia Minor. It captures the scent of the island, with its signature note distilled from the famously fragrant wild anise that grows around **Lisvorio**. It also suits the island's palate; ouzo's delicate sweetness is the ideal counterpoint to the briny thrill of fresh fish and seafood. But most of all, the way locals enjoy ouzo on Lesvos is an expression of their

Bring Your Bathing Suit

Atmospheric Ottoman-era baths and toasty thermal springs offer another way to connect with the island. Of Lesvos' five springs, only **Therma Spa** at the Bay of Gera and the newly refurbished **Hippocrates Thermal Springs** near Polyhnitos were open at the time of writing.

Top left Mytilini Town
Top right Salted sardines from Lesvos
Bottom left Ouzo for sale, Mytilini Town

enviable talent for embracing the moment – a reason in itself to visit.

Ouzo, Mezedhes, Parea

Ouzo is a casual drink enjoyed with refined customs. There's always food – usually mezedhes (a selection of small dishes), but a handful of olives and some *ladotyri* (a sheep's-milk cheese ripened in oil) do very nicely. Much more importantly, ouzo is always enjoyed in the company of friends, known as the *parea*.

Ouzo glasses in the North Aegean are slender and tall, to encourage delicate sips. Adding water softens ouzo's bold flavours and keeps its effects at an enjoyable minimum, extending the pleasures of the moment. While drinking ouzo is a graceful ritual, sharing mezedhes is delightfully anarchic. Replacing a hierarchy of courses, mezedhes are shared communally from the centre of the table.

The ouzo experience centres on connecting the group: people serve their companions

Enjoying Ouzo like a Local

At the picturesque harbour of **Skamioudi**, near Lisvorio (where the anise for ouzo grows), fisherfolk bring in their catch from the Gulf of Kalloni. It's the perfect place for enjoying ouzo.

Add cold water – avoid ice – to your *kanonaki* (the special glasses we use for ouzo on Lesvos).

In cooler months, savour fresh mussels *(chavara)*, clams *(kidonia)* and scallops *(chtenia)*, grilled or raw. In summer, try sashimi, Aegean-style: *papalina* are delicate fresh sardines cured with local salt. Eat while drinking – small sips, small bites.

The essential ingredient: *parea*, or friends to share ouzo with. Toast with *'Eva!'*

■ Recommended by Maria Kaplanelli, *Lesvos Food Fest* coordinator @theotheraegean

Far left Greek mezedhes
Below Lesvos street

first, and everyone raises a glass together to enjoy the first sip. Light-hearted conversation, laughter and lots more toasting follow.

Experiencing the Amanedhes

Lesvos has an eastern soul. Ouzo is a taste of it, and the *amanedhes* its voice. 'Aman, aman!' – an expression of anguish – lends the deeply emotive genre its name. A repeated rhythmic sequence creates a dreamy, timeless space. Then the song unfolds. Each fluid note slides into the next as they ascend; the vocals of the *amanedhes* share more with the call to prayer of the muezzin than with an aria. You don't need to understand Greek to relate to the depth of feeling; as ouzo brings the soul to fuller expression, so do the *amanedhes*. Its singers are increasingly rare. But with luck, you may find one in the cafes of **Mesotopos** or **Plomari**.

Celebrate Women, Celebrate Love

The works of Sappho, the lyric poet of Lesvos, so evocatively express a passion for women that she's honoured in the word 'lesbian'. In the beach town of **Skala Eresou**, today's lesbians – and indeed everyone – will find a warm welcome. The highlight is the **International Eressos Women's Festival** (*womensfestival.eu*), combining a spirit of pilgrimage and community with stellar DJs and various activities and events each September.

By Amber Charmei
Amber's favourite aspect of life in Greece is the graceful way locals embrace the beauty of the moment; enjoying ouzo on Lesvos conveys it perfectly.

Practicalities

ARRIVING
240

GETTING AROUND
242

SAFE TRAVEL
244

MONEY
245

RESPONSIBLE TRAVEL
246

ACCOMMODATION
248

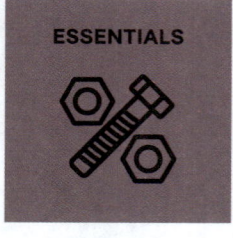
ESSENTIALS
250

LANGUAGE
252

Right Athens

EASY STEPS FROM THE AIRPORT TO THE CITY CENTRE

Most travellers arriving in Greece come through Athens' Eleftherios Venizelos International Airport, located approximately 33km from the city centre (a 30-minute drive). The airport was renovated in 2021, and you'll find a variety of shops, restaurants, cafes and hotels. There are also currency exchange points, ATMs and car rental offices.

AT THE AIRPORT

SIM CARDS
Although you can buy Vodafone SIM cards at the airport, they're double the cost of those in the city centre. Cosmote, Vodafone and WIND are the country's major operators; you'll find several branches in every city.

CURRENCY EXCHANGE
There are four Onexchange offices in the airport to change currency. Rates are more or less the same as those at places in the city centre; you can also exchange money in any bank branch.

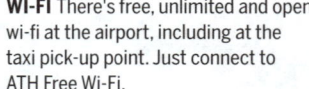

WI-FI There's free, unlimited and open wi-fi at the airport, including at the taxi pick-up point. Just connect to ATH Free Wi-Fi.

ATMs There are many ATMs across arrivals and departures; all accept foreign Visa and Mastercard cards.

CHARGING STATIONS Charging stations are available at numerous points throughout the airport; they're free and work with EU plug types.

CUSTOMS REGULATIONS
Greece follows Schengen customs regulations. The maximum non-declared monetary allowance is €10,000. For duty-free goods from outside the EU, the maximum allowance per person is 1L of spirits or 2L of wine, and 200 cigarettes or 250g of tobacco.

GETTING TO THE CITY CENTRE

Metro Metro line 3 connects the airport to the city centre (Plateia Syntagmatos) half-hourly from 6.30am to 11.30pm. The journey takes 40 minutes and costs €10 (or €18 return). The station is located across from the airport and connected by a bridge.

Rental car There are two dozen companies with service desks in the arrivals hall. Be sure to book well in advance for the best price.

Rideshare You can use either the Uber or TaxiBeat apps. There won't be any difference in cost, as this route is fixed price.

Bus There are four bus routes tickets can be purchased outside the arrivals hall. Bus X95 takes you to the centre in about 60 minutes, and bus X96 takes you to Piraeus port. Tickets cost €6.

Taxi Queue outside the arrivals hall. Don't let your driver rip you off – airport taxis are a flat rate, with different costs during the day or at night (between midnight and 5am). To the centre it's €40/55, to Piraeus €50/70, and to Rafina port €30/40. You can book taxis in advance through *welcomepickups.com*. Note that not all taxis accept cards.

OTHER POINTS OF ENTRY

The other major mainland airport is Thessaloniki's Makedonia International Airport. Crete, Santorini, Rhodes, Kos, Corfu and Mykonos all have airports receiving international and chartered flights from Europe.

The majority of ferries for the Cyclades, Dodecanese, northeastern Aegean, Saronic Gulf islands and Crete leave from Greece's busiest port, Piraeus in Athens. Some Cycladic and Sporadic islands are serviced by the Rafina port. Igoumenitsa has boat services to Italy and some of the Ionian Islands, while Alexandroupoli and Kavala ports service some of the harder-to-reach northeastern Aegean Islands. Rhodes and Kos in the Dodecanese are connected by catamaran to Mamaris and Bodrum in Turkey respectively. For further information see *openseas.gr*.

There is a daily train service connecting Thessaloniki with Sofia, although you'll have to transfer to a bus for the short section between Kulata on the Bulgarian side of the Greek border and Strimon on the Greek side.

From mid-June to mid-September there is also a train service between Belgrade and Thessaloniki via Skopje. In Belgrade you can connect to trains to other parts of Europe.

 TRANSPORT TIPS TO HELP YOU GET AROUND

On the mainland and larger islands like Crete or Naxos, you'll definitely want a car. Car rentals and fuel are expensive (especially in summer) but nothing beats the freedom of going at your own pace. On smaller islands, you can get around by moped or motorcycle (you'll need a special licence). For all vehicle rental you need an International Driver's Licence.

ROAD CONDITIONS The main highways in Greece are in good condition, but note that in major cities there are plenty of potholes. On smaller islands, expect dirt roads, and just about anywhere you go, there will be hairpin turns.

BUS
The bus network is comprehensive. All long-distance buses, on the mainland and the islands, are operated by the regional collective known as KTEL (ktelbus.com). Fares are fixed by the government; bus travel is reasonably priced and has good safety records.

CAR
You can easily rent cars in towns across Greece; the largest selection is available at airports and ports. If you're planning on doing some off-road driving, it's best to rent a 4WD. If you're driving in the mountains during the winter, make sure the car has snow tyres.

CAR RENTAL COSTS

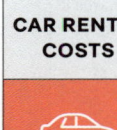

Car rental
€35–60 per day

Motorcycle rental
€25–50 per day

Petrol
€2 per litre

INSURANCE Make sure you have insurance that covers damages to vehicles and personal injury from your insurance company or credit-card company at home.

DRIVING ESSENTIALS

 At a roundabout, cars entering have the right of way.

 Speed limit: highways 100km to 120km; residential areas 50km unless otherwise noted.

 On the islands, wildlife can jump onto the road, especially at night.

 The blood alcohol limit is 0.05% (roughly two drinks).

 Children under 12 years can't be in the front seat.

ROAD SAFETY
Greece has the highest level of traffic accidents in the EU. Drivers are aggressive, road signs are treated as suggestive rather than imperative, and people often drive over the speed (and alcohol) limit. Exercise extreme caution while driving, especially in the Peloponnese and on the islands. In places like Crete, don't cut off another driver with your rental car – this could be taken as an invitation to start a fight.

MOTORCYCLE Few images are more romantic than that of a couple zipping along a beach road at sunset on the back of a motorcycle. And while it's one of the most practical ways to get around the smaller islands, note that if you've never driven one before, a Greek island is not the best place to try. You'll need a motorcycle licence to rent any two-wheelers, including a low-CC moped.

FERRY Greece has an extensive ferry network – the only means of reaching many islands. Schedules are often delayed due to weather, and timetables change before each summer season; see *ferryhopper.com* or *greekferries.gr*.

PLANE The majority of domestic flights are serviced by Aegean Airlines, Olympic Air, Astra Airlines or Sky Express. Greece has 14 airports, seven of which are located on various islands, including Crete, Santorini and Mykonos.

KNOW YOUR CARBON FOOTPRINT A domestic flight from Athens to Thessaloniki emits 53kg of carbon dioxide per passenger. A train would emit 22kg for the same distance, per passenger.
There are a number of carbon calculators online. We use Resurgence at resurgence.org/resources/carbon-calculator.html.

ROAD DISTANCE CHART (KMS)

	Athens	Delphi	Epidavros	Ioannina	Kalamata	Kavala	Meteora	Thessaloniki	Volos
Delphi	185								
Epidavros	140	255							
Ioannina	445	315	380						
Kalamata	285	355	180	465					
Kavala	680	535	770	415	380				
Meteora	360	235	485	105	575	380			
Thessaloniki	515	380	620	360	715	155	225		
Volos	325	205	450	270	520	385	145	215	
Xanthi	705	580	820	430	930	55	430	205	410

SAFE TRAVEL

Though generally a safe country, one of the biggest threats in Greece can be other people – whether that be drunk drivers, tourists trying to spike your drink, or men harassing you on the street.

EARTHQUAKES There's a lot of seismic activity in Greece, and earthquakes happen regularly across the mainland and some of the islands. Most are quite low on the Richter scale – just a small tremor you may not even notice – but occasionally, there are larger earthquakes that result in significant property destruction and some deaths.

WILDFIRES A sad but common experience of summer is at least one major wildfire. Extreme heat, climate change, poor government response and human activity have all contributed. They cause unimaginable destruction and can happen without any warning. Do your part to keep the environment safe – never litter, don't throw cigarette butts near wooded areas, and always properly damp out your campfire.

EXTREME WEATHER In the past years, weather has become increasingly extreme in Greece. Summers get hotter earlier and for longer, winters are colder and snowier than ever. Expect soaring temperatures and very little rainfall; be sure to keep hydrated and wear a sunhat during the peak of summer.

Cannabis Greek drug laws are among the strictest in Europe. Recreational cannabis is illegal and getting caught possessing or consuming weed is likely to lead to fines and/or imprisonment.

Tap water On smaller islands, tap water is not drinkable, so you'll need to buy bottled water, drink boiled or bring your own filter.

INSURANCE
Emergency care is provided free of charge to everyone at public hospitals. For EU citizens, a European Health Insurance Card (EHIC) covers most medical care (not emergency repatriation or non-emergencies). Non-EU citizens can get travel insurance for private hospitals

PHARMACIES
A dime a dozen in Greece, and most pharmacists speak fluent English. Most medications are available over the counter and are much cheaper than elsewhere in Europe.

QUICK TIPS TO HELP YOU MANAGE YOUR MONEY

CREDIT CARDS Accepted in cities and most tourist places. Most businesses now have contactless and Apple Pay, but cash is still king – especially in taxis, outdoor markets and some cash-only spots. There are ATMs in all towns and on most islands (except for the smallest ones). Visa, Mastercard and American Express are accepted in nearly all ATMs.

PAYING THE BILL
Unless you're getting takeaway, it's common to pay at the table. If paying by card, you'll occasionally be asked to come up front.

TIPPING
While completely optional, it's always a nice idea to leave an extra euro or two on the table.

DISCOUNT OR TAX?
The VAT rate in Greece is 24%, and businesses are obliged to give you a receipt. However, in order to save taxes, some businesses will offer you a 24% 'discount' if you pay in cash. This just means you won't get a receipt and the transaction is under the table. Though obviously not legal, it's a common practice.

CURRENCY
Euro

HOW MUCH FOR A...

Gyros
€3-4

Freddo espresso
€4

Taverna meal for 2
€40-50

BANKS & ATMs The major banks include Ethniki Trapeza, Piraeus Bank and Alpha Bank. You will find at least one branch and ATM in town; some smaller islands may only have a local ATM.

VAT REFUND
Those with permanent residency outside the European Union may claim a refund of the VAT on certain items purchased in Greece.

MONEY CHANGERS
Changing foreign currency is usually no problem at banks. ATMs will always prompt you to choose whether you want to be charged in euros or your home currency.

DISCOUNTS & SAVINGS
Most sights, activities and public-transport services are offered at reduced rates (or free of charge) to seniors, students, young children and families.
An Athens Museum Pass (€69) gets you entry into nine of Athens' top attractions, including the Acropolis, the Acropolis Museum and the Panathenaic Stadium.

RESPONSIBLE TRAVEL

Tips to leave a lighter footprint, support local and have a positive impact on local communities.

ON THE ROAD

Calculate your carbon There are a number of carbon calculators online; try resurgence.org/resources/carbon-calculator.html.

Choose more ecofriendly transport in cities Opt to walk or catch the bus for short distances as opposed to taking a private car.

Remember to save water Keep showers short and don't have a bath – on the islands, water is a precious commodity.

Consider opening the windows or turning on a fan Air-con is one of the leading causes of temperature changes in urban spaces in Greece.

Hold onto your rubbish (including cigarette butts) Until you find the nearest rubbish bin, whether you're at a campsite or on the beach.

Recycling It's basically nonexistent in Greece, so try to keep your single-use plastic to a minimum.

GIVE BACK

Support local businesses Greece suffered through a decade of economic crisis and austerity measures. It's always a good idea to spend money on locally owned businesses and leave tips in restaurants, cafes and taxis.

Help migrants and refugees Since 2015, a huge influx of refugees and migrants have arrived in Greece. You can volunteer with NGOs if you have the right skills, or donate money. Some NGOs on the ground are Humanity Crew, Za'atar, Second Tree and Lesvos Solidarity.

Donate for reforestation To help reforest Greece, donate to Plant Your Roots in Greece foundation, dedicated to reforesting burnt-down parts of the country.

Volunteer for wildlife conservation The Sea Turtle Protection Society of Greece operates a rescue centre in Glyfada near Athens, plus other projects around the country for which it's possible to volunteer.

DOS & DON'TS
Do learn a few words of Greek Even just a greeting in the local language will go a long way.
Don't be disrespectful in a church If entering one, keep your shoulders and knees covered and take off your hat.
Do eat up It's considered rude to refuse food (or a drink!).

LEAVE A SMALL FOOTPRINT
Pick a spot It's tempting to travel far and wide across Greece, but instead of island hopping, consider choosing one or two spots to visit and explore locally.

Go off-season Greece is inundated with tourists in high season, and it's creating a physical toll on both the landscape and people. Consider visiting in low season.

Don't clog the pipes Anywhere you go, make sure you throw toilet paper and any other products in the rubbish bin – never down the toilet!

SUPPORT LOCAL
Eat locally It's easy to do so in Greece – you can always find a green market or a local taverna for fresh produce and regional ingredients.
Spend consciously Purchase locally made souvenirs, crafts, food products and items from small brands as opposed to international chains.

CLIMATE CHANGE & TRAVEL
It's impossible to ignore the impact we have when travelling, and the importance of making changes where we can. Lonely Planet urges all travellers to engage with their travel carbon footprint. There are many carbon calculators online that allow travellers to estimate the carbon emissions generated by their journey: try resurgence.org/resources/carbon-calculator.html. Many airlines and booking sites offer travellers the option of offsetting the impact of greenhouse gas emissions by contributing to climate-friendly initiatives around the world. We continue to offset the carbon footprint of all Lonely Planet staff travel, while recognising this is a mitigation more than a solution.

RESOURCES
thehellenicinitiative.org
lesvossolidarity.org
zaatarngo.org
archelon.gr

UNIQUE & LOCAL WAYS TO STAY

Whether you're looking for a five-star resort perched on a cliff, a restored stone cottage in the mountains or a caravan by the sea, Greece has it all. With some of the most interesting architecture and stunning landscapes around, you'll be hard-pressed to get a bad night's sleep.

COST PER NIGHT AT A...

Campsite €50

Luxury resort €200

Apartment €60

CAMPING
There are dozens of campsites scattered across Greece, some of which happen to sit on some of the country's nicest coastline. There's parking for campers, space for tents (you can also rent), and some even have semi-permanent bungalows and small homes for rent. There are all sorts of services and amenities on site.

VILLAS
Greece has no shortage of villas for rent, and they make the ideal accommodation for larger groups of friends or families. Though some are more luxurious and expensive, you can find good deals through local realtors. Some owners may insist on a minimum stay of a week.

SELF-CATERING
Renting a studio, apartment or villa is great for space-cravers, families, small groups and privacy seekers. Naturally, furnishings and decor vary widely, from traditional to modern-minimalist, but all are invariably clean and often in lovely locales. Cooking facilities range from kitchenettes with a microwave, kettle and a fridge to fully furnished kitchens with stove and oven.

CYCLADIC-STYLE ACCOMMODATION

One of the most emblematic images in Greece is a white cube of a structure with blue shutters and doors set against that sparkling Mediterranean sky. Painting these houses blue and white was actually a decree under the 1967 military dictatorship, but the stone structure underneath is authentically Greek. Cycladic-style architecture – which apparently inspired none other than Le Corbusier – can be found across the island chain of the same name, and makes for a particularly atmospheric architectural experience. Based on simple lines and natural materials, these buildings form an organic part of the landscape: it's a true wabi-sabi aesthetic. Thick stone walls, flat roofs and built-in, curved furniture round out the design.

Across the islands, you'll find hotels, villas and B&Bs that make use of this Cycladic style of architecture. On volcanic Santorini, you'll find these sorts of lodgings built into caves on the caldera, while on windy Mykonos, the entire island is covered in these sugar-cube constructions. The fanciest Cycladic-style hotels will have infinity pools and linen curtains, but you can also find simple stone homes that will fit a much more modest budget.

BOOKING

You'll want to book well in advance for the peak summer season (June to August), especially on the most popular islands. In the shoulder and low seasons, you can usually find good discounts on hotels, including the fancier ones.

Lonely Planet (lonelyplanet.com/greece/hotels) Find independent reviews, as well as recommendations on the best places to stay – and then book them online.
Hipaway Villas (hipawayvillas.com) For the most unique bohemian villas in Greece, perfect for groups or families.
My Greek Villa (mygreek-villa.com) Family and beach villas for rent, romantic getaways and more.
Campsaround (campsaround.com) Comprehensive map and booking site for campgrounds and hostels across the country.
Panhellenic Camping Association (greececamping.gr) A comprehensive list of campsite locations.
Greek Youth Hostel Organisation (higreece.gr) Covers 18 properties across the country including guesthouses and hotels as well as traditional hostels.

MOUNTAIN REFUGES

Around the mainland, Crete and Evia are all sorts of mountain refuges, from sparse huts with outdoor toilets to comfortable modern lodges. Run by the country's mountaineering and skiing clubs, they're an excellent (and cheap) way to sleep in nature.

ESSENTIAL NUTS-AND-BOLTS

HOSPITALITY
Greek culture is one of extreme hospitality. Paying for the bill, inviting you over for a meal, or insisting on giving you a free drink is common and should be accepted.

STRIKES
A frequent occurrence, strikes usually don't last more than a day but can seriously impact your travel. They are sometimes announced in advance in Greek media.

SMOKING
Most indoor places prohibit smoking (there are some exceptions) but it's permissible in outdoor areas.

FAST FACTS

Time Zone
GMT+2

Country Code
+30

Electricity
220V/230V/50Hz

GOOD TO KNOW

 Citizens from more than 90 countries don't need a visa (*mfa.gr/en/visas*).

 A 24% VAT is added to all goods and services.

 You'll pay a tourist tax of up to €10 per night/room in hotels.

 To buy alcohol you must be 18 but there is no legal drinking age in private residences.

 Stay on the right when driving, cycling and walking.

ACCESSIBLE TRAVEL

Greece is not very accessible. Footpaths are tiny, cars often park on them, and drivers barely stop for pedestrians. People with wheelchairs or strollers will find it frustrating to navigate Athens and Thessaloniki.

Hotels Some hotels and all all-inclusive resorts are wheelchair-accessible. Check *disabledholidays.com* to see which ones.

Public transport Metro stations have ramps and elevators; buses have wheelchair lifts.

Islands The most accessible are Corfu, Syros and Crete. Several beaches have the Seatrac (*seatrack.gr*) independent access system.

Ferries If you require special assistance getting onto the ferry, contact the ferry company 48 hours in advance to make arrangements.

Sights Not all archaeological sites are accessible, particularly the smaller ones in more rural places. The Acropolis has one wheelchair-accessible entrance.

GREETINGS
When meeting someone for the first time, it is customary to shake hands.

BREASTFEEDING
Though it's acceptable to breastfeed in public, few people do, so you may get a few stares.

HAND GESTURES
Thrusting your hand palm-up in someone's face is considered an offensive gesture.

FAMILY TRAVEL
Restaurants and cafes Greeks love children, and will happily take care of your little ones. Highchairs are readily available, waiters will heat up a formula for you, and special food might magically appear at your table.
Transport Children under the age of four years travel for free on ferries, buses and the metro.
Sights and attractions Most sights and museums are free or half-price admission for kids and teens.

MAPS
Outside major cities it's not uncommon for Google Maps to get a little, well, fussy. Don't be afraid to ask locals for directions, and when all else fails, bust out that old paper map.

RELIGION
Most Greeks are Orthodox Christians, and the church still plays an important role in society – the church bells are an inescapable sound! Some 14% of Greeks are atheists, and there are a smaller number of Greeks who are Muslim or Jewish.

KOSTAS KOUTSAFTIKIS/SHUTTERSTOCK ©

LGBTIQ+ TRAVELLERS
Marriage In 2024, same-sex marriage was legalised in Greece. However, the Orthodox Church still has an outsized influence on the culture, so you may encounter conservative attitudes outside major cities and gay-friendly islands.
Gay Hotspots Athens has a huge gay scene, and Athens Pride in June draws people from across Europe. Mykonos' XLSIOR (*xlsiorfestival.com*) is one of Europe's best summer gay circuit festivals.
Lesbian Hotspots The western side of Lesvos is popular with lesbians, and Skala Eressos hosts the International Women's Festival (*womensfestival.eu*) in September.

LANGUAGE

All Greek words of two or more syllables have an acute accent (´), which indicates where the stress falls. In our pronunciation guides, stressed syllables are in italics.
Masculine, feminine and neuter forms of words are included where necessary, separated with a slash and indicated with 'm', 'f' and 'n' respectively. Polite and informal options are indicated where relevant with 'pol' and 'inf'. To enhance your trip with a phrasebook, visit *shop.lonelyplanet.com*.

TIME & NUMBERS

What time is it?	Τι ώρα είναι	ti o·ra i·ne
It's (two) o'clock.	Είναι (δύο) η ώρα	i·ne (dhi·o) i o·ra
It's half past (10).	Είναι (δέκα) και μισή	(dhe·ka) ke mi·si

morning	πρωί	pro·i
afternoon	απόγευμα	a·po·yev·ma
evening	βράδυ	vra·dhi
yesterday	χθες	hthes
today	σήμερα	si·me·ra
tomorrow	αύριο	av·ri·o

1	ένας	e·nas (m)	4	τέσσερεις	te·se·ris (m&f)
	μία	mi·a (f)		τέσσερα	te·se·ra (n)
	ένα	e·na (n)			
2	δύο	dhi·o	5	πέντε	pen·de
3	τρεις	tris (m&f)	10	δέκα	dhe·ka
	τρία	tri·a (n)			

BASICS

Hello.
Γειά σας./ Γειά σου. ya·sas (pol)/ ya·su (inf)
Goodbye.
Αντίο. an·di·o
Yes./No.
Ναι./Όχι. ne/o·hi
Please.
Παρακαλώ. pa·ra·ka·lo
Thank you.
Ευχαριστώ. ef·ha·ri·sto
Excuse me.
Με συγχωρείτε. me sing·kho·ri·te
Sorry.
Συγγνώμη. sigh·no·mi
What's your name?
Πώς σας λένε; pos sas le·ne
My name is ...
Με λένε ... me le·ne ...
Do you speak English?
Μιλάτε αγγλικά; mi·la·te an·gli·ka
I don't understand.
Δεν καταλαβαίνω. dhen ka·ta·la·ve·no

EMERGENCIES

Help!	Βοήθεια!	vo·i·thya
Go away!	Φύγε!	fi·ye
Call the police!	Φωνάξτε την αστυνομία!	fo·nak·ste tin a·sti·no·mi·a
I'm lost.	Έχω χαθεί.	e·kho kha·thi

Index

A
accessible travel 9, 250
accommodation 248-9
  Athens 49
  central Greece 101
  Crete 165
  Cyclades 189
  Ionian Islands 143-59
  Thessaloniki 79
Achilleion Palace 159
Acropolis 17, 50-3
Aegean Islands 34-5, 234-7
Aegina 137
Agapi 197
Agios Lavrentios 107
Agios Spyridon Church 175
airports 240, 241, 243
  Athens 48, 101
  central Greece 101
  Crete 164
  Cyclades 189, 192, 198, 200, 202
  Dodecanese 216, 220, 224, 226
  Ionian Islands 143, 151
  northern Greece 78
  Peloponnese 119
Aitoliko 111
Amari 37, 177
Amygdalokefali 177
Ancient Agora 57
Ancient Mycenae 16
Ancient Olympia 16, 33
Andritsena 125
Angistri 137
Antiparos 13, 201
Antipaxi 12, 38, 145
Apiranthos 203
Apollo Coast 71

Apollonia 195
Arahova 103
archaeological sites 16-17, 206-7, **16-17, 30-1**, see also temples & sanctuaries
  Acropolis 17, 50-3, **53**
  Acropolis of Lindos 232
  Ancient Akrotiri 191
  Ancient Corinth 132
  Ancient Dion 85
  Ancient Gortys 126
  Ancient Messini 132
  Ancient Mycenae 16, 133
  Ancient Nemea 133
  Ancient Olympia 16, 33, 132
  Ancient Thira 191
  Androusa Castle 129
  Angelokastro 159
  Bastion of St George 219
  Delos 17, 199, 206-7
  Delphi 16, 31, 102-3, **103**
  Despotiko 201
  Gortyna 183
  Kastro, Methoni 133
  Knossos 17, 37, 168-9
  Mystras 132
  Nestor's Palace 133
  Odeon of Herodes Atticus 53, 57
  Old Town of Rhodes 219
  Palace of the Grand Master 219
  Palamidi Fortress, Nafplio 132
  Paleohora 137
  Parthenon 50-3, 56
  Pella 97
  Phaestos 183
  Roman Agora 57
  St Anthony's Gate 219
  St John's Gate 219

Theatre of Epidavros 133
architecture 57, 126-7, 148-9, see also castles & fortresses
Argyrades 159
Argyroupoli 177
Aristotle 93
Arkadia 124-7
Arkoudilas 147
art 68-9, 206-7
art galleries, see museums & galleries
Assos 158
Astypalea 228-9
Atatürk, Mustafa Kemal 86
Athenian Trilogy 57
Athens 20, 31, 36, 44-73, **36-7, 46-7, 51, 53, 57**
  costs 48, 216
  drinking & nightlife 66-7
  festivals & events 53
  itineraries 46-7
  practicalities 48-9
Athens' First Cemetery 54-5
Athens Riviera 70-1, **70**
Azogires 177

B
bathhouses 83, 86
beaches 8-9
  Crete 37, 171, 172-3
  Cyclades 191, 192-3, 199, 201, 202-3, 205, 210-11
  Dodecanese 221, 230, 232
  Ionian Islands 145, 159
  Saronic Gulf Islands 137, 139
  Thessaloniki & Northern Greece 93
birdwatching 121, 223, 235

boat trips 93, 144-5, 183, 211, 222-3, *see also* ferry travel
books 42
breastfeeding 251
bridges 89
budgeting, *see* costs
bus travel 241, 242
business hours 40

C

camping 248
canyons & gorges 37, 109, 133, 170-1
car travel 241, 242
carbon footprint 243
castles & fortresses 130-1, 151, 167, 175, 227, 230-1
cats 41
caves 109, 127, 131, 134, 135, 139, 145, 227, 232, 233
cemeteries 54-5
Central Market 58-9, **59**
chemists 244
children, travel with 251
churches
 Church of Agios Georgios 103
 Church of the Annunciation 197
 Church of the Seven Martyrs 194
 Moni Agios Nikolaos 139
 Panagia Ekatontapyliani 201
 Panagia Paraportiani 211
climate, *see* weather
coffee 40, 152
Corfu 32, 144-59, **147**, **153**, **155**
costs 48, 78, 164, 188, 216, 245, 248
Crete 9, 13, 17, 29, 36-7, 160-83, **36-7**, **162-3**, **173**, **177**
 beaches 172-3
 food 167, 178-9, 182
 itineraries 162-3
 practicalities 164

000 Map pages

currency 240, 245
customs regulations 240
Cyclades 13, 17, 29, 184-211, **186-7**, **205**
 ferry travel 188
 food 210
 itineraries 186-7
 practicalities 188

D

Delos 17, 29
Delphi & Central Greece 16, 31, 98-115, **100**, **103**
 food 114-15
 itineraries 100
 practicalities 101
Diakofto 120
Diaporos Island 93
Dimitsana 125, 135
discounts 245
diving & snorkelling 93, 183, 211, 222-3, 224-5, 231
Dodecanese 34-5, 212-33, **214**
 food 221, 233
 itineraries 214-15
 practicalities 216
dogs 41
Donousa 205
drinking & nightlife 40
 Athens 66-7, 73
 Cyclades 198-9
 Dodecanese 232-3
 Ionian Islands 158-9
 Lesvos 234
drinks
 beer 201
 coffee 40
 ouzo 234-7
 water 244
 wine 22, 115, 208-9

E

earthquakes 244

Easter 27, 156-7
Emborios 225
Epidavros 39
etiquette 41, 247, 250
events, *see* festivals & events
Exanthia 144

F

Fakistra 107
Falasarna 36, 173, 177
family travel 251
Faros 195
ferry travel 164, 188, 216, 241, 243
festivals & events 20-7, 65, 83, 103, 107, 134, 156-7
films 23, 43, 83, 107
Fira 191
food 14-15, 49, 58-9, 72-3, 90-1, 179-80
 bean soup 90
 gyros 78, 81, 245
 honey 15
 olives & olive oil 23, 56-7, 103, 119, 124-5, 148-9, 178
 souvlaki 48, 164, 216
 tours 135
 tsipouradhika 104-5
Fortezza 175
fortresses & castles 130-1, 151, 167, 175, 227, 230-1

G

Gerolimenas 135
Gorianades 109
gorges & canyons 37, 109, 133, 170-1
Greek language 41, 252
Gythio 135

H

Halcyon Islands 120-1

Halki 223
Halkidiki 92-3, **93**
Hania 37, 166-7, **167**
hiking 18
  Athens 65
  Crete 170
  Cyclades 194, 205
  Dodecanese 223, 233
  E4 103
  Ionian Islands 147
  northern Greece 89
  Peloponnese 121, 123, 134
Hippocrates 227
history, *see also* archaeological sites
  economic crisis 66-9
  Knights of St John 219, 227, 231
  Minoan 17, 168-9, 180-1
  Ottoman era 86-7
  travel itinerary 30-1
  Venetian 148-9
Hora (Mykonos Town) 199
Hora (Naxos Town) 203
Hora Sfakion 177
horse riding 10, 126, 147, 183
hot springs 83, 235
hunting season 7
Hydra 12, 20, 39, 137, 138

I

Innahorion villages 177
insurance 242, 244
internet access 49, 79, 189, 217, 240
Ioannina 30, 94-5, **95**
Ionian Islands 12, 32-3, 140-59, **142**
  food 154-5
  itineraries 142-59
  practicalities 143
Iraklia 205
Iraklio 37
Ithaki 32, 145, 158, 159

J

Jewish culture 183

K

Kalamaki 107
Kalamata 129
Kalavryta 120
Kalymnos 35
Kampos 197
Kapani Market 81
Kardamyli 135
Kardiani 197
Karitena 125
Karpenisi 108-9
Kastoria 87
Kastro 194
Kataraki, Vasso 111
Kavala 87
Kefallonia 12, 38, 158, 159
kitesurfing & windsurfing 10, 200-1, 211, 233
Kioni 158
Kita 131
Klima 193
Klisova Lagoon 111
Knossos 17, 37, 168-9
Koryshades 109
Kos 34, 226-7
Kosmas 134
Koufonisia 205
Kritsa 177
Ktikados 197

L

Lagia 131
Lake Korission 147
Lake Kremasta 109
language 41, 252
Lefkada 33, 144, 158
Leigh Fermor, Patrick 122
Lecnidio 135
Lesvos 34, 234-7, 251

LGBTIQ+ travellers 198-9, 237, 251
Liapades 147, 158
Lisvorio 235
literature 42
Litohoro 85
Loggia 175
Lykavittos Hill 64-5

M

Mamma Mia! 107
Mani, the 130-1, **131**
Mani: Travels in the Southern Peloponnese 122
maps 251
marble 197, 202, 211
markets 58, 81
Meganisi 145
Meronas 177
Messolongi 110-11, 112, **111**
Meteora 31
Milos 12, 192-3, **193**
Minoan culture 17, 168-9, 180-1
Minos 181
Mohlos 177
monasteries & convents
  Emialon Monastery 126
  Evangelistrias monastery 225
  Filosofou Monasteries 126
  Mon Repos Estate 159
  Monastery of St John the Theologian 232
  Monastery of the Apocalypse 232
  Moni Agias Varvaras Rousanou 114
  Moni Arkadiou 183
  Moni Chrysopigi 211
  Moni Megalou Meteorou 114
  Moni Mega Spileo 121
  Moni Taxiarhou Mihail Panormiti 229
  Prodromos Monastery 126
money 240, 245, *see also* costs
Monodendri 89

monuments & statues 53, 55, 193, 206-7, 227
mosques 95, 167
motorcycle travel 243
Mt Athos 93
Mt Helidona 109
Mt Helmos 121
Mt Kaliakouda 109
Mt Olympus 84-5
Mt Pantokrator 147
Mt Zeus 203
museums & galleries 19, 49
  Acropolis Museum 52, 56
  Ali Pasha Museum 95
  Ancient Corinth Museum 134
  Ancient Mycenae Museum 134
  Archaeological Museum 83, 232
  Archaeological Museum of Ancient Olympia 134
  Archaeological Museum of Chania 167
  Archaeological Museum of Melos 193
  Archaeological Museum of Naxos 203
  Archaeological Museum of Patra 134
  Archaeological Museum of Rethymno 175
  Art of Silk Museum 97
  Athens 69
  Basil & Elise Goulandris Foundation 69
  Benaki Museum 72
  Bouboulina's Museum 139
  Byzantine & Christian Museum 72
  Delphi Archaeological Museum 103
  Deste Foundation 138
  Heraklion Archaeological Museum 183

000 Map pages

Historical Archives Museum of Hydra 138
History & Art Museum 111
Kerameikos 72
Lazaros Koundouriotis Historical Mansion 138
Maria Callas Museum 72
Maritime Museum of Crete 167
MOMus Museum of Contemporary Art 83
MOMus Museum of Modern Art 83
Municipal Ethnographic Museum 95
Museum of Byzantine Culture 83
Museum of Marble Crafts 211
Museum of Prehistoric Thera 211
Museum of the Kalavryta Holocaust 120, 134
Museum of the Olive & Greek Olive Oil 134
National Archaeological Museum 56
National Gallery 56
National Museum of Contemporary Art 68-9
Nikolopoulos Andritsena Library 125
Onassis Stegi 68
Open-Air Water Power Museum 125
Public Library and Museum of the Greek School 125
Public Tobacco Factory 72
Silversmithing Museum 95
Studio of Panayiotis Tetsis 138
Technopolis 72
Vergina Royal Tombs Museum 97
Victoria Karelias Collection of Traditional Greek Costumes 134
White House 159
music 42, 66-7
Mussolini, Benito 22
Mykonos 28, 198-9, **199**

Mylopotamos 107
Myrthios 177
Mystras 39

N
Nafplio 33
Naoussa 201
national parks & reserves
  Arcturos Bear Sanctuary 97
  Samaria Gorge National Park 171
  Tzoumerka National Park 97
Naxos 21, 29, 202-3, 209, **203**
Nemea 22
nightlife, see drinking & nightlife
Nike of Samothrace 207
Nikea 225
Nisyros 35, 224-5
nymphs 7

O
Oia 191
Old Perithia 158
Olympia 16, 33, 130
ouzo 235

P
Paleohora 177
Panathenaic Stadium 56
Papingo Rock Pools 97
Pappadiana 177
Parikia 201
parks & gardens
  Stavros Niarchos Park 60-1
Parliament 56
Paros 13, 28, 200-1, 208, **201**
Parthenon 50, 56
Patmos 34
Patra 25
Paxi 12, 38, 145, 159
Pelion Peninsula 7
Peloponnese 32-3, 116-35, **32-3**, **188**
  food 127, 135
  itineraries 118

practicalities 119
Pera Gialos 229
pharmacies 244
phones 240
Piraeus 24, 70-1, **71**
Plaka 193
planning 6-19
Polyaigos 192
Prespa Lakes 97
public transport 48, 78, 241, 242
Pyrgos 197

R
religion 156-7, 251
responsible travel 246
Rethymno 37, 174-5, **175**
Rhodes 35, 218-19, 230, 231, 232, 233, **223**
Rimondi Fountain 175
rock climbing 233
rock pools 97
Romans, see archaeological sites

S
safe travel 242, 244
sailing, see boat trips
Samaria Gorge 37, 170-1, **171**
sanctuaries, see monasteries & convents, temples & sanctuaries
Santorini 29, 190-1, 208, **191**
Saronic Gulf 136-9
Saronic Gulf Islands 136-9
Schinousa 205
Serifos 209
shopping 40, 73, 153, 183
Sifnos 28, 194-5
silk 97
SIM cards 240
Skamioudi 236
skiing 107, 114, 183
Skyros 25
smoking 250

snorkelling, see diving & snorkelling
Soufli 97
Spetses 137, 139
Spinalonga Island 183
Stagira 93
statues & monuments 53, 55, 193, 206-7, 227, see also archaeological sites
Stemnitsa 125, 135
strikes 250
sustainability 223
swimming 106
Symi 34-5, 228-9, 232, 233, **229**
synagogues 95, 183

T
tap water 244
Tarabados 197
taxes 245, 250
taxis 48, 241
Telendos 231
television programmes 43
temples & sanctuaries, see also monasteries & convents
  Sanctuary of Poseidon & Amphitrite 211
  Sounion Temple 71
  Temple of Aphaia 137
  Temple of Epicurean Apollo 125
  Temple of Demeter 203
Theatre of Dionysos 51
Theatre of Epidavros 131
Theriso 177
Thessaloniki & Northern Greece 23, 32, 74-97, **76-7**
  itineraries 76-7
  practicalities 78-9
Thronos 177
Tilos 35, 222-3
Tinos 39, 196-7, 209, **197**
tipping 245
tombs 97

Tourlida 111
train travel 120-1, 241

U
Unesco World Heritage Sites 16-17, 30, 32

V
Vathy 195
Venus de Milo 193, 206
Vergina 31
Vikos 89
villages 11
visas 250
Volax 197
volcanoes 190-1, 224
Vouraïkos Gorge 33, 121
Vourvourou 93

W
walking, see hiking
water (drinking) 244
weather 20-7, 48, 78, 101, 143, 164, 188
wi-fi 49, 79, 119, 217, 240
wildfires 244
windsurfing & kitesurfing 10, 200-1, 211, 233
wine & wineries 14-15, 22, 33
  Attica 58-9
  Crete 169
  Cyclades 191, 208-9
  Meteora 115
  Peloponnese 125, 127
World Heritage Sites 16-17, 30, 32

X
Xanthi 87

Z
Zagoria 88-9, **89**
Zagorohoria 30, 89
Zahlorou 135

'Cruising to Tinos on the huge open deck of an old-style ferry at sunset while sipping a beer defines joy.'
RYAN VER BERKMOES

'Comprising bucolic landscapes and home to the fabled Pan (of human body with goat legs), the mountain area of Arkadia has forests, wildflowers and spectacular gorges.'
KATE ARMSTRONG

'There's nothing quite like walking a village lane and meeting a chatty yia yia who's willing to speak with me in Greek and discuss the minutiae of the day.'
ALEXIS AVERBUCK

'Volos' tsipouradhiko ritual is the antidote to stress-filled urban banality. It represents the epitome of living spontaneously, as only Greeks know how.'
HELEN IATROU

Although the authors and Lonely Planet have taken all reasonable care in preparing this book, we make no warranty about the accuracy or completeness of its content and, to the maximum extent permitted, disclaim all liability arising from its use.

All rights reserved. No part of this publication may be copied, stored in a retrieval system, or transmitted in any form by any means, electronic, mechanical, recording or otherwise, except brief extracts for the purpose of review, and no part of this publication may be sold or hired, without the written permission of the publisher. Lonely Planet and the Lonely Planet logo are trademarks of Lonely Planet and are registered in the US Patent and Trademark Office and in other countries. Lonely Planet does not allow its name or logo to be appropriated by commercial establishments, such as retailers, restaurants or hotels. Please let us know of any misuses: lonelyplanet.com/legal/intellectual-property.

THIS BOOK

Commissioning editor
Daniel Bolger

Production editor
Graham O'Neill

Cartographer
Bohumil Ptáček

Book designer
Virginia Moreno

Coordinating Editor
Michael Mackenzie

Cover researcher
Kat Marsh

Thanks James Appleton, Imogen Bannister, Melanie Dankel, Felicity Hughes, Rachel Imeson, Anne Mulvaney